Wilma Martin Turner

He Heard His Brother Call His Name

A Memoir

PATSY DORRIS HALE with
WILMA MARTIN TURNER

ISBN:1491275162
ISBN-13:9781491275160

DEDICATION

My story is dedicated to my precious four children, grandchildren and their families. I know we are all uniquely and wonderfully made and that God has a special plan for each one. May we grow in wisdom and grace.

Patsy Dorris Hale

CONTENTS

PROLOGUE

Have you ever felt the need to tell your story? I have felt that need but have hesitated. Many of my friends who lived through this story with me, and people who have come to know me, have shaken their heads and said, "Patsy, you should write all this down."

"All this" resides in a private room in my heart. I used to go there occasionally—but I would rather keep the door locked; pain is still in there. But you, dear friends, have coaxed me to write. I reach for the key… Pray for me.

A few people in this account, for various reasons, have asked that they not be identified. To honor their requests, I have changed their names and the names of children.

1. CHRISTMAS EVE

The ghosts of our future are out of control.
~ Anonymous

My name is Patsy Hale. The account I am about to give is my story, and it is true.

I am sure you have had a pivotal day in your own life; something happens and things are never the same. Christmas Eve 1977 was such a time for me and my husband, Bill. That is the day we started down a road that changed our family's history. Who is accountable for the nightmare years that followed? We all sinned. Omission or commission—which is worse? Tell me if you can, for after thinking it through a thousand times, I still don't know. I can, however, relate the facts. I remember them clearly.

As I begin, allow me a moment to tell you a little about that crucial day: of the Christmas setting, of our proud history, and of our beloved family heirlooms and possessions—handmade by relatives both living and dead, the kind of things that ground families and confirm their heritage, things our family cherished.

Fort Worth, Texas 1977

I wake early this morning, this happy Christmas Eve, 1977, roll over and feel for my watch on the nightstand. Its little glowing face blinks 4:46—almost five a.m.—so much to do in the next twelve hours. By five p.m. Virginia, Billy's Mother will arrive, heralding the start of our evening festivities. She will bring her Christmas heirlooms and family treasures. I love the yearly ritual of unpacking and displaying these things and hearing the stories that accompany them. My heart starts to race with excitement. I lie motionless for a minute more, listening to my sweet husband sleeping softly beside me, and I smile with pleasure.

This is Billy's favorite day of the year, and he spares no effort to make Christmas Eve wonderful. Nor do I.

I slip out of bed quietly in the dark and feel my way to the door, open it, and close it carefully behind me. Inching down the hall, I pull the children's doors shut. The house smells wonderful already, filled with the aroma of yesterday's baking. I don't want the additional smell of my morning coffee to trigger any waking response. I can get a lot done this morning with my active family asleep. I chuckle at the thought of our Allison—"Ears," we call her. She will wake at the slightest sound from me. She is our oldest child and the one who loves to help Mommy. Almost nothing goes on in our household that escapes little Miss Ears.

The lights from below blink and beckon on the staircase as I tiptoe down.

Pausing to watch the twinkling tree, I am soon mesmerized by the holiday environment. The sharp conifer scent of nature and the sweet brown smell of baking, together with the colors and lights, affect me deeply. Standing by the tree, quiet and at peace, I let the spirit of Christmas move through me.

I notice that one string of lights on the tree is dark. Probably only one light is burned out, but each bulb will need testing to find the culprit. I will let Miss Ears do this job and save Billy the aggravation. She likes that sort of thing. She will love it when the burned-out bulb is finally found and the whole string lights up.

One of our family traditions is that we always go Christmas tree shopping on December 13, our first son, Will's, birthday. Buying and putting up the Christmas tree is a festive occasion for us, and it adds excitement to Will's birthday celebration. We then spend many loving hours decorating this tree. Because everything has to be perfect for

Billy, we took the tree to a nursery this year and had each branch carefully flocked to look like a light snow had just fallen. Then we hung all the old ornaments on the tree as well as the special new one that we add each year. The roping is all silver; even the Christmas cookies, hanging from the branches, are glazed in silver. I bake these elaborate cookies as tree ornaments and as evening treats for the children. Every night, for one week before Christmas Eve, the children and I gather around the tree—the children especially interested in the cookies. They carefully admire the pale decorations beneath the silver glaze and choose one cookie each for munching. This custom is a fun gathering together, and, I admit it, a chance for me to satisfy the child in myself. As we sit around the tree I, with affected mystery, shake the wrapped packages, especially any new ones I have added, and give hints as to what is inside. This is a guessing game my mother played with me as a child, and I still enjoy it as much as my children do. The nightly gathering is also a countdown to Christmas Eve.

As I reach the kitchen and ease the door shut, plans are already racing through my head: of course first of all put the coffee on, then make cornbread and chop celery and onions for dressing. The dressing recipe is from one of my dad's cousins. It is the best we have ever had, and I use a special secret ingredient to make it even better. But before the chopping, I must start the turkey giblets simmering with spices, for broth and gravy. Busying myself with this preparation, I begin to reflect on my evolving role in our extended family.

Some years back, Billy's dad, I.B. Hale, divorced his mother, the legendary Virginia Kingsbery of Sherman, then Fort Worth, Texas. Since that time, the responsibility for this yearly gathering has fallen largely to me. Feeling very much "the keeper of traditions," I enjoy this matriarchal role. It is my job now to keep up with all the old family customs and recipes. I think of the Kingsbery family fruitcake, and its long soaking requirements, and realize that I have spent literally weeks in preparation for tonight. This traditional fruitcake, so the story goes, has been served every Christmas Eve for at least five generations. This is the first year that Virginia has given me the recipe and trusted me to make this cake. In surrendering the ancient recipe to me, she took one more step toward relinquishing her role. The thought fills me with melancholy.

I love the family history and honor it. In past years, on Christmas Eve, Virginia's Mother, Belle, would tell us stories of her husband's family, the Kingsberys from Atlanta, Georgia; stories handed down for more than a hundred years. She told us that the tradition of grand Christmas Eves had come over with the Kingsbery family from England to Virginia and from Virginia to Carrollton, Georgia. When Virginia's grandfather, Joseph Kingsbery Sr., a young decorated veteran of the Civil War, moved from the family plantation in Carrollton—which our family visited and, last I heard, is still standing—to Atlanta, he and his wife took the tradition with them. In Atlanta, wealth and influence further enhanced the Kingsbery Christmas Eves. Belle told us how her father-in-law had prospered in Atlanta after the Civil War. His ideas and influence played an important part in Atlanta's "rising from the ashes," she said. He had been influential in bringing the Cotton States and International Exposition to the city and was made president of that endeavor. This exhibition gave Atlanta its big boost toward becoming the primary trading hub of the Southeast. Mr. Kingsbery also helped found, and was president of, an elite gentlemen's club, the Piedmont Driving Club, in Atlanta. The driving involved the new contraption, cars, not golf balls. The beautiful young socialite, Belle Birge of Sherman, Texas had met her future husband, Joseph Kingsbery Jr., at his dad's club. The couple would go driving in Joe Jr.'s automobile around Atlanta and were as happy and carefree as two well-born young people could possibly be. The club still thrives today as one of the most prestigious country clubs in the South. In 1927 *The Atlanta Constitution*, the city's premier newspaper, then and now, dubbed Joseph Kingsbery "the father of Piedmont Park," the park where the Exposition was held and where the club stands. Some years ago, Billy and I visited friends from college who live in Atlanta. Happily, we were able to find the graves of Joseph Kingsbery and his wife. They are resting in a family lot in Oakland, one of Atlanta's historic cemeteries.

Thinking of Joseph Kingsbery, I feel a surge of pride in these family ties. Tonight I will be hostess of the ritual Kingsbery dinner with three generations of Mr. Kingsbery's grandchildren—Virginia, Billy, and our children. We will be using some of the same china and silver serving pieces that were used by the Kingsbery family in Atlanta more than a century ago. Our family's custom is still to dress in our most formal and festive apparel for this occasion. Billy will read the Christmas story, remember the good things about the passing year and say a prayer of gratitude for our Lord's birth and for our many blessings. Then, with carols playing, we will sit down to our feast.

I don't say "feast" lightly! Remember, counting the fruitcake, I have spent weeks preparing this spread. So with the dressing ingredients cooking—cornbread baking and onions and celery sautéing, I sip my coffee and start writing this evening's menu. In the past I have been known to let some lovingly prepared dish get lost in the refrigerator and go unserved. After a couple of these disappointing omissions, I learned to carefully list every item and check each one off at serving time. First, the turkey, and I will serve it on my favorite platter, the one my mother painted. She does lovely hand-painted ceramics, and this platter has a beautiful rim of holly and cranberry design. There will be dressing, gravy, and my mother's fresh cranberry salad. Mother will also bring the famous green bean casserole, now a holiday staple all over America. I will make the creamed potatoes and Lucerne peas with plenty of butter and black pepper. My recently divorced friend, Leigh, is bringing a broccoli casserole—over my protest that there will be plenty of food without it. We will also have my signature dish and the family's favorite, Texas beef brisket. I put that in the oven late last night, as it needs several hours to slowly simmer and bake. As a matter of fact it should be ready to take—

Suddenly my reverie is shattered by the piercing ring of the telephone! This kitchen phone is kept at top volume so it can be heard all over the house and into the yard. Nothing could have shocked me into faster action at this hour—I leap across the room and snatch the receiver in the middle of the first ring. "Hello?" I whisper, my heart going wild. Nothing from the other end. "Hello?" I ask again in a low, deliberate voice. I hear the careful click of a hang-up. Stunned, I replace the receiver, turn the ringer to its lowest volume, and listen for any sound from the children overhead. To my surprise, there is no stirring. With any luck, they will sleep another two hours. I refill my coffee and stare out the kitchen-door window, my heart returning to calm. Switching off the inside light, I stand at quiet attention, watching the dark morning.

Okay, where was I? Listing the menu items, and now the brisket is ready to come out of the oven. It smells just right, tangy and delicious. I wrap the baking pan in foil and put it on the back porch. Because the weather is cold, the meat will be fine until I reheat it this evening. Our friends Stan and Anna are coming for dinner. She will bring two pans of her special yeast rolls to be baked at the last minute and served piping hot. As for sweets, I have prepared nearly every kind of candy, cookie, cake and sweet bread that both sides of the family traditionally make during the holidays. I have sweets in Tupperware or plastic wrap stored all over the house and porch. And the real centerpiece, the Kingsbery family fruitcake, is ripening in the buffet. There is no way the dessert table will hold all these baked goods, but that's fine because I'm going to save the sweet breads— strawberry, pumpkin, banana walnut, and zucchini—for Christmas breakfast and for any drop-in guests on Christmas Day. I will put out the prune cake, Billy's favorite, and the fruitcake for tonight. And I will display the candies on one of my mother's hand-painted ceramic trays; they will include chocolate fudge, pecan divinity, pralines, rum balls, and millionaire candy—a recently invented concoction of caramel, chocolate, and pecans. Then there are cookies: pecan tassies, my grandmother's recipe; my mother's sand tarts; Hello Dollies, a recipe from my mother's lifelong friend; and the old Irish cookie called kippling. The kippling recipe had come from Virginia's maternal grandmother. Finally, I will make pecan pies and Dutch apple pies this morning. Okay, is this everything? No, I forgot the sweet potato soufflé. Now that's it.

I am just fitting the pie crusts into the pans when little feet begin to patter about in the bedrooms above. I hear Billy call out, and all four pairs of footfalls thunder toward our bedroom. With my family squealing, and laughing upstairs, I think of the busy day before us and am grateful for my head start.

At five o'clock in the evening we hear Virginia pull into the driveway, exactly on time as always, and we are ready for her—Christmas carols playing throughout the house and the whole family dressed in our best attire. I have even swept my hair up into a formal cascade of curls, a style that provides maximum display for the diamond and garnet earrings and necklace that my father designed and made for me. Garnets are my birthstone, and I love their look more than that of rubies. Dad is an exceptional jeweler and owns one of the most respected jewelry stores in town. He also did custom work for individuals and for other jewelry stores, Haltom's Jewelry being one of his regular customers. Daddy gives me jewelry on at least one occasion every year. This dazzling set of necklace and earrings was his special gift to me six years ago, on my twenty-seventh birthday.

When Virginia rings the doorbell, the children and Billy run, loud and laughing, to greet her and get their hugs and kisses first.

Virginia is still as elegant and gracious as any woman in Fort Worth. Her beautiful jet-black hair had grayed prematurely and now, in her early fifties, she wears it blonde and brushed back in a stylish bob. She has the languid sea-green eyes that the Kingsberys are noted for, and she is as trim and straight as a girl. Observing her, one would not be surprised to learn that she had been one of Fort Worth's most beautiful debutantes.

Billy carefully carries the boxes of Virginia's things in from her car. These contain the family heirlooms and treasures that amaze and thrill us.

Virginia has a creative talent that is incomprehensible to me. She not only has a keen eye for art but is patient and dexterous and can turn her imaginary visions into things of great beauty. Some years ago

Virginia had spent nearly twelve months creating an "egg tree." Let me tell you how she made this amazing and, to my knowledge, totally unique, work of art: She had carefully emptied eggs, saving their shells. She had broken small perfect openings in the front of the shells. She had also made miniature figures and landscapes of paper and wood and painted each tiny piece. Tediously maneuvering these impossibly small forms through the tiny door of each eggshell, she had fashioned little Christmas-like scenes and glued them securely in place. Finally, she had painted beautiful scenes on the eggshells' exterior to reflect the theme inside. After gluing tiny hooks on each egg, she had hung them on a hand-carved wooden tree. Virginia had found this beautiful tree, with seemingly impossible hand-carved branches, in a boutique in Houston. The tree, she said, was her inspiration for the eggs. Every year I have the same reaction to this egg tree—it simply takes my breath away. We display this very carefully; the higher it sits off the floor, the safer I feel.

Virginia also made a brass tree. Brass trees are commercially popular at this time, but Virginia wanted something special. So she wove her own brass wire into a wild and satisfying shape, then cut and formed birds, angels, and even tiny leaves of brass and soldered them onto it. This tree, too, is exquisite.

Next, we unpack the Christmas stockings. When Billy and his twin, Bobby, were infants, Virginia's Mother, Belle, had made her precious grandsons their first and only Christmas stockings. These were sturdy and lined, hand-beaded and beautiful. Made with exquisite care, these stockings were intended to last a lifetime of Christmases. Not to be outdone, Virginia also crocheted and lined and hand-beaded stockings for her own grandchildren. As we've seen, she is a perfectionist, and she spent months making them. They are almost equal to Belle's creations. Virginia delighted our four children last year when she presented all of them with their own Christmas stocking. We hang these stockings from the brass hooks on the bottom of the large antique mirror my mother gave me when we moved into this house.

Next, from soft tea towels, I reverently unwrap the old items from Atlanta: two serving bowls and two small platters, still in perfect condition; a gravy boat with a tiny chip on the rim; several silver serving pieces, including spoons, forks, and a ladle; and a small ornate silver pot—the original purpose of which we never knew, but I use it as a cream pitcher for coffee. I hear there had once been a cup presented to and used by President Cleveland when he was in Atlanta to celebrate the cotton exposition and also when he returned to visit in the Kingsbery home. I understand it is somewhere in Atlanta now, but I don't know where.

Finally, Billy brings out what he considers to be the star of the show: The Tablecloth—and though it makes me very nervous, with our young children, Virginia insists that we use this tablecloth every Christmas Eve. Virginia's Mother, Belle Birge, had started an interesting tradition: When her family members were getting on in age, she bought a large, very heavy, white linen tablecloth. Everyone who dined at her home was asked to sign and date this tablecloth. Then, with red thread, Belle embroidered the signatures and dates.

Virginia inherited the tablecloth from Belle and continued the tradition. There are the names of long dead family members, such as Robert Allen Birge and others of the well-known Birge family of Sherman, Texas, as well as those of us still living. In addition, there are the names of politicians and civic leaders, some dead, some alive; Davy O'Brien and a couple of other Heisman Trophy winners; and, one of the most intriguing, J. Edgar Hoover, head of the FBI and a good friend of I.B., Billy's father—who was once an FBI agent and one of Hoover's favorites.

A giant of a man at 6 foot 4 inches tall and definitely a leader, I.B. was one of the FBI's most valuable agents. He was often put in charge of large numbers of men on important, and always secret, operations. I.B. was also known as one of the world's most accurate sharpshooters, and he gave many demonstrations, intended to awe, both here and abroad. In addition to his other responsibilities at the FBI, he trained the agents to shoot. Even after I.B. left the FBI and was made head of security at General Dynamics in Fort Worth, Hoover had continued to give him special assignments. I.B. never spoke to anyone, not even Virginia, about these assignments; he would just go away for a while. One of I.B.'s friends had dared to wonder out loud if the security position at General Dynamics, a major military contractor, had been another special FBI assignment.

After I.B.'s untimely death at fifty-four, the family learned some surprising things about his activities. We learned that he was present at Parkland Hospital when President Kennedy's body was taken there after the assassination. (To this day, my cousin, a reporter at the *Fort Worth Star-Telegram* at the time, is still asking why—with St. Paul's Hospital so close by, with a state-of-the-art trauma unit—Kennedy was not taken there. It would have saved crucial minutes in transit.) We also learned that I.B. was standing by when Lee Harvey Oswald was shot. The family found out about these apparent involvements only when we saw photographs and news tapes played on television years later. It was even rumored by certain people in Dallas and Fort Worth that I.B. had been involved in helping to change the Kennedy parade route through Dallas. If this were true, we wondered, why had he been chosen for that? Had he been unwittingly used? And we questioned later why, because of his sudden death, at a young age with no history of heart problems or hypertension, an autopsy was not performed to determine the cause of his death.

I went to I.B.'s house the week after his burial to visit his wife, and after such a shocking, sudden death, to help in any way I could. Billy's stepmother was in her reading chair, grieving and in tears. Her maid was there to help her organize I.B.'s clothes and his other things into what she would keep and what she would give away. I could see they had all the small stuff out on the kitchen counter. The maid gave a motion of her head for me to come over, and when I did she held a bottle of pills. "Miss Patsy, we found these in Mr. I.B.'s medicine cabinet. We don't know what it is. He didn't take medicine. Miss broke down, like you see in there, when she saw it because she's never seen it before." But I was young and pregnant and busy, and I forgot about the pills. Many years later, I asked Billy's stepmother if she remembered those pills and if she had investigated them. She did remember them, vividly, but for whatever reason, she had let it drop. We were never quite able to put all these things together. In the phrase commonly used today, we were not able to connect the dots.

Finished with the unpacking, I reverse the cassette tape of carols, and we all get busy preparing the dining and dessert tables for the evening.

At six o'clock, my parents arrive, both dressed elegantly. There are no words to describe how much I love Mother and Daddy. They are an adorable couple. He is medium height, about 5-foot-11, and Mother is 5-foot-3. They are pretty much a contrast—Mother with naturally blond, short, curly hair, and Daddy with dark hair (now salt and pepper) parted straight down the middle and brushed back, unusual but very attractive on him, and he has always worn it that way. Dad has the beautiful clear-blue eyes of the Irish, whereas Mother's eyes are light hazel. Mother is a beautiful woman with radiant skin and is noted for her lovely smile. She is good-humored and laughs a lot. Mother is very giving and is always doing for others. She also adores my dad.

Daddy loves to tell jokes and is good at it, keeping people around him laughing and in a good mood, especially Mother, to whom he is totally devoted. He is a sincere Christian, honest and kind and, like Mother, very giving. His motto—I've heard him say it a hundred times— is "A good name is worth more than great riches."

Within a few minutes, Stan and Anna arrive. They, too, are a great couple and interesting to be around. Stan has an operatic tenor voice and Italian good looks. Anna is beautiful, with shining brown hair and the figure and gait of the dance choreographer she once was.

Right behind them Leigh comes in carrying a huge dish—her broccoli casserole. Leigh, too, has a beautiful voice and, like Stan, often sings solos at our church. "Leigh," I say, giving her a big hug, "I'm so excited! With you and Stan here, we will have some incredible music tonight!"

After all the typical hustle and bustle of greetings, exchanging compliments, taking food to the kitchen, and hanging up coats, the men settle down to conversation. Dad is already telling a joke, and the men are laughing heartily. As I pour drinks, the women compliment me on everything from the children to my appearance to the house—especially the house.

This is the first time my parents, or the others for that matter, have seen our house since we finished the renovations. The children want their grandmothers to see their bedrooms, and before we know it we have a full-scale inspection going on.

Billy and I loved this house the first time we spotted it from the street. There was a beautiful tree in the front yard with low twisting limbs, shady and perfect for climbing. The children would love that. The property had a large, fenced-in backyard, big enough for the children's swing set and games, and for Billy to have his dog run. As a huge bonus for us, behind and on one side of the house, a couple of lots were empty. We could entertain friends and Sunday school classes with cookouts in the yard and ball games in the empty lots. One of my favorite features of this house was a country-style roofed and open back porch.

Inside, the house was large and comfortable with three bedrooms and two baths upstairs. Downstairs were the kitchen and its alcove breakfast area with picture window, the pantry, a half bath, and a large living room/dining room area. The crowning feature was an oversized, separate den with sliding-glass doors onto a patio in the backyard. The house was in beautiful condition when we bought it—but even so, it wasn't good enough for Billy. To a greater or lesser extent, he and the contractor he hired worked on every room.

We proudly show our guests the beautiful kitchen cabinetry Billy installed and finished. The men are amazed at his skill, and the women are impressed with how much storage I have. "If you think the kitchen is nice, take a look at our den," I tell them. I lead everyone into the den and am rewarded with their gasps of admiration.

We were so pleased to have a big den in our new home that merely painting the walls wasn't sufficient for Billy—he upholstered the walls of the entire room in genuine suede! The suede is a soft beige color, and for contrast Billy changed the doorframes, toe trim, and crown molding to natural, dark barn wood. Billy is like his mother, a perfectionist, and he paid merciless attention to every detail—the work is without flaw. To do the expensive walls justice, we needed fine furnishings. I bought a quite pricy three-piece sectional sofa and matching chair all upholstered in suede a few shades darker than the walls, and two large contrasting ottomans. I found the perfect carpet, pillows, and lamps in the various light and dark earth tones popular in the 1970s. We spared no expense—Billy never does—and also put in a game table, bookshelves, and a new television.

This is our favorite room, and our family gathers here for all activities: homework, reading, TV, and devotion. We love this room, and I must say—a friend who is an interior designer did say—it looks like a page out of *Better Homes and Gardens.*

When the children grow restless, Billy calls out, "It's time to get serious about Christmas, folks!" As the others follow Billy, I glance at the dining and dessert tables. They both look properly impressive. The turkey and dressing are on hold in the oven, and the brisket and warm dishes are covered. I turn the carols down low and hurry to join the children and guests in the living room.

Billy is standing, ready to read the Christmas story. Our eyes meet, and we share a tantalizing moment of joy and pride. I know the proverb well—"Pride goes before a fall," but regarding Billy, I am heedless of this caution. I am especially proud before my parents, who had been rather hesitant about our marriage. I am proud that he is not only a good-looking man but also a good man: good husband, good father, ambitious and hard-working. As he stands poised before us, I drink in every perfect feature: his shining black hair combed back smooth; black brows, perfectly framing his green Kingsbery eyes; his dad's nose, small and slightly upturned, youthful and disarming; symmetrical mouth and strong jawline narrowing to his chin—he is perfection to me.

Billy's beauty and his rich, Texas voice have all of us engrossed in St. Luke's account of Jesus' birth; the reading of it is over too soon, then we rise on cue.

As we bow our heads for our prayer of gratitude and commitment, some of us notice that Billy has become distracted. He walks over to the back window and stares out into the dark. Following his gaze, we notice what are possibly car headlights bobbing around in the empty field behind the house. As we watch, the lights move straight toward our backyard.

"It's probably Christmas carolers," I say, a little irritated—but singers rarely carol on Christmas Eve, I think to myself.

Billy turns to me, a puzzled frown on his face, "You all just stay here for a second," he orders. "Let me check this out." The next instant, he bolts toward the kitchen and out the back door.

2. UNEXPECTED GUESTS

"...is it not to share your food with the hungry and to provide the poor wanderer with shelter, when you see the naked to clothe him, and not turn away from your own flesh and blood?"
~ Isaiah 58:7

"I'm sorry," I say to our guests. "Why would anybody come around at dinner time on Christmas Eve?" I shush the children and motion for them to stay put. "Let's don't break everything up, kids. Just stay here a second, folks, and let me see what's going on." I go to the kitchen door, but the bobbing lights have disappeared.

Then, out of the night, I hear a call—"Billy!"—and my knees nearly buckle. Again the familiar voice calls, "Billy!" A feeling of dread fills the pit of my stomach. It is Bobby, Billy's twin, and my nightmare. I remember the mysterious phone call early this morning, well before dawn, and the careful click of a telephone hang-up. Of course that was Bobby, just like some mischief from his checkered past.

"Billy!" he yells, "It's me, your long lost brother! I'm over here in the dark." Billy turns, and with emotional outcries he and Bobby run into each other's arms. There has been a six-year absence between these identical twins.

I hold the door partially open against the cold and watch them rejoice in their reunion. As I listen now to the brothers' happy laughter, all misgivings leave me.

Stepping back into the room, I announce loudly, and with genuine joy, "Bobby is here!" Virginia claps her hands and lights up with happiness. Her son has been missing for years with only second-hand word from friends. An instant later, both brothers burst through the kitchen door and into the room.

What do you say and do when a loved one shows up and is completely changed? All of us, including Billy, stare in disbelief at this reverse metamorphosis. I cannot help comparing the stranger we behold now with the handsome, well-dressed Bobby I had last seen six years ago—stepping out of his flashy Corvette, smiling, always an electrifying presence. "Mr. Neiman Marcus," our friends called him.

Now stands before us what appears to be an undernourished mountain man. His hair is long and turning gray, and he has a graying, scraggly beard. He is dressed in what amounts to rags. His limp pants fall above his ankles, and most alarming, his feet are bare.

We have not yet gained our composure, nor has Bobby greeted his mother, when he spins around and calls over his shoulder, "Stay here, everybody! I want you to meet my family." He vanishes into the darkness as quickly as he appeared.

His family? We had heard from one of his friends in Fort Worth that Bobby was traveling with a girl named Kurina. Is she a part of this additional surprise—his family? Not knowing what to say, we say nothing, each of us lost in thought. I dearly want to speak to our children. The older children barely remember their Uncle Bobby, and Ben, the youngest, has never met him. Our friends have only heard of Bill's glamorous and mysterious twin brother. Now there is no time to talk or explain or even ask questions.

Abruptly, Bobby swings the door open and, with his old elegance, ushers his "following" into the room. He declares, with as much dignity and confidence as a king, "I would like you to meet the Morning Star family." At this point Bobby becomes very animated—motioning grandly to each of his family members in turn, and introducing them by what we later learn are their gypsy names: "This is Running Cub; Lotus—Billy and Patsy, you remember Lotus—our little girl, Spring Flower; our baby boy, JaJa; and Starlight, my wife."

Then he looks at Starlight and turns his attention to us. "And this is my Texas family I've told you so much about: Billy, my brother, and his wife, Patsy, and my mother—" but my thoughts wander–

Starlight/Kurina, the girl "he's been traveling with." I've heard it said that "you never have a second chance to make a first impression." In Kurina's case, that saying holds true for me. The vision of the innocent-looking young woman who stepped out of the darkness that Christmas Eve, and into my home is stamped indelibly on my mind. Thirty years and unspeakable heartache later, that first impression is still Kurina to me. She is a big woman, as tall as Bobby. Her flaxen hair, parted straight down the middle, hangs long behind her shoulders. I have the impression that she has just combed it smooth in preparation for our meeting. Her skin is a robust pink, probably from the cold. She wears a long skirt made of brightly printed cotton. Below the skirt her feet are bare and rough. Her blouse is also printed cotton, different from the skirt, with a bright flower pattern, and is gathered at the sleeves and at the shoulder-width neck in the peasant fashion. She has large breasts, partly from nursing the young child in her arms, I reason. Kurina's pale blue eyes are unknowable as we study each other for long seconds. What does she think of me: my platinum hair, formal dress, jewels and makeup? And what does she think of my comfortable home, shining with lights and smelling of Christmas? I can't contain these thoughts of comparison and consider them shameful. I feel a veil of distrust fall between us.

I turn my attention to the children: Spring Flower is a cute two-and-a-half-year-old girl, with blue eyes and blond hair, barefoot and dirty. The baby, JaJa, is a beautiful boy, about nine or ten months old, I guess. His little nose is crusty and dirty from dripping and the cold. I think how satisfying it will be when I get the chance to take a warm washcloth to those grimy hands and pretty little face.

Then there is Lotus. I haven't seen Lotus in six years. She is a beautiful Eurasian child with black eyes and black hair and is the daughter of Bobby's third wife, Connie. She is about the same age and size as our eight-year-old, Katie. But I wonder, if she is with anyone other than her mother at Christmas, why not her own father?

Why Bobby?

Running Cub is another puzzle. Somewhat older than the other children, he is small-framed for his age, which I guess is nine or ten years, and rather thin. His hair is brown and shoulder-length with a fine texture. His eyes are deep brown and intelligent, and he seems bright and completely at ease. How does Running Cub fit into this gypsy-like family, I wonder. This is not the time to ask.

Virginia has been as patient, and well behaved, as a mother could be under the circumstances, but she finally surrenders to her longing and rushes over to kiss and hug her son and grandchildren. As Virginia chokes back tears, I announce, "Bobby, you're just in time for dinner."

I run to take the turkey and dressing out of the warm oven and put the rolls in. My mother and friends, eager for distraction, scramble to help me with the last-minute preparations.

Billy and the men find the card table and chairs and set them up for the children. Our children are used to sitting at the "big" table and are not completely happy with this arrangement. Billy explains to them that the older cousins will sit at the small table together, and the younger children will sit at the big table. "That way your mother and Starlight can help the little ones with their meal." The children are content with this explanation, and the adults, with affected normalcy, talk loud and laugh loud.

It's not long before I clap my hands together. "You know what?" I shout over the commotion, "We've got all this delicious food getting cold." Billy and our children run playfully past me, through the arched doorway, and into the dining area.

Within minutes we are seated and Bill is saying the blessing. Thank goodness he makes it short, for Bobby's little ones are already climbing, unchallenged, onto the table.

The meal is chaotic. Bobby has brushed off Billy's suggestion that they wash up for dinner, so the entire Morning Star family is eating heartily, dirty hands and all. They look as if it has been a long time since their last meal. Despite the chaos, I feel compassion for them and am glad we have plenty of food.

When dinner is over, the table and floor look like we have been sabotaged by wild bears. What a mess!

I can't deny that it bothered me a lot when Bobby allowed his young children to sit on top of the table, grabbing for food in every direction. So much for Bill's statement that "Your mother and Starlight can help the little ones with their meal." The little ones helped themselves. I was forced to take some dishes safely back to the kitchen and bring them out only for refills. The whole hectic undertaking kept me busy and anxious. It seems silly now, but during all this commotion I thought more than once of the family's patriarch, Joseph Kingsbery. I wondered, with some amusement actually, if he had ever had a Christmas Eve like this.

Understandably, there has been an uncomfortable sense of things going amiss from the minute this unrecognizably new Bobby showed up in our living room. Mother is the first to verbalize her feelings. "Baby," she whispers sympathetically when she meets me in the kitchen as dinner is ending, "they've made a circus out of all your efforts."

She looks at me with great compassion, and I feel the sting of tears gathering in my eyes. "Mother, please, I can't break down now. With or without Bobby's permission, I've got to bathe these babies—before all that dirt and food makes its way onto my furniture."

Her look immediately changes from compassion to determination. "Absolutely," she says. "Get Allison to help you, and we women will take care of cleaning up."

Little Miss Ears, of course, is standing right with us and hears the plan. Allison lifts baby JaJa off the table, and I take Spring Flower. "Starlight, we're going to bathe these babies." I catch a quick glance of approval from Billy. "And I've got plenty of clothes for them." We are on the stairs before I finish the sentence and Billy is loudly ushering the men and Starlight into the living room, with Virginia close behind. Virginia is not one to help much with cleanup anyway, and certainly not with her long-lost son here.

Running Cub chose to stay with the adults, and I get the feeling that he is a lot like our Allison—nothing much gets past him. Lotus and Katie come up the stairs holding hands. Lotus wants to take a bath too, which makes me happy.

I start the bathwater, then let Allison and Katie and Lotus bathe the babies while I change from cocktail dress and heels to hostess pajamas and flats. And while I'm up here, I think, turning out the bedroom light so I can see outside, let me find that truck that I heard Bobby say they came in. I look down into the backyard and there it sits: a big, dark hulk of a truck parked directly behind the house outside the fence. He had found his way around to the back and across the empty field. That accounts for the lights bobbing around as the truck took the bumps. It's so much like Bobby, ever the drama king, to park out of sight and prolong his big entrance.

Will and Ben are busy finding some of their old, good toys to wrap for the new cousins for Christmas. I look in on the baths then hurry to find clothes to fit JaJa and the girls. I find a pretty toddler's dress adorned with butterflies for Spring Flower along with some little-girl slippers. Pajamas with feet are for JaJa. Katie gives one of her dresses and a blue sweater to Lotus.

My mother and girlfriends are still cleaning and vacuuming when Allison and I return downstairs with Bobby's beautiful babies, clean and dressed. We find everyone else in the living room. They are lounging contentedly in the glow of the tree, engrossed in some story Bobby is telling. Allison gives the clean, happy JaJa to Kurina. Spring Flower helps me put the four gifts I have wrapped for her and her siblings under the tree. "She's a precious child," I whisper to Kurina.

I walk over and take a seat on the piano stool. I had planned to play the piano and, since Stan and Leigh have exceptional voices, I wanted them to sing for us. But one and all are paying strict attention to Bobby; so I just sit for a few minutes and watch my friends and family. But I am disappointed and pay little attention to Bobby's story. He is in his element, the center of attention. Even if he knew what my plans were and that we have remarkable talent in this room, he would much rather have everyone focused on him. I am still seething at Bobby's lack of respect for me and for his mother at dinner. He knows very well from years past—in fact, his whole life— the elaborate planning and hard work his family invests in Christmas

Eve. And he is well aware of the historical and sentimental value of Virginia's tablecloth. Now his babies have spilled, and sat in, food on the cloth, and it is stained beyond cleaning.

Oh, Patsy, stop it, I think. Don't make yourself miserable. After all, the tablecloth is Virginia's, and she didn't open her mouth. (She didn't ask anyone to sign it either. Maybe with all the turmoil, she forgot.) Think of it this way, Patsy: This family loves to tell stories about itself, and the stains will be fodder for another interesting family story. I am a master at this type of logic. It's a great mental exercise that usually puts me in a better frame of mind. It works this time too; almost instantly my spirits lift. I'll just consider this whole unforgettable dinner experience as a big favor from Bobby.

It's already getting late, and I still have to serve coffee and dessert. Afterward the children, as a sort of pre-Christmas treat, will get to open one gift each, as is our custom on Christmas Eve. "I hate to interrupt," I call, "but I've got coffee ready, and some delicious desserts." Our usual practice is to sit around the tree and enjoy our dessert and coffee. But in light of the mess made at dinner, and hoping to avoid a similar living room disaster, I decide we will sit at the dining table again—this time without the famous tablecloth.

Our children are not interested in dessert, but they are very interested in the one gift each child is permitted to open. They are running back and forth picking up everything under the tree. They shake and listen and comment loudly on each package—such a major decision to pick just one. From our seats at the table, we adults can easily watch their excited performance. The children have so much advice for one another and act so silly about these gifts that we are all howling with laughter—all except Bobby.

Amid the fun and frivolity, I notice Bobby, bent over his coffee, glaring at the riotous scene before him, mute and pensive. (No sane person could have ever guessed his future plans for these harmless toys.) His children run up to him and excitedly show him their gifts: a doll apiece for the girls, and a couple of cars and stuffed animals for the boys. Bobby draws back from them and mockingly comments, "Well now ain't y'all got some pretties."

Oh, Bobby drives me crazy! Not more than thirty minutes ago I used my special twisted logic and made peace with his thoughtless behavior. Now this. I think to myself, if you didn't want your children to experience Christmas, why did you bring them to my house on Christmas Eve? Everyone hears his disapproving remark and sees him shrink back from the toys. Once again we are all on guard.

Very shortly, Stan and Anna announce that they must be going as they are driving to Arkansas early in the morning to spend Christmas weekend with Stan's family. That announcement is good enough for the others, and they start leaving for their own homes too. I open the door for Leigh, my sweet friend, and she pauses on the porch for a minute. She looks worriedly back at me, trying to read my take on the predicament my family is in. I close my eyes for a moment and sigh. "I'll call you soon, Leigh. Merry Christmas."

"Please do, Patsy," she says glumly. "And Merry Christmas to you."

Mother and Daddy are slow to leave, and I know Mother wants a moment alone with me. "I want to give you and Daddy a piece of my banana bread and some fruitcake for your coffee in the morning," I say louder than necessary as I lead them into the kitchen. Billy, obliging me, becomes engaged again with Bobby and the children.

"Patsy, baby, how are you going to manage all this?" Mother whispers.

"We'll be okay," I assure her. "We've got plenty of room. Bobby, Kurina, and JaJa will take the guest room. The old twin mattresses are perfectly good, and we can put them on the floor for the kids. We'll figure it out and be fine. But I guess we won't be coming to your house for dinner tomorrow after all?" I question halfheartedly, knowing full well the answer.

"No," Mother agrees, shaking her head. "But we will bring the ham over here, and I've got some other things. Let's talk in the morning."

"Okay, but late morning, Mother. And let me call you. I have a feeling we'll be up all night." I wrap my arms around both my parents and am almost overcome with love for them. I think they have given me an upbringing that every child should have—in a secure, loving, and godly home. If anything goes wrong in my life, it won't be because of them. I kiss Mother in the spot I love to kiss, on her neck under her right jaw. In my whole life I have never heard her raise her voice to my dad; for that I am grateful. I love him so much I think I would die if he were hurt. In fact, if my parents ever had a quarrel, I don't know about it. They leave quietly without further goodbyes.

It's peaceful again in the kitchen, my little refuge. Needing a break, I open a coke and sit alone at the table. What a wild ride this day has been. It seems like a long time since I sat here this morning, sipping coffee and making plans. It's nearly ten o'clock now and we still have lots to do. The children must go to bed soon so Billy can put their toys together. Maybe Bobby will give him a hand. Virginia and I will finish wrapping gifts.

Virginia loves our late-night ritual of gift-wrapping. She will get a cigarette and a fresh cup of coffee and, with great ceremony, start planning her strategy. She likes to glue wrapping paper to every box and lid individually; sometimes she uses the same paper on the lid and box, and other times she will match or contrast the patterns. It seems that Virginia's love for beautiful, handmade things knows no limit. To me—far, far less artistic than Virginia—all this detail is a great excuse to prolong the evening. She and I will laugh and talk till nearly daylight. Since her divorce, Virginia always spends a few days with us during the holidays, and her stay is just one more thing that makes Christmas wonderful.

I think back to when I first met Virginia. It was fifteen years ago when Billy took me to meet his parents. I can still smell the wonderful, spicy aroma that filled their house that day. What a coincidence—Virginia was making the family fruitcake. It was a few weeks before Christmas, and she told me how the cake had to be wrapped in cheesecloth then put in brown paper and stored in a dark place; that dark place was her antique buffet, inherited from her mother, Belle. Opening the brown paper every week, and adding brandy through the cheesecloth, caused the cake to "ripen" in time for Christmas. I was just a teenager then and very impressed with the elaborate ritual she described.

I didn't meet Billy's father that day because he was sleeping, having gotten in only a little earlier from one of his "special assignments." But by the time Billy and I left the house, I felt I had been in the presence of the most gracious woman I had ever met. I think I came to love Virginia that very day.

Earlier this evening, Virginia whispered to me that she was thinking of getting a hotel room nearby since we might be crowded with Bobby's family. Actually, because Bobby and his family are here, I want more than ever for Virginia to stay. Thinking quickly, I said, "You can have Allison's bed, and Allison and Katie will sleep together." She happily accepted my plan.

Finishing my coke, I feel considerably better, refreshed enough to rejoin my unexpected guests.

3. KING OF THE GYPSIES

"…be careful what you say for we make each other."
~ Graham Greene

I find both families in the den, still listening to Bobby. He is spinning some fantastic, uncensored tale about leading hundreds of gypsies, on horseback, through mountains in South America.

"Ten thirty, kids," I call out. "If Santa Claus is coming tonight, we had better go to bed." The adults will be glad to leave this bedtime chore to me, I think to myself, since, no one but Virginia even bothers to look up.

I am immediately distracted by Running Cub, who comes over rather cautiously and whispers up at me, "Aunt Patsy, I've got some firecrackers. Can we pop them?" He is so cute and precocious I know immediately that I am going to go along with him. In my refreshed mood, I instantly make plans of my own. I am dying to investigate that mysterious-looking truck parked behind the house. This might be my chance.

I bend down and say quietly to Running Cub, "It's so late; won't we wake the neighbors?"

"These firecrackers are not very loud," he assures me.

He is so funny I almost laugh. "That is good enough for me, Running Cub."

The other adults are focused on Bobby, and my girls, ignoring me

25

completely, are playing with Spring Flower and Lotus. This is a perfect opportunity for my plan. So, to the boys' delight, I conspire with them. "Put your coats on, and I'll get Running Cub and me a jacket. I'll get a flashlight and matches, and we'll meet on the back porch—but be quiet," I whisper secretively. "And don't let anybody see you."

The night is still and cold, and to our delight, a soft snow is falling. "We will have a white Christmas, boys," I say. "It will be the first time in years." I tell the boys to stay quiet and keep the snow a secret until after the firecrackers. I give the matches to Running Cub and tell him and my boys to go over to the right side of the yard. They can safely shoot the firecrackers there. "I'm cold," I say. "You be careful. I'm going to stay close to the house."

The minute the boys' backs are turned, I scoot behind the house, out the gate, and practically run up the thick plywood ramp that gives entrance to the back of the truck. Steadying the long flashlight with both hands, I push the switch.

The first pool of light falls on a sight that seems so staged and unreal that I freeze with disbelief. The answer to a troubling old mystery is solved in that instant. Lying here and there like worthless rags are my grandmother's quilts, six or eight of them, scattered around, stained and dirty. I shine the light closely on a couple of my former treasures and realize that the abuse these beautiful heirlooms have suffered cannot be mended.

Bobby, pretty much as far back as I can remember, helped himself to about anything he wanted. But my quilts? I had missed them years ago, and the loss had puzzled and saddened me. But more important, that loss had broke my mother's heart:

On my twenty-fifth birthday, my parents gave a "milestone" dinner party for me. That evening, Mother ceremoniously gave me ten of my grandmother's quilts. Mother was always proud to tell anyone that she grew up on a cotton farm, in a family of eleven children. She had a great time that night at the party telling us stories about the heritage and art of quilting and particularly the history of these quilts. As a young girl she had watched her four older sisters and her mother— with needle and thread dancing over the quilting frame—pull each tiny stitch of the beautifully patterned quilt tops perfectly into place.

Mother's favorite was a quilt of many circles. The circles were fashioned from pieces of her and her five sisters' outgrown clothes. Even as adults the six sisters had fun recalling the various dresses and blouses represented. "Ruby, remember that dress," Mother said, pointing at a piece of navy-blue material with white polka dots. "Aunt Bernice made it for you, and you wore it Easter Sunday. The rest of us were so jealous we could die." The sisters could tell a story about almost every scrap, not only in that quilt but the others as well.

At any rate, the quilts reminded Mother of her girlhood, and when she asked about them later, as I knew she eventually would, it was with shame and guilt that I had to admit they were missing—and furthermore, that I had no idea how they had been lost. Looking at them now, I know I will not tell Mother the quilts had been stolen by my brother-in-law. Nor will I tell her that I found them in his filthy truck.

The shocking discovery of my heirlooms, stained and cast aside, seems to symbolize something—I don't know what—but it has brought me lower than I have been all evening. Even the babies climbing on the tablecloth couldn't match this sight. I do, though, glance briefly around the floor and sides of the truck, dreading what else I might find. I am mindful enough to realize that the truck is not a van type, with solid walls and a top, as I had thought, but only a frame holding a huge tarp over the top and sides.

I'm not much surprised to see hens roosting in the truck and straw scattered over the floor. Also traveling in the truck is a horse—a beautiful mare—and her colt. I had seen them tied to a tree beside our porch when the boys and I went outside. That didn't surprise me either, because earlier in the evening I overheard Bobby tell Billy that the horse he traveled on in South America is here with them. Bobby and the mare are devoted to each other, so he said, and have not been apart in years. They obviously all share these cramped quarters: animals, children, and adults.

There are a few cedar posts added in the center, apparently to hold the tarp higher for standing and walking around inside. The truck is incredibly junky and crowded. A generous number of nails have been driven into the truck frame, and it appears that every nail holds something: beads, and lots of them; wooden imagery, like a sun and moon and star, perhaps having to do with their gypsy names; a dog's leash; pieces of brightly colored clothing; a primitive wreath of twigs and feathers; several bunches of dried flowers and leaves; some towels; and even a couple of plastic grocery-store bags of, what I assume, is food.

I am inside the truck for four or five minutes when the first firecrackers go off. I hurriedly step back outside, turning off the flashlight. It's not a moment too soon, for Bobby comes crashing out the back door yelling something about startling the horses.

As I run inside the gate and toward the boys, I toss the flashlight into the wintry-looking hydrangea bush at the back corner of the porch. "It's not the children's fault," I call out. "I told them they could shoot the firecrackers. I forgot about the horse."

Bobby's yelling has set a terrible-sounding dog to barking. I was not aware now that the family had a dog. It has been perfectly quite, even during my break-in. No doubt Bobby had told it to "stay" when they first arrived, and the dog had not moved till it heard its master's shout. That kind of obedience is not unusual for Bobby's animals. His unnatural ability to train and control animals, almost any animal, is legendary among our family and friends—an uncanny gift he and Billy share. Bobby makes a strange, soft chirp and the dog hushes instantly. "What's his name?" I ask as I approach the hundred-pound, silver-and-fawn-colored beast, untied and well behaved.

"His name is Sebastian," Running Cub says as he and my boys run past me to pet the dog. The snow is still falling, making the yard light and wintry as the children and the big dog romp. I want to tell those in the house to look out and enjoy this rare snow scene. Instead I step over to where Bobby is soothing the mare and her colt.

"I forgot about the horse," I repeat apologetically.

"No harm done," he says. "Meet Sheba. She and I have been through a lot together."

Bobby had flipped on the porch light when he came out, and it is when I draw closer that I realize the horse is not tied to the small tree, as I had thought, but is loosely tied to a supporting post of our back porch.

"Sheba is beautiful, Bobby, but she could certainly have done some harm, tied like this to the porch. If she had spooked, she might have broken this post loose." He made no reply. "Can we tie her somewhere else?" I ask.

"The horse is fine," he says. "It's people that cause animals to act crazy."

"Let's just tie her to this tree and be sure."

My icy stare and reasonable request mean nothing to Bobby. "I said the horse is fine," he repeats.

I won't win this dispute, not even on my own property. I know, from years past, that once Bobby declares something, he will get irrational defending himself. I don't have the will or energy to waste on him. It's too late and too cold.

"It's cold out here," I say to change the subject, still doubtful that our porch will escape damage. "Let's go inside where it's warm."

"It's not that cold," he contradicts me. He is without a jacket and standing barefoot in the snow. He tosses his head toward the truck. "Let me show you our home. He walks over to the bush and—I wasn't prepared for this—retrieves my flashlight. "We can use this to look around," he says, his voice matter of fact, as he shows the flashlight to me and snaps it on to check the light. I am dumbfounded. Bobby's old talents are not diminished. He is still as observant as a police investigator—and just as knowing. I make no excuse for the flashlight. What can I say? We keep our flashlights out here in the bushes?

"Sure, I'd love to see it," I say with a rasp in my voice, my throat tight with humiliation. Not only did he find my flashlight but my snowy footsteps will still be visible around the truck and on the ramp. Well, as sure as my footprints will reveal my curiosity, the quilts will reveal Bobby's theft. I'm sure he hasn't forgotten that the quilts are in plain view in the truck; but he knows I won't mention them. This is some sort of fools' game we have played many times before: no questions, no confrontation, no involving other people. *What was I thinking, over the years, never confronting him? But no one ever did, it seems—so that even his involvement in a tragic death had gone unchallenged.*

29

"Come on." He jerks the flashlight in little jumping motions from my feet to the path he is taking, the idea being to follow him behind my house, through the dark, out to his gloomy "home." I don't like being alone with Bobby, but the boys have gone back inside, and apparently Billy is too busy to notice our absence. When I hesitate, Bobby turns to face me. He cocks his head and juts his bearded chin forward, questioningly. With a touch of sadness, I remember how seductive that mannerism had once been. I trail behind him despite my uneasy feeling.

Bobby, leading our little two-man parade, looks like a shabby drum major marching along in the dark, picking his bare feet straight up and down off the snow. What a shame—those feet should be in designer shoes. With that thought, a most pleasant memory surfaces:

I am walking with Billy and Bobby, and we are approaching luminous, beveled glass doors. We are in the main hall of their parents' country club. The boys are seventeen. They look and smell wonderful. Bobby holds the door open for Billy and me, and as we enter the warm glow, people around the room are watching us, unashamedly. They continue to watch as Billy and Bobby swagger in with an uncertain young elegance; they watch as the boys walk around, greet friends, laugh their warm laughs and smile their electrifying smiles—dazzling the entire room. The boys' pedigree: twin sons of the popular I.B. and Virginia Hale. The couple's friends are beaming with goodwill. There is so much hope for the Hale boys—many expectations, endless possibilities.

But in only a few months, a young girl's death will bring misery to this family, and suspicious questioning to the lips of those smiling friends.

The soft thud of Bobby's footsteps on the ramp brings me back to the present. He is at the top of the ramp now, waiting for me to come up. I look at the dark entrance and start slowly climbing toward him, slipping backward a little in the snow with each step. He studies my progress but doesn't offer a hand. I'm glad he doesn't.

Bobby flashes the light around, and I see pretty much the same things I had seen earlier, only this time it looks even more like a junky storage room.

My eyes follow the light around, looking for something to break the silence. "What's this?" I ask, picking up the wreath of twigs and feathers I had noticed earlier.

"That's one of Kurina's nature arrangements. The feathers are from a bird that died at our last camp in Arizona. Kurina and the girls felt real sorry for the bird, and this little wreath is its memorial." He points out several bunches of dried flowers and what looks like herbs hanging upside down from nails. "Kurina likes to pick flowers and plants from around our favorite camping sites." A string of leaves hangs from a nail near the bird wreath as well as some pieces of dried cactus with the flowers attached.

"Kurina sounds tenderhearted, Bobby, and she must love nature," I say.

"Yes she is, and yes she does," he confirms.

"Do you all sleep in here?"

"Almost never." He shines the light on a large folded tent hanging on some hooks. "That's our bedroom. And this is our kitchen." The light reveals a large galvanized bucket and a galvanized dishpan that holds eating and cooking utensils.

"How do you cook? Do you have a camp stove?"

"No, we build fires. You have to know a lot about survival, living like this, and we've learned about all you need to know about camping and cooking and building fires. Kurina enjoys building cook fires. She knows how to make every kind of campfire—depending on what she wants to cook."

"That takes a lot of skill. Billy always built our campfires. Do you remember, Bobby, when you hated camping? Billy and I loved it, but you never wanted to go."

"Well, yeah, there came a time when I didn't like hunting and camping anymore; I didn't like the inconvenience. Getting dirty and sleeping in bags didn't appeal to me. You know how I was back then. I wanted to dress up and take my dates to swank places."

"Yes, Mr. Neiman Marcus, I remember well," I say with a laugh.

"Yep, I was pretty sharp back then. But I've changed a lot over the years. I've experienced a whole lot of things too—things I'll tell you and Billy about later."

I want to change the subject. "Do you put the tent up every night?"

"No. As a rule we just leave it up. We usually stay in one place for at least two weeks, sometimes more. Ordinarily our stay has a lot to do with what's going on in that particular area. We just came here from the Rainbow Festival in Arizona. We were there for close to three weeks."

"Is that a problem, Bobby, staying so long? I mean you've got horses and a dog?"

"Not a problem. When we find a place we like—maybe it's got a stream and some grass—if I can find the property owner, I'll tell him we're just passing through and need some time out. I ask him if we can stay a few days—tell him about the animals, tell him we're careful with fire; nobody's ever turned me down yet."

"How long have you been living out of this truck?"

"Pretty much since we met. Kurina calls it our honeymoon truck. Both babies were born in it."

I shudder at the thought of childbirth in this chaotic jumble. "Kurina is so young. Does she like living like this?"

"She loves it, and so do I. It's freedom. No bills, no bosses, no jobs; I guess we're just gypsies at heart."

"Are you really gypsies, Bobby?" I think of the two children traveling with them: one belonging to a former wife and the other, Running Cub, so far unidentified. "I mean in your minds and hearts? Do you believe in their beliefs? I heard you tell Billy and Virginia that you were leading a large band of gypsies in South America."

"Yeah, leading and teaching. And they taught me a lot of things."

"Well, from what I've heard, Bobby, and from a movie I saw recently, if you were actually leading them and they looked to you for direction, then that means you were king of the gypsies."

"Really." I can feel him stare at me in the dark. "You actually sound concerned."

"I don't know if I'm *concerned*... Well, maybe a little."

"Oh, come on, let's go," he says dismissively. "We're losing the light."

4. NO COMPROMISE

"People will forget what you said, people will forget what you did,
but people will never forget how you made them feel."
~ Maya Angelou

When we step outside the truck, the snow has stopped falling.

"Well, I was hoping this would be a white Christmas," I say, "but it won't be very white."

"No," Bobby answers, "the snow will be nearly gone by morning."

When we walk by the mare and colt, to my relief, Bobby unties the mare. "Sheba's used to the place now," he informs me. "She'll be fine without tying." He talks softly to the horses and to Sebastian. I shake my head in amazement. Not twenty minutes ago we had nearly had a standoff about the mare being tied to the porch; now she's fine. Well good! I climb the steps and go inside.

In the kitchen, Billy has fresh coffee brewing—fragrant and welcome after the cold yard. He is in a good mood and dancing around. Billy is hardly ever still anyway. "I thought I would have to come after you." He flashed me a huge grin, what he calls his "Hale smile." I love that big grin; it shows me he is happy and content. He looks out the window and sees Bobby still with the animals. "Bobby showed you the truck?"

"Yes; he wanted me to see it. He calls it their 'home.'"

"They've been living out of that truck for three years. Can you believe it?"

I don't want to be negative and spoil the mood, so despite what I really think, I answer offhandedly, "I bet it's a blast, like a three-year camping trip."

Bobby pops through the back door. "Did you know it's been snowing?" he asks.

"Yeah, the boys told us. We went on the patio about the time it stopped. We noticed the light and figured you were showing Patsy the truck. I think she likes it. She says you've been on a three-year camping trip, and you know how she likes camping."

Well, maybe not quite, I think. There are still questions I want to ask at some point. For instance, is it hard to always have drinking water for such a big family—out in the wilds? I know the streams are polluted, if only by grazing or wild animals. From what we were told in school, drinking slow-moving stream water is a good way to get sick; I guess they have to boil the water. I also wonder about the simple convenience of a chair for Kurina and a table to eat on. Cooking and eating picnic-style on the ground, in all kinds of weather, through two pregnancies, and while nursing two babies, actually goes beyond my idea of camping fun.

I leave the men in the kitchen and go to the den. The door is closed, but on the other side I can hear Kurina talking with Virginia. I alert them with a light knock and go in. Virginia's wrapping paper, probably two dozen rolls, is laid out on the floor. I watch as she crawls around, sorting through the rolls for patterns and contrasts. It's always entertaining to watch Virginia transform plain boxes into works of Christmas art. Tonight she has more to wrap than the typical Christmas Eve: the gifts she brought and at least a dozen gifts we've come up with for Bobby's family. I'm especially excited about my gift for Kurina. It's a beautiful warm shawl I've never worn, and I asked Virginia to secretly wrap it for her. The shawl is brightly colored and Kurina likes to wear color. I think she will love it.

I watch this young, vibrant girl, chatting continuously and nursing her baby boy. The two of them make a lovely sight. I tell her,

"Kurina, you look like a Christmas Madonna." She pauses just long enough to smile up at me and continues talking. I had noticed early that Kurina, though young, is outgoing and likes to talk. She has a hearty, loud laugh too, and laughs often.

"The kids are upstairs?" I ask during a pause in the conversation.

Virginia answers, "We need to get started wrapping soon. I sent them up to get ready for bed. Allison said she'll get pajamas for everybody."

"I'll run check on them—and get them to bed as soon as Billy and Bobby take the mattresses up." I had explained the sleeping plans to Kurina earlier, and she seemed to be in agreement.

Upstairs I find the children brushing their teeth and changing into pajamas, but they are moving slow. It's well past the typical bedtime frenzy, and I can tell they're tired. "Allison, keep the children up here, and we'll be back in a minute with mattresses."

When I get to the kitchen, the coffee is made and Bobby is spraying whipped cream out of a can into his. I had learned earlier, when I served dessert, that Bobby now likes not just cream but whipped cream in his coffee; and he learned that I have only the pressurized kind. Billy has filled cups for his mother and Kurina.

"Billy, can you and Bobby help me?" I ask. "I need the twin mattresses out of the garage for the kids. They are really tired, and it will only take a minute."

Billy is already walking toward the den balancing the two cups of coffee, and Bobby is right behind him with two cups, not even trying to keep them from splashing. "Can we just enjoy our coffee first?" Bobby said over his shoulder in an irritated voice. His tone soured my mood and I didn't answer. Knowing those two, they can "enjoy their coffee" all night long, I fumed silently, as I poured my own and tore off paper towels to blot Bobby's sticky spills.

I take my cup to the den and, to emphasize our situation, say to Virginia, "I know we've got a lot of packages; we can start wrapping as soon as the children are in bed. Billy and Bobby will put the mattresses out when they finish their coffee." I sit impatiently on the edge of a straight chair at the game table.

As soon as I take my seat, Bobby starts up. "I don't know what you've got planned, Patsy, but the Morning Star family will be just fine right here in this den."

Staring speechless at him over the rim of my cup, I recall Bobby's words: "We usually stay in one place for at least two weeks, sometimes more." I remember, too, the dining table and floor after dinner, and just a minute ago I watched Bobby carelessly spill sweet, creamy coffee on the new carpet. If they stay two weeks, our carefully renovated den will be wrecked. The fastidious Mr. Neiman Marcus once kept his person and his surroundings immaculate, but immaculate is a thing of the past. As a couple, he and Kurina are a disaster. I can't think how to respond, and Billy, as though there is nothing pressing on earth, sips his coffee.

Then, so he could be perfectly sure that I understood, Bobby, still staring directly at me, jabs his finger at the floor for emphasis. "Right here is where we plan to stay."

His hateful words fly at me, and I feel my breathing quicken. "Oh, is that right, Bobby? Well, I've got my own plans, and they don't involve you spending a single night in this room." *Those were my thoughts, but they were never expressed. If I had had the courage to take a stand, right then against his further abuse, who knows? It might have changed our lives. I'm just not sure how.*

I glance at Billy for some clue that he might support me if I object. His lack of immediate approval tells me he is not in favor of this arrangement; but his face is blank. I judge that he is waiting for me. Maybe I can try persuasion. "Bobby," I finally say, "you're calling this room a den, but it's more like Grand Central Station. You and Kurina will have no privacy whatsoever. In fact, we don't use this as a den; we use it as our family room. We are in here all the time. Before Billy gets home from the clinic, the children and I are in this room at least two or three hours every day. I wish we could let you stay here, since you like it; but I'm sorry, we have to have this room. It's the only place to do the children's homework and their school projects."

"That's great. We'll love the company," Bobby says.

"Bobby, we spread out all over the room! I do all kinds of chores in here, like pile clothes and fold them on the sofa, and iron—so I can be with the children. And sometimes they have a TV show to watch."

"Sounds fine to me. So what's the problem?"

"Well, one problem is that we get up at six o'clock in the morning. This room is a regular beehive from that time till eight o'clock, when I take the children to school and Billy leaves for the clinic. I really mean that. As soon as we're dressed, we gather right here under our Peace Maker sign." I pointed out Billy's beautiful art project on which each of us had, painstakingly, carved our favorite Beatitude from the book of Matthew. "We also make plans for the day. Billy likes to know what each child will be doing: taking music lessons, playing ball—that's our private family time. And, Bobby, that private time is important to us. After we have breakfast, we come back in here to gather up books and homework. I don't think you want to wake up that early and be right here in the middle of our family activity."

"I'm telling you it will be fine. We don't mind getting up early—in fact, we usually do."

"And I'm telling you, Bobby, our mornings are frantic. With twelve of us in this room at the same time, we'll be running all over each other. I don't think we can manage it. Honestly, upstairs I have a beautiful queen-size bed for you and Kurina. It will be comfortable and private, and you'll only have to share the bathroom with Billy. I want you to come up and see it."

"All that would be real nice, Patsy, but we like it here." He punches his thumb toward the patio. "And we've got our animals right outside this door. Besides, we've got a fireplace in here—this room is perfect. And look at this sofa; just about all of us can sleep on it."

Yes, look at this sofa, I think. I bought it through a designer and paid quite a lot for it, not that you would care. This arguing back and forth is maddening. I wish Kurina or Bill, or even Virginia, would help me convince Bobby that when six people drop in to stay—for no telling how long—sleeping arrangements and preserving privacy are important.

When Billy finally spoke up, he had a cheerful sound of discovery in his voice. "Patsy, you forgot something—school doesn't start back for another ten days. Why don't we try Bobby's plan till then and see how it goes?"

No, I didn't forget about school, but, defeated, I answer, "Fine. Sure. We can try it till then."

Virginia lights her cigarette with a quick, loud scratch and strolls into the kitchen for fresh coffee. I follow her, carrying a clean ashtray. We look at each other and shrug our shoulders. I muster a little laugh for her benefit and say, "You know Virginia, this evening feels like Yogi Berra's 'déjà vu all over again.' Every time I get my bearings, I'm in another conflict with Bobby."

"Yes, he's good at disrupting things, Patsy. We both know that. I wish there was something I could do or say. But if I had, it would have just caused more trouble. He would have been as obstinate to me as he was to you. He was going to strong-arm his way into having your den, regardless. "

"I know it. In light of the way things have started, probably the whole visit will be like this. He's not going to accept any suggestion I make. If I had told him that their only choice was the den, he would have been indignant. I can hear him now: 'Aren't we good enough for your guest room?'"

Virginia laughs but says, "He won't take orders from anybody, and certainly not from a woman. Sometimes I think Bobby really doesn't like women. I wonder if he even likes me, his own mother. He never agrees with me about anything either—just like with you. One good thing, though: At least he and Billy aren't fighting. My boys are volatile, you know that, and I was expecting that any minute Billy would have enough of Bobby. I'm keeping my fingers crossed."

Virginia continues in a reflective voice. "Billy and Bobby have been fighting all their lives, Patsy. Did I ever tell you about the terrible incident when they were recovering from scarlet fever? They were about two years old."

"I don't think you did, Virginia. Seems like I heard somehow that they had scarlet fever; probably Billy told me. But that's all. I guess he didn't remember anything about it."

"Then I'll tell you. You already know that the twins were born in Boston. I.B. was working for the FBI at the time, and we were living there. We lived in Boston for several years. While we were there the twins, when they were about two years old, contracted scarlet-fever. When the doctor diagnosed their symptoms as scarlet fever, it nearly scared I.B. and me to death. Scarlet fever in the early forties was dead serious, and these were barely two-year-old toddlers. The doctor admitted them at once to the hospital, and as soon as we could drive there, our babies were put in isolation. They were also put in the same bed—the nurses said so they wouldn't cry. At first I could only look through the glass at my poor little boys. After a couple of days I was allowed into their room, but I had to wear a lab coat–type cover-up and a mask. It was interesting to me, and also troubling, that Billy would reach out and want me to hold him, but Bobby would turn away from me.

"They eventually recovered. And when we got them home, I put them in one of their baby beds with tall side railings. I was thinking they would like to be together, as they were in the hospital. That was a mistake. I went back in the room a little later to check on them and was horrified by what I saw. Those barely recovered babies were fighting for all they were worth. One of them had the other by the eye and ear, digging in with fingernails. The other twin had practically the same hold on his brother. They were so young and looked so much alike, I don't remember who was who. I think one thing that made this episode so shocking was that neither of them uttered a sound. They both had bloody scratches and black eyes and even bites—and they had inflicted all that damage to each other in grim silence. After that, it was back to their separate beds. I didn't dare leave them alone together for fear they would hurt each other."

"You mean they started fighting that young? That's incredible, but I'm not surprised. Since we were young teens, the twins used to alarm me and their other friends with how loud and violent they would become with each other, sometimes for no reason that was apparent to us. But, you know, they stopped actually fist-fighting when they were sixteen or seventeen. Do you remember? Bobby really got the best of Billy in one fight, and after that Billy declared, 'I am the lover and Bobby's the fighter.'"

"I do remember that," Virginia says, "and what a relief it was."

"All of us friends were glad when it happened," I say. But, I think to myself, that incident didn't stop their loud verbal abuse of each other. The fact that they have been together for more than six hours now without a cross word is unprecedented.

Virginia and I walk back to the den, realizing that we need new plans. "Where are we going to wrap the packages?" Virginia spreads her hands toward the cluttered floor. "In the living room we might wake the children."

"Well, I guess that's a problem now," I answer, looking at Billy, half expecting him to ask Bobby what to do next.

"No problem on this end," Bobby declares. "We'll stay out of your way. You wrap and build right here as planned. Our kids don't believe in this Santa Claus thing."

I don't answer his insulting remark. "Speaking of the children..." I say, heading for the stairs.

I find Allison, Spring Flower and Lotus together in the big guest bed. The two little guests are asleep, but Allison is still awake. "Can we sleep here, since Uncle Bobby doesn't want it?" she asks.

"Of course you can, my darling Ears. Thank you for helping Mommy." This little blond-headed doll heard all that argument, I think, and she figured things out for herself.

In the other rooms, my two boys are asleep in Will's bed and Running Cub is in Ben's. Katie is in her own bed, leaving Allison's for Virginia. These kids are more capable than their contrary parents, I think. Considering this sudden change of plans, they have done everything just right and without our help.

I bounce downstairs and announce, "Good news. All of our wonderful children are fast asleep." I spread my hands toward the floor. "We can start this job anytime."

Billy springs to his feet with excitement. "Okay, Bobby, let's get this wagon built."

"Another thing," I add, tapping my watch. "It's midnight." I pull the door shut and yell softly, "Merry Christmas!"

5. THE DAY AFTER CHRISTMAS EVE

"And merry Christmas to you." Billy hugs me and becomes animated and silly, grabbing me and dancing around. Bobby and Kurina laugh out loud at him and do their own little do-si-do. Virginia produces a plate of cookies and turns the radio to Christmas carols to work by. We sing along with the carols—I am surprised at how much Bobby and Kurina enjoy singing—and we get busy with the task at hand, which is to finish all this Christmas stuff before the sun rises. All of us, including Bobby, are jovial and in the Christmas spirit, mostly thanks to Billy. A big part of Billy's charm is that he can make any occasion fun—in this case, putting toys together—so that even loose screws bouncing under the furniture make us laugh uncontrollably.

At last, well past two in the morning, all the gifts are wrapped and toys put together and we are winding down this incredibly long day. I think we all feel good and of one accord, and I'm looking forward to some rest.

I hurry to the linen closet and return with clean blankets and pillows for Bobby and Kurina. But Bobby has one more surprise for me: "What are you doing, Patsy?" he asks in a concerned voice. "We wouldn't think of putting you to all this trouble. We've got plenty of quilts in the truck. We'll use them!"

I drop the bedding on the sofa and turn to Bobby, my second appeal of the evening racing through my mind. "Bobby, I've seen those quilts," I begin, "and they're not very clean. I honestly prefer that you use my blankets."

"Don't be ridiculous. They're perfectly fine; we use them all the time." He looks at me with such questioning innocence I almost wonder if I'm mistaken; maybe they are fine. I feel he is taunting me. He can't be serious.

"That's actually my point, Bobby. Outside is one thing, but I really don't want them in the house."

"Well," he says as he walks toward the kitchen, all of us but Kurina following him, "we're used to them, and we want to use our own quilts." He grabs the flashlight off the counter and goes out the door—Billy right behind him.

I turn to Virginia. "Do these decisions just spontaneously pop out of his head to drive me crazy? Every time I think things are okay, he comes up with some new harassment."

"Weren't we just talking about this earlier, Patsy? He's my son, but I'll say it again: He's a disruptive force. And he probably can't help it," she adds softly.

Oh, he probably can help it too, I think. I recall our teenage years and remember how Bobby liked to make girls cry. I think it made him feel important. Maybe that's what he wants from me. If I break down and just bawl my head off, will he let up?

"Bobby's obviously going to do whatever he wants, regardless of me, Virginia. He knows now that Billy, for some reason I don't understand, won't object to anything he says. I've had enough of it. I'm going to bed."

"Please do, Patsy. I'll stay up till Bobby gets settled with whatever it is he's dragging in."

"Quilts. Just be looking for quilts, dirty and stained."

"They must be special," she says with a grin. "I may have to borrow one myself."

"They are very special," I say, starting to laugh, but withholding the information that they are actually mine. "In fact, I noticed one that had a lot of circles—I think it's the Wedding Ring pattern—and it smelled like gasoline. Tell Billy to bring that one up for me." We are both dead tired but laughing.

When Billy comes to bed, I am still awake, and despite my good laugh with Virginia, I'm still angry with Bobby. "I guess you brought in those same filthy quilts that I saw lying around in the truck?"

"Yeah. It's for sure they weren't sanitary." Billy sounds annoyed. "The flashlight burned out, but even in the dark I could see him pull one out from under a hen. I almost said something. I don't know why he's acting so crazy."

I know why, I think to myself—to further show me he'll do anything he wants to do in my house. It's a power play.

"But you know," he continues, "I'm determined not to fight with Bobby. I've become a Christian since I saw my brother last. I want to be an example for him. I'm resolved to see this as a test."

"Well, your efforts haven't gone unnoticed. Your mother and I have been amazed. I guess I'm proud of you, especially for her sake, because she has been on pins and needles with all the tension Bobby is causing."

"We'll make it," Billy says, chuckling softly and settling into his pillows.

"Billy, I must ask one thing of you, though."

"What?" he asks, barely audible and sounding tired.

"Did you recognize those quilts?"

"What are you talking about?"

"I mean, Billy, those are the quilts Mother gave me. Remember my twenty-fifth birthday? My grandmother made them. Men may not notice things like that, but every quilt is different. I recognized them instantly."

He lies so quietly that he could have stopped breathing. I turn toward him in the dark. "Mother is coming tomorrow. She must not see the quilts. She thinks they were lost years ago. As a matter of fact, so did I. We really don't want Bobby exposed to my mother and dad, or to your mother, for that matter, as a thief—because my mother will say something if she sees them."

Billy continues his silence until I think he has fallen asleep; then with a long sigh, he says simply, "They'll be out of the house by noon."

I wake to the muffled sound of the boys rummaging for their coats in the hall closet below, and rolling the new bike and wagon outside. It will be cold this early. I'll check in a little while to be sure they're warm enough. Our quiet street will have little or no traffic on Christmas morning, but other children will be out with their new Christmas things—and some parents too.

Our children expect us to get up late on Christmas morning. When they get hungry, they have milk and whatever holiday breads and cookies I leave out for them. The children also know that, as is our custom, they can play with the things that "Santa brought" but must save the wrapped packages until after brunch and we will open them together.

I prop on my pillows, listening absently to the faraway sounds of the children; but my thoughts turn inward.

For probably the first time in my life, I am waking up on Christmas morning in less than a buoyant mood. I guess I'm overwhelmed by all that went on here last night. I wonder what today will hold. From the time Bobby surprised us before dinner last evening, I've been overruled by him on every decision I've tried to make. No doubt that's the way it will continue. He is contrary and immovable, and he's not going away for some time. I wish Kurina would encourage him to cooperate with me, but she might as well be one of the children. Furthermore, my husband is practically his accomplice. Oh! This line of thinking will only make me feel worse. Stop rehashing your grievances, Patsy, I think. Who was it that said, "It is a sin to rise up early and drink the cup of sorrows?"

Coffee! That's what I need, and soon. I'll stretch out in the living room with the girls and a fresh hot cup—sounds good. I ease out of bed and let Billy sleep.

Downstairs the three older girls are playing quietly. As usual, Allison is in control. They all let out happy little yelps when they see me. I pull the footstool over so I can be right at their level and give each girl, in turn, a good tight hug and snuggle my face into each little warm neck. Lotus responds lovingly to me, and I know she needs a mother's affection. Surely Connie is somewhere missing her little girl on Christmas morning. I smooth the child's dark hair away from her beautiful face. You little doll, I think to myself. Why are you here with this strange couple?

I've got to stop thinking things like this now. We've got to get through today. If I'm going to worry, I'll worry about it tomorrow. "Did you girls eat something?" I ask.

"We ate some cookies," Katie says.

"Well," I say, goosing her under her arms, "I'm going to eat a cookie myself."

The Morning Stars are still asleep, I notice as I pass the closed den door. I think the satisfying thought: "You love that room so much, Bobby. Just stay in there for the rest of this miserable trip." But thinking can be risky; Bobby's so creepy, he'll sense me standing here and pop through the door.

After checking on the boys outside, I go to the kitchen and start the percolator.

Alone in the kitchen, thoughts of the children traveling with Bobby return to me. The most complete accounting he has given for them goes something like: "Running Cub is our friends' kid, and Lotus is my wife's kid. We're taking care of them for a while." It seemed to be a sore point, and as the children are apparently fine, I left it alone. But the memory of a curious phone call, one that I haven't thought of in a long time, keeps dragging at my attention:

"I have a call for this number from a Mr. Bobby Hale," the operator announced, *"And he would like to reverse the charges." Not having heard from Bobby in several years, I eagerly took the call.*

But a voice, not Bobby's, answered the phone, "Hello, my name is Judge X, and I'm calling from my courtroom in Hawaii. Is there a Dr. William Hale at this number, and if so, can I speak with him?"

"Judge, this is Mrs. Hale and my husband is on call tonight. I don't know when to expect him. Can I help you?"

"I see no reason why I can't talk with you, Mrs. Hale. Does your husband have a brother?"

"Yes he does—a twin brother, Robert Allen Hale."

"Well, I have before me a man claiming to be Robert Allen Hale, but he has no identification. Do you know his voice?"

"Yes, I do."

"Then I want you to talk with him and identify him for me. Can you do that?"

"Yes, sir, I can."

"Good. I can't proceed until I know who he is."

Bobby came on the phone and said urgently, "Patsy, I need to speak to Billy."

"Bobby, I don't expect him here till tomorrow sometime. What's going on?"

"Give me his phone number. I've got to talk to him. He needs to come out here!"

No, I thought. No! Billy will probably get mad at me, but I refuse to let him get further embroiled in Bobby's unending problems. Only last Monday, Billy and I had spent all day trying to help one of Bobby's former wives, and their child, through a very intricate situation and it troubled Billy deeply. "This is Bobby's child," he had whispered to me with concern. "He should be here, dealing with these issues himself."

Into the phone I said, "It's not possible to give you that number, Bobby. Please tell me what's happening. I'll tell him as soon as he gets home."

"That'll be too late!" he yelled. "I've been picked up on some crazy kidnapping charge, and I need my brother!"

I could hear some talking and scuffling on the other end. It sounded like the judge told the deputy to give him the phone. "Mrs. Hale, this is Judge X again. Is this man your brother-in-law?"

"Yes sir, he is."

"He told me that his father is an FBI agent. Is that true?"

"He was for years, Judge, but now he is head of security at General Dynamics."

"He also says he was married to the governor of Texas, John Connally's, daughter?"

"They were married when they were young teenagers, before Mr. Connally was governor."

"If I remember correctly, that girl was shot—and killed?"

How in the world, I wondered, did Bobby think this information was going to help him? "Yes sir," I answered. "It was ruled an accident."

"Well, ma'am, you can tell your husband that his brother is being charged with child abandonment. A young girl was picked up on the beach; and after

46

considerable investigation, the child care worker found Mr. Hale. The child identified him as her mother's boyfriend. We are looking for the mother. Hopefully she won't press charges against him and turn this case into a kidnapping."

"Judge, I pray not. My husband can't possibly go out there at this time. He's only been with his new position for a few months."

"Mrs. Hale, I can tell you with ninety-nine percent certainty that things will work out. We've got so many of these people wandering around this island; you know it's warm in Hawaii and they like it here. I'm going to continue this case till we find the mother, and that, most likely, won't be long. If she cares for her daughter, she will come to us. Hopefully we won't have to take custody of this child."

"What about Bobby?" I asked.

"He'll be with us until the mother shows up. If things don't go well, we'll be forced to call you again; otherwise you probably won't hear from us. I'm going to let you go now."

I toyed with the idea of not telling Billy about this call, but if things escalated, how could I explain myself? When he got home the next day, I put an especially good lunch on the table, then, as much as I dreaded it, started to explain Bobby's latest misadventure.

Always ready to take his brother's side, Billy turned on me. "What are you saying about my brother? You don't even know what's happening. There's bound to be a logical explanation."

"Well, I don't know what that explanation would be. Just look at this mess. What is he doing in Hawaii? And how did he get there—with no identification, and escorting a child he can't account for? Maybe I should have asked him, but he was in a courtroom."

"He did account for her. She was his girlfriend's child. Right?"

"Well, if he was responsible for her, he sure wasn't taking care of the little thing. Imagine abandoning a terrified child on a crowded beach."

He dropped his head into his hands. "Patsy, I miss my brother so much I can hardly stand it. My very soul cries out for him. If I could have heard his voice, it would have helped."

I tried to put my arms around him, but he sidestepped me. "I sympathize with you, darling," I said. "I know how it is with twins. But believe me, hearing his voice would not have helped you in this case. He was so irrational. He insisted

47

that you drop all of your own interests and go straight to Hawaii to take care of him. You would not have liked his tone. Billy, I just felt led to spare you the heartache."

"I don't mean to be harsh, Patsy. It's like you say, just look at this mess— Bobby in trouble in Hawaii, of all places! And insisting that I drop everything here and go straight to him? Bobby and his problems require too much attention. I don't have the time. I ought to call that courthouse, but I'm not going to."

"I'm glad you're not." I said. "The judge said they will call us if things aren't soon resolved. It's been close to twenty-four hours now, so I think he's home free."

We found out later that the abandoned child was Lotus, the daughter of Connie.

The scent of fresh coffee drifts through the house, and the adults start drifting toward the kitchen.

"I might as well fix brunch, don't you think?" I call this out to no one in particular but get a whole chorus of, "Yes!"

Everyone loves my Christmas brunch casserole, a truly decadent dish with sausage, eggs, hash browns, butter, cream and cheese. And, by tradition, I make it only on Christmas morning.

With the quilts in mind, I give Billy a meaningful look and say, "While I cook, maybe you all can straighten up a bit before Mother and Daddy get here."

I say this even though I know they will not be over until later. I phoned Mother just a while ago and she told me, "Considering you have such a crowd, Patsy, we are going to skip brunch this time and bring the ham over about four o'clock."

The important thing is that Billy takes the bait, and by the time I finish cooking, there is not a quilt in sight. Not only that but things are almost tidy. This bit of cooperation lifts my spirits considerably— it doesn't take much.

We have a leisurely brunch and a hurried cleanup, then playfully scurry to the living room to open presents. By tradition we let each child take turns picking a package and handing it to its owner. That way we can all admire one another's gifts as we open them one at a time. There are even some very nice things that we pulled together last night for our unexpected guests. In fact, the most elaborate gift of the day turns out to be the beautiful suede hunting shirt that Billy gave to Bobby.

In one of what I call Billy's "creative fits," he purchased a length of fine suede and also a leather sewing tool—an awl, I think it's called. We have a Tandy leather shop somewhere in town, and he probably got them there. He drew his own shirt pattern, freehand, on brown paper and cut the pieces out. Then he pinned the pattern pieces to the suede, cut the suede pattern pieces out, and then sewed the pieces together by hand. The zipper up the front was fitted flat and clean, and the collar and pockets and cuffs could not be more professionally perfect. He even sewed darts in the front and back to fit only his physique. This shirt is a work of art.

I think Billy not only inherited his mother's artistic ability but his grandfather's as well; for when Bobby opened the shirt, Virginia herself pointed out that her father had been a tailor.

I already knew the story: Joseph Kingsbery Jr. had founded and owned The Kingsbery Manufacturing Company, which designed and manufactured the King B Best Made brand and at least two other brand names of men's play and work clothes and uniforms. Joseph Kingsbery Sr., after his wife's death, moved from Atlanta to Texas and worked for his son's company, as treasurer and credit manager, until he was ninety years old.

Anyway, last night Billy, without my knowledge, put the suede shirt in a gift box and had Virginia wrap it.

Now Bobby is unwrapping his gift. Virginia is so excited that she shushes all of us in the room to be sure we watch. I see Bobby, with great care, pull the hunting shirt from Virginia's beautifully wrapped box, lifting his arms high to expose the shirt's full length. It is a surprise, all right, and it almost makes me sick. I am not happy with Billy. I can just see this stunning hunting shirt—the only one of its kind, testament to my husband's talent, and what should have been an heirloom for one of our boys—hanging neglected on a nail in that ragged truck.

My dim view of Billy's giving his shirt away is soon overshadowed by Bobby's jubilant spirit at receiving it. Bobby hastily unbuttons his old flannel shirt and drops it in Kurina's lap. He puts the soft new shirt on and, whooping with glee, dances around the room modeling for us. "Billy, my brother! This is perfect for my lifestyle. You did a super job. And look at this stitching—a tailor couldn't do better. You need to hire out to Neiman Marcus." Billy is smiling his biggest Hale smile ever.

"And look at this," Bobby says, pulling the zipper up and down. "Who would believe it—the zipper really works."

Virginia gets the twins' attention and obviously wants to give them further reason to believe in Billy's talent: "You already know that your grandfather, Joseph, was a tailor, but you don't know about Belle's side of the family." She continues to tell more family history: Her ancestor, William Bradford, before he came to America on the Mayflower, had worked with fabric. He was a weaver of fine cloth, and he also dyed silk. She says she thinks we can trace Billy's talent all the way back to the 1600s.

"Three hundred years? Mother!" Billy jumps up and is dancing around with Bobby as we all, especially Virginia, laugh our heads off.

When my parents come over in the afternoon for Christmas dinner, we have a much less dramatic repeat of Christmas Eve, and a much reduced menu—mainly ham sandwiches and leftovers.

6. VIRGINIA'S DEPARTURE

"Things that matter most in this world can never be held in our hand."
~ Gloria Gaither

Today is Wednesday, the day I've been dreading, the day of Virginia's departure. She has been with us since Christmas Eve. Now relatives along her route home to Austin eagerly await her annual visit with them.

Before Billy leaves for work at six in the morning, Virginia has coffee with him. She expresses her concern about leaving. "Billy, please continue to get along with your brother. You know I hold my breath when you two are together for long."

"We're grown now, Mother. The fistfights are over."

"You do know they may be here awhile. From what I was able to get out of Bobby, they have no definite plans."

This news sounds dismal to me, but Billy replies, "I hope they do stay, at least through January. I have a job lined up for Bobby, upholstering walls. He says he'll take it."

"Can he do that?" she asks.

"I'll be with him on this first job. He'll learn in no time. I'll get the word out, and there'll be jobs lined up if he'll take them."

Virginia walks Billy to the door for their goodbyes. When she returns to the kitchen, she looks at me with a hopeful smile but gives her head a little shake. I understand her sentiment and share it with her—neither of us is convinced that everything is going to be fine.

While I prepare the usual full breakfast for the children and the Morning Stars, which today includes chicken-fried steak and gravy and biscuits, Virginia gets dressed and packed for her trip home before coming down to eat with her grandchildren.

When Virginia comes in for breakfast, she is dressed in a tailored navy-blue pantsuit and small turquoise earrings. She is a modern-day study in elegance. Later I watch her as she walks through the living room, looking at herself approach the antique mirror—a noticeable spring in her step now. I watch her flip her hair back with her fingers and smile at herself in the mirror, and I realize that Virginia is already thinking of those other relatives, a cousin and a favorite aunt, and I know she is happy to be leaving here.

As I watch her carefully remove the old handmade stockings from the mirror's hooks and put them back into their boxes for next year, I think of her busy life. I hope she will fit this unstable situation with her sons here in Fort Worth into a small corner of her memory, to be dwelled on as little as possible. Maybe that's what will happen, for Virginia seems to be infinitely resilient. After she and I.B. divorced, though she had never labored outside the home, Virginia decided to give the work force a try. She took the Texas Civil Service exam and scored the highest grade ever made on that test. She was hired into Human Resources, where she interviewed and tested job applicants and placed those who passed the tests. At one point, Virginia interviewed Lee Harvey Oswald, the future accused presidential assassin, and placed him in a job. Before long, she was recruited to the State Capitol in Austin, where she was appointed by the governor as head of the Personnel Department for the Texas Employment Commission, where she has thrived. Virginia will return to her demanding job in the State Capitol next week, and it can easily be another year before we see her again.

I would like to add here that Virginia's encounter with Lee Harvey Oswald was the subject of a visit to her office by the Warren Commission investigating President Kennedy's assassination. Actually, my own and Lee Harvey's paths crossed in our youth and again, in a remote way, after his death. When he was young, his family lived in Fort Worth in the West Ridglea area on Ewing Street. Our good friend Milton lived next door and went to school with Lee. Milton had a close friendship with Robert Oswald, Lee's older brother. Their mother, Marguerite, moved her family frequently, enrolling Lee in twelve different schools. At one point the family moved back to Fort Worth, and he attended Arlington Heights High School, where Billy, Bobby and myself also attended. The Oswald family lived on Thomas Place, four blocks from Tremont, where my family lived. In school, Lee was quiet and preoccupied, seemingly in his own world. After a brief time, he dropped out to join the Marines. He was seventeen years old.

My close friend Jana's older sister, Jo Rae, was dating Robert Oswald and became engaged to Robert—who, by the way, was a well-liked and much respected young man. Jo Rae had some insights herself: When Lee joined the Marines, no one in the family expected him to last. After all, Jo Rae said, "He had pretty much been raised to be a drifter." Robert and Jo Rae's engagement was called off, but they remained friends. Robert continued to live in the Fort Worth area, and so did his mother.

Lee Harvey, as his family had predicted, left the Marines, and following a long-standing ambition, he defected to the Soviet Union. He fell in love there with a Russian girl, Marina, and married her on April 30, 1961. Soon she was pregnant and gave birth to a daughter, June. Lee's work and what he wanted for himself in the Soviet Union was short-lived and displeasing to him. Shortly after his daughter's birth and without saying anything else about his goals, Lee flew to Texas with Marina and the baby. It was while the family was in Fort Worth that Virginia, my mother-in-law, interviewed Lee and placed him in a welding job.

It seems to have been common knowledge that Marina and Lee had struggled to keep their marriage together from the first. All the hardships and moves, plus Lee's work habits, greatly affected the Oswalds' relationship. Now they had left Fort Worth and were back in Dallas. In her loneliness, Marina soon decided to move in with a Russian couple there. Lee left Dallas and went to New Orleans, where, in the summer of 1963, he became involved with a young woman he had met when both were hired at Reilys Coffee Company. This job was a cover for Lee—he was involved with making a biological weapon that he was to smuggle into Cuba, according to Judith Vary Baker. He fell deeply in love with Baker that summer, even though he was married and she was engaged to be married.

She, too, was involved with the biological project.

Lee flew back to Dallas a time or two to see his daughter, June, and his wife, Marina. Eventually Lee moved back to Dallas, where he had his final job at the Texas School Book Depository. After he moved back, their second baby girl, Audrey Rachel, was born at Parkland Hospital—within six weeks of the Kennedy assassination. Lee was never able to bond with this second child, for soon he, too, was killed by an assassin's bullet.

I think of the old saying "What goes around comes around." Years later, Jo Rae lived in Bedford, a suburb between Fort Worth and Dallas, where Marina had moved with her new husband. Jo Rae's own girls went to school and played with Marina and Lee Harvey's children.

After all the years of Christmas visits, today is the first time I feel I might lose my composure at Virginia's leaving. I walk her to her car, helping to carry a last armful of things. Although she is not usually an emotional person, she hugs me tight and says, "Patsy, you've got your hands full with my sons. I wish I could stay, though I've not been much help."

"Virginia, what would I have done without you?" I can say nothing more. I am already so choked with loneliness that my voice fails me.

Now I watch miserably from the front stoop as Virginia lets the engine run for a few minutes to warm before turning her car around in the driveway. She rolls the driver's window partway down and throws me a kiss, then drives away—picking up speed as she turns the corner and heads toward Camp Bowie Boulevard and Highway 35 South.

My children and the Morning Star family, having had breakfast with Virginia and having kissed her goodbye at the door, are already busy with their various activities.

With Virginia gone, my mindset is that I'm settling in for the duration of Bobby's visit and bracing myself for whatever that holds.

Feeling almost lost, I wander into the den, which is Bobby's domain now, and stare out the glass doors into the backyard. The older children are in the yard. It looks like Will and Ben are teaching Lotus and Running Cub to play a game that, to my knowledge, only our family knows—Frisbee golf. This game of Frisbee golf is another brainchild of my creative husband: More than two decades before the game's popularity started to spread across the United States, Billy had devised Frisbee golf for our children to play in this big, new backyard.

As if in a dream, I can barely hear Will giving animated instructions. I love watching him. I can see Billy clearly in his body movements and in his sincerity as he explains the rules of the game. Like Billy, he insists on exactness and getting things just right. My eyes follow the sound of our youngest son's clear, high-pitched voice, chiming in with a question, as he runs closer. Ben is running and pulling up his pants as he runs, his elbows pointed out to the side in an unconscious mannerism—the same mannerism his granddad, I.B., had exhibited all his life. Sometimes Billy and I laugh in wonder at this little genetic indicator.

In what feels like slow motion, I turn my attention back to the cluttered room and notice, again, the strange new odor. It moved in with the Morning Stars and increasingly permeates everything in here. It's not an unpleasant smell, just peculiar, a little like almonds. My grandmother's dirty quilts have been permanently removed to the truck, a safety measure against my mother dropping in and spotting them, but clothes, I guess clean and dirty, are piled on the floor and furniture. Several used coffee cups are arranged neatly around the stove. I suppose Bobby will finally have every cup and mug in the house sitting there. Feeling uncharacteristically stubborn, I decide I'm not going to move them again. What happens when he—or, worse, Billy—can't find a clean cup? It seems silly to ponder something so trifling, but I'm curious.

Bobby is sitting quietly on the floor with his legs crossed, yoga style. This pose irritates Billy; I think because it reminds him that several years ago Bobby was associated heavily with a well-known Maharishi in Spain and spent more than a year with him—as the driver of his gold Cadillac and as his right-hand man—learning all the while. When Bobby was sufficiently trained, he was sent back to Texas and, in Billy's assessment, wasted his time teaching transcendental meditation in Dallas and Fort Worth. Bobby also carried this teaching to the Northwestern states before finally giving it up. I can't tell whether he is meditating now, but I figure he must be. Kurina is lounging comfortably, nursing JaJa. They spend a lot of time on these two activities.

I slide my ever-handy comb out of the table drawer and turn my attention to little Spring Flower. She and JaJa are beautiful babies. I could become seriously attached to these children if I weren't afraid of losing them to Bobby's habit of abandoning wives and children, basically never to be seen again. We sit for a while, pretty much in silence, me talking softly to Spring Flower and combing her baby-blond hair. I need to pull myself together after Virginia's leaving, and it's good to sit here communing with this child, thinking mundane thoughts—like what to cook for supper, and whether I need to buy groceries.

Bobby unfolds himself and slouches toward the stove. My comfortable reverie is immediately disturbed. It is already toasty warm in here, but, as is tiresomely predictable by now, he is going to start another fire, or in this case, stoke the fire that is already going. He will drive me out of the room with the heat. The stove was one of the reasons Bobby gave for wanting to occupy our den, and we quickly learned why—he is obsessed with the stove and the fire. When Virginia was here, she wouldn't come into the den because of the heat.

The stove sits in the corner on a two-tiered brick platform, and if Bobby isn't sitting cross-legged on the floor playing his guitar or meditating, he is sitting on the first tier of that platform as close to the stove as possible, usually drinking coffee; I don't know how he bears the extreme temperature. He wants a fire regardless of the weather, which for the past couple of days has been fairly warm for December. Bobby's obsession with the fire is just one more point of constant irritation, not only to me but to Billy as well:

It was only yesterday—Virginia was still here—that Bobby had the fire going

56

so hot that Billy slid open the patio doors to cool the room. That gesture didn't even register with Bobby, for as soon as the stove wasn't red hot, he started to add more wood.

Billy, finally becoming impatient with this ritual, said, "Hey, man, what are you doing? We're not going to have enough firewood to get through the next cold spell."

Bobby, ignoring him, laid the piece of wood on the grate and slid it back into the stove to burn. Billy walked over to him, almost confrontationally. That's when I went into the living room where Virginia was reading, but we could still hear them and I could see them. "Are you cold?" Billy asked, sounding disgusted. "I thought you had been living in the wilds and going barefoot in the snow. It's hot as blazes in here."

Bobby looked back at him and replied, equally confrontational, "Maybe it is a little warm, but I like a fire."

"Well, yeah, I do too, but we're burning up. I'm afraid we'll all be sick. Besides, we're running out of wood."

"Where do you get this wood, Billy? I'll be glad to replace it."

"We get it off the ranch, and I cut every stem myself. It takes hours."

"Tell you what," Bobby said, "Kurina and I will drive out there in the truck, and I'll cut you a cord."

I don't know how he reacted to Bobby, but Billy walked through the living room and muttered at us, "If he actually cuts a cord of wood, he'll probably take down our only pecan tree."

He stepped back to the den and said, "Bobby, that offer to cut wood— forget it. I'll drive out with you this weekend. We're pretty selective about what we cut."

Billy headed for the front door, and I knew he was going to the clinic. "I'll miss supper tonight," he said. "Just leave me a plate."

I could tell he was mad and wanted some time to pass before he saw Bobby again.

Because I have no influence when it comes to Bobby, I felt a sense of satisfaction when Billy finally spoke up yesterday about the fire. It seems to me that Bobby is trying to push Billy's patience right to the limit. I'm almost sorry about this, but Billy is resolved to see the trials of this unexpected visit as a test of his new self-control. I just wonder if Bobby is conducting his own test. Knowing their history of competitiveness, it could be that Bobby sees Billy's every act of tolerance as a sign of weakness that he can exploit. In one of our discussions about the twins, Virginia confirmed my suspicion that Bobby has always tried to be one up on Billy. I think this rivalry accounts for Bobby pushing as far as he can safely push toward running Billy's household his own way. Bobby has created a tense atmosphere in our home—and for whatever reason, he is working to keep it that way.

On Monday, the day after Christmas, there was yet another example of Bobby's deliberate provocation: I had gone to the store for more groceries. Billy was at work, and I left the children in the care of Virginia. I thought surely that everything would be fine for an hour or so. But I am discovering that things are never fine when Bobby is around. When I returned home and walked inside, bags of groceries hanging from both my arms, Bobby's huge dog, Sebastian, was stretched completely out on my sofa—Bobby on one end of him, like a challenge to me, and Kurina on the other. Because Virginia never went into the den thanks to the heat, she had no idea the dog was there. "Bobby, Billy doesn't even let our own big dogs in the house, much less on the furniture," I protested. (Bobby already knows this rule because on Christmas Day he had brought Sebastian inside and Billy then put the dog out, saying, "There's too many of us, Bobby, and this dog is way too big to be in here.")

Bobby answered me, "Sebastian wants to come inside. I'll put him out in a while." He didn't even offer to put the dog on the floor. I just stood there staring at him, biting my tongue to keep from saying the angry things I was thinking. But I didn't need to say anything, as it turned out—he had already anticipated my argument. "Patsy, stop worrying about your furniture and how much you paid for it. All this stuff," he says, flipping his hand at the furniture, "is so unimportant in the scheme of things. Sebastian won't do a bit of harm to this sofa."

My throat was tight with anger while I finished unloading the car. Bobby, lounging comfortably with Sebastian, didn't move a muscle to help me, even though all the extra groceries were necessary for him and his family.

When Billy came home that evening, he was in a good mood and happy to see Bobby. I knew then that I would not mention the dog, Bobby's disrespect, or anything else negative that happened in Billy's absence, which in days to come would be considerable. Billy is more protective now of Bobby than he has ever been. The couple of times I dared complain, Billy found excuses for Bobby and accused me of questioning his brother's motives—whatever that means. If I am to get any cooperation from Billy, he will have to discover Bobby's infractions himself.

I am thinking all this stuff about how "I'll just be brave and bear up by myself," but the truth is, with Virginia gone and me even more vulnerable to Bobby's bullying, I need emotional support. What I really need is Billy's support, but I am not likely to get it. Reflecting on the deteriorating situation, I decide it's time to call our good friends Roland and Trish and invite them over. I want Roland, especially, to meet the Morning Stars.

Roland is an evangelist and preaches at many churches. Though much in demand and usually booked for weeks in advance, he nevertheless visits our church several times a year. That's how Billy and I met him and his wife, Trish, and we became great friends. We love being with them and have gone on several trips with them, including taking our children to Israel on one of Roland's annual guided tours.

It is only natural that I turn to Roland now, not only because he is a friend but also because I value his counsel. Roland has advanced degrees in theology and behavioral psychology and years of experience in clinical counseling. Because he is well known in our community, our church members who want personal counseling—marriage, child-rearing, depression, or other problems—are often referred to Roland's office. He is also one of the few counselors who have training in dealing with religious cults and the people who have been lured into them. Cults were a particular threat to young people in the late 1960s and '70s, and we're still not free of them.

When I reach Roland on the phone, he is eager to meet Billy's brother, and we make plans for him and Trish to visit us late next week when she returns from her mother's. I need a boost, and the promise of fellowship with our good friends gives me comfort.

As it turns out, so many things happen in the next week that Billy decides he, too, wants Roland to meet Bobby, and soon! He tells me that during their talks at night, Bobby has started arguing with him about some strange beliefs and theories he has picked up in the past few years. "I'd like to get Roland's take on this situation," Billy says. "I can't just take Bobby to Roland's office, which would be way too obvious, but you can invite him and Trish to the house."

"Oh, I'll be glad to," I answer. This is good! Billy will be much more receptive—thinking the visit I've already planned is his idea.

By Saturday our firewood, as Billy feared, is too far gone to last the week. I overhear Billy say, "Bobby, let's go to the ranch and cut that wood. The little bit we have left won't last you till evening."

I have not been to the ranch in months, and I want to go out and look around. The weather is not cold, so I say, "Billy, why don't we all go? We can have a hot dog roast and let the kids run wild." I look at Kurina, and she is smiling and nodding her approval. I knew she would be game for getting out of the house and onto some open land. My suggestion excites everybody, and in no time we have the portable grill, folding chairs, and everything we need for a romping good afternoon.

When we get to the ranch, we follow Billy and Bobby around until they find their cutting site, then the children want to explore the ravine and play. Kurina and I search for a picnic spot and decide to set up near the beautiful old oak grove.

The oak grove is where Daddy and I used to sit in the shade when I was a child. It is also the very spot where some of my young male friends from high school, including Billy, had buried a gambling machine—the kind known as a one-armed bandit. They kept that bandit a secret between themselves, and I didn't learn about it until two decades later, when the device, which had not been buried very deep, begin to surface. That's when I heard an interesting tale:

In the 1950s and early '60s there had been a ranch, with a dubious reputation among the adults in the locality, not too far down the road from here. This mysterious place was a popular party destination for the elite in the Dallas/Fort Worth area. Because of its clientele, it enjoyed the protection of the local sheriff. Growing up, I remember seeing the house many times as we drove to Daddy's land. When viewed from the road, the house, which sat on a rolling Texas hill, presented itself as just another great, sprawling ranch house. One of our high school friends—let's call him Eddie—had worked at this establishment as a young man. After the bandit surfaced, Eddie told us about what was politely called "the restaurant," and his work experience there.

When turning off the main highway, the fashionable guests drove through the ranch house entry gate and down a winding, two-lane drive. The drive curved around the bottom of the hill, where the trees had not been cleared away. In these trees stood a gatehouse with a large iron gate. "At the gatehouse," Eddie said dramatically, "you met the gatekeeper. He either knew you or didn't know you. If he did not know you, he checked with Mr. Arigo, the manager, and you were either told to leave or invited in."

Because of the height of the hill and the size of the house, there was not a better view in this part of the county. Most of the trees had been, tastefully, cleared off the hill, and no one could approach without being seen. This was a good thing for all involved, for even though a very good time could be had, much of it was illegal: gambling and drinking. Not only was gambling not permitted in the State of Texas but also the county was dry at that time.

The ranch was actually a prestigious gambling establishment with the best food in two counties. To get around illegally selling alcohol, the owners made drinks complimentary with the meal. The gambling ranch was modeled after the celebrated, illegal casino in Galveston and was owned by the same man and wife. This shrewd couple—let's just call them Mr. and Mrs. John Jones—had arranged for the ranch property to have at least the appearance of a working ranch. They also owned a couple of businesses in a small nearby town as a front for their money.

As Eddie was a good and reliable employee, one evening Mr. Arigo selected him for a special assignment.

He put his hand on Eddie's shoulder. "Eddie, son," he asked, "do you think you can drive Mrs. Jones's Lincoln Continental to Love Field? You will be picking up two gentlemen from Chicago. Remember their names, Mr. Arlotta and

Mr. Oggioni. You will drive them straight here."

"Yes, sir. No problem, sir," and Eddie was on his way.

When Eddie brought the Chicagoans into the club, there was an uneasy interest among the staff in the men, with their polished, typically Chicago look. One of the waiters, probably from Chicago himself, whispered to Eddie, "Boy, those men are Mob-wired from head to toe." Eddie just shrugged, not knowing for sure what the waiter was talking about.

Within four hours, Eddie was again summoned by Mr. Arigo. "You will be returning our guests to Love Field," he said. "The car is waiting." He motioned his head toward the door. The two well-dressed men stepped out of the shadows toward Eddie. This time he was paying closer attention and thought it strange that they, flying in from Chicago, had nothing in their hands, no suitcase, no briefcase, nothing. They smiled, real friendly, at him and followed him to the car. On the drive back, the men were more chatty and exchanged pleasantries and small talk with Eddie. When he dropped them off at the airport, he had the feeling that "those were really nice men."

His next special assignment was as a courier—or, as Mr. Arigo put it bluntly, "We want you to be our bagman." Every Saturday afternoon Eddie was handed a black bag to deliver to a club in Dallas. Mr. Arigo never told him what he was carrying, but he was almost sure it was money. After a few weeks, Mrs. Jones saw Eddie with the bag and asked Mr. Arigo, "How old is he?" After hearing Eddie's tender age, she told him, "No more! Find somebody else to do this job." So that ended his stint as bagman.

Eddie was afraid he would be fired, but Mr. Arigo found other jobs for him, one of them being gateman. One night he was on the gate and Mr. Arigo called him, saying, "Mr. Jones says he is expecting a Mr. Case to come here tonight. When he reaches the gate, simply tell him: 'Mr. Jones says to leave it in the car.' That's all you need to say."

So when Mr. Case gave Eddie his name, he said, "Mr. Jones says for you to leave it in the car."

The man's whole demeanor changed; he told Eddie menacingly, "Don't touch it; don't look at it; I don't want it moved."

He told Eddie too late because he had already looked at it as the man removed the object from his jacket and laid it on the seat. It was a chrome-plated revolver.

At the time, all the employees thought it odd that the club got away with gambling and drinking. None of them ever said a word outside the restaurant, but the law must have known what was going on in that place. Of course it was "protected," but they still had to at least pretend to keep up appearances, and the vice squad would drop in every now and then. They must have given plenty of warning, because by the time they got inside, the place was clean. Mr. Jones would welcome them and give them the best food in the house. Everybody smoked back then, so there wasn't even the smell of alcohol over all that smoke. Conveniently, the "vicers" didn't nose around much.

Then one night all the fun stopped. Eddie was not on the gate, but they all got the news: Mr. Jones told Mr. Arigo, "Leave the gate open and get everybody out!" He had been tipped off that the Texas Rangers were raiding that night. By the time the Rangers got there, everyone was gone—but they pulled all the one-armed bandits out of the house. The Rangers closed them down for three weeks. By the time three weeks were up Eddie had found another job and was starting a new semester at TCU. But during the shutdown, several of the one-armed bandits went missing as word got around that the ranch had been raided. Teenage boys in the area, hearing about the shutdown, and being naturally curious, went snooping around. Billy and some of his friends were among them. When they came across the "bandits," they hauled one out and stored it in Mr. Dorris's barn under the hay. Later, they realized your daddy would run across the bandit sooner or later, so they buried it in the only spot that was soft enough to dig in: the area near the oak grove.

Years later, when the bandit began to surface, due to some slight erosion, Billy told me his part in the story—which was interesting to me, and had been a huge adventure for him and his teen age friends. I still have some of the nickels from the bandit.

In the early '60s, vice and anything smacking of the Mob fell seriously out of favor—and the Texas Rangers were vigilant. "The restaurant" never recovered. One morning, as traffic flowed by on the highway below, it could be seen that, during the night, the beautiful ranch house had burned to the ground.

7. ROLAND'S FIRST VISIT

"Nothing in the whole world will ever be able to separate
us from the love of God."
~ Romans 8:39

Today is the day Roland and Trish are coming to lunch. I am in a happy mood, bustling around preparing for them, when the phone rings. I'm surprised to hear Roland on the other end: "Patsy, I should have called earlier. Trish didn't get in last night as planned. Her mother still can't be left alone. Trish will be staying with her a few more days."

"This is bad news, Roland. I'm so sorry that Mrs. Logan is still sick." Without waiting for his reply, I continue, "Why don't you come on, though? I bet you could use a home-cooked meal, and Billy is going to be here for lunch. No telling when you'll be free again, and we want you to meet Bobby."

"I've blocked my schedule till three… Okay. Don't hold me to the minute, though. I'm expecting a new client this morning. I might be half an hour early or late."

"Either way is fine. See you when you get here."

Sooner than I expect, I hear a car door slam, and I run to the window. Roland is walking toward the front door. Considering his position in life, as a counselor and evangelist, his looks are a little surprising. He has silver-white hair and looks uncannily like actor/comedian Steve Martin. It amuses him because people often, especially on airplanes, mistake him for Steve Martin. The persona suits him too, because Roland, despite being direct and plainspoken when serious, is also witty and loves to joke and laugh. He is always well groomed and immaculately dressed, whether casual or formal. He is well educated, with several degrees and a huge vocabulary. Roland is one of the most intelligent men I have ever known, and I have never heard a subject brought up, in any setting, that he is not well acquainted with.

Not ten minutes ago, Bobby borrowed my car and took all the Morning Stars to the grocery to buy his whipping cream. I like their trips to the store because they usually stay gone a while. With any luck, Bobby will take them somewhere for lunch. They will still be back in plenty of time to meet Roland.

"Roland, I'm glad you're early. We'll have a few minutes to talk before Bobby gets back. By the way, I didn't tell him you were coming today."

"Why not?" he asks as he hands me his jacket.

"Well, actually, I did tell Bobby that you and Trish would drop in sometime this week; I just didn't say when—the reason being I can never tell what Bobby might do. I just want you to meet him without him, uh, being prepared. I just want him to be himself."

"Are you saying he's not always perfectly genuine?"

"I don't mean that—well, yes, I do mean that. Billy told him what you do, and I don't want your meeting to be compromised by his put-ons. Oh, by the way, you've seen his picture." I point to the decade-old studio photograph of Bobby on the credenza. "Forget that; you won't even recognize him."

"Yes, you told me he came back a changed man. From the way you're talking, apparently not changed for the better?"

"No! For the worse, if that's possible."

"I thought I heard stress in your voice on the phone last week, and here it is again. Is this visit going well?

"Not very well, I'm afraid. For Billy's sake, I try hard to put up with his brother, but sometimes I can feel my nerves starting to crack. It's hard to keep my spirits up with Bobby constantly dragging me down."

"Constantly dragging you down? I'm sorry to hear this. Sounds like he got off on the wrong foot with you—and can't get his balance."

"That's putting it mildly, Roland. He's not trying to…get his balance. The truth is the opposite. The harder I strive to make things go well, and make this precious time together enjoyable—as Billy says, fruitful—the more Bobby does to drive me crazy! You wouldn't believe—"

"Patsy, don't," Roland interrupts. "We can talk, but I'd rather not get emotionally involved before I even meet him." Roland says this with a smile—to soften his reprimand, no doubt, but I know he already understands that I need his counsel.

Roland looks toward the kitchen. "Do I smell coffee?" he asks.

"You sure do! I completely forgot to offer you anything, even a seat." I motion him to the breakfast alcove, where the large, center pane of the bay window has been broken, then put back together with long, jagged strips of gray duct tape. "Forgive my bad manners."

"You've got a lot on your mind," he says distractedly, peering sideways through the duct tape at the horses outside. "That's a beautiful mare and colt. They must be Bobby's."

I wish he would ask me how the window got broken. "Yes, they are his. The mare has been with him for several years. He got her in South America when he was traveling with gypsies there; he said everyone in the clan rode horses."

"You don't say. Gypsies in South America?" He drums his fingers on the table, and I figure he would rather have heard that from Bobby.

"I'm sorry, but it's true. He'll tell you all about it. In fact, he'll be happy to tell you all about it."

"Well, anyway, I bet it was a mess, getting a horse from South America into the U.S. Did Bill help him with that?"

"No, he didn't. Actually, we didn't even know Bobby's whereabouts."

"That's right, you told me that." Roland positions himself on the alcove bench so his view of the backyard is unobstructed. In no more than a second, he has a surprised look on his face and his eyes lock onto the old truck parked just outside the fence. Roland's obvious fascination with the thing surprises me, and I watch with interest as he scrutinizes it through narrowed eyes. All of a sudden he laughs out loud and says, "I can't believe my eyes! The last time I saw one of those old camouflaged trucks, I was driving it piled with troops. We were roaring toward Fort Benning, Georgia. What do you know about that truck, Patsy?"

I put a mug of black coffee in front of him. "Of course that, too, is Bobby's. It's what they came here in."

"Is it? Wonder where he got it." Roland is rubbing his chin in thought and still staring at the truck. "I bet there's a story behind that."

"Well, part of the story is that that's what they've been living in for three years. Both their children were born in it."

"Three years and two kids," he says, lifting his eyebrows. "It sounds like they are true vagabonds. But," he adds quickly, "I'm not being derogatory at all. You've got to be pretty tough to live like that."

He continues, "I believe that truck was built in the 1930s; it's forty years old at least—and still running!"

"It doesn't run all the time, unfortunately," I reply. "In fact, something's broken on it now. Bobby says it breaks down frequently. Conveniently, it stopped running right after they got here."

Roland obviously hears the annoyance in my voice, for his next sentence is, "Do you think he contrived the breakdown? I doubt he would do that, don't you?"

"No," I answer matter-of-factly, "I don't doubt it. I think Bobby uses the truck's breakdowns as an excuse to stay where he is until he thinks of something better. They can't go anywhere until it's fixed and, in his own words, 'it's like a scavenger hunt trying to find parts.' No telling how long it'll take. On the other hand, no telling how convenient and quick it might be. He said something about using a banana peel to keep some part running on it, I don't remember what. So when he actually gets ready to go, chewing gum and Gem clips might work! Roland, I hope you don't think I'm being mean."

"I'd say you sound pretty cynical. Parts would be hard to find, though. But come to think of it, I might have an idea where he could find old parts. I might take him. I'd like to rummage around myself."

"Good!" I said. "He'll love to talk to you about his truck. He's crazy about it, and so is Kurina."

"You're saying they won't sell it to me?" he says with a laugh. "Do you think Bobby would mind if I had a look at it? I used to drive those trucks. I'd like to climb into the driver's seat again—just for old time's sake."

"Goodness no, he won't mind at all. He would want you to see it. I think he considers that truck an extension of his proudly wacky personality. Let me get our jackets, and we'll just have a look right now."

The uplift I feel, stepping out into the fresh air on this bright January day, lasts only a moment. I haven't had occasion to come out here for a couple of days and am unaware that the horse has been chewing the main post that supports the roof of the porch. If it chews another inch, the whole roof will fall in. This sorry sight deadens my spirit, but it doesn't surprise me. After all, didn't I predict, on Christmas Eve, that damage could easily be done to the post?

"Bobby, tied like that to the support if she spooked she could do some real damage... Can we tie her somewhere else?"

"The horse is fine. It's people that cause animals to act crazy."

What a stupid statement that was. What did *people* do to make a teething colt—come to think of it, it must have been the colt—chew the post in two? Bobby is the *people* responsible, as usual. With him here, I cannot relax a single minute. I obviously need to inspect my house for damage every day, without fail, top to bottom and front to back; this is really getting old.

I want Roland to see this ruined post, but when I turn around, he is already walking toward the horses.

"I like other people's horses, but I don't know much about them," he says as I approach. It seems to me this girl is special. Tell me about her."

"Well, her name is Sheba, and her color is a light sorrel," I answer. "And with her black mane and tail and white blaze, she *is* special. But look at her colt. To me, he is even prettier than his mother." The colt looks like his mother but lighter red and with four white stockings. "And you're going to love this Roland—his name is Goethe."

"Great name! They're beautiful, but I wouldn't want to care for one myself."

"Well, how would you like to care for one of *these*?" I ask as Bobby's dog trots over. "His name is Sebastian."

"Sebastian, are you a bear?" Roland laughs and scuffs the dog's massive head with both hands. "What breed is he?"

"Great Pyrenees; he's the rascal that jumped through my window; I'm sure you noticed all the duct tape."

"This big dog jumped through that window? I can't imagine him jumping that high." Roland looks at Sebastian with real admiration. "Sebastian, you're a fine fellow," he says, petting him with new respect.

I can't help giggling at the picture of this one-hundred-fifty-pound dog jumping all the way up and through the alcove window.

Roland adds, "It seems like he would have broken the table when he landed."

"No, no, no, it didn't happen like that," I say, laughing. "He jumped from the inside to the outside, not from the outside in."

"You mean you're keeping this big dog in the house?" he asks incredulously.

"No—at least we don't want to. We don't want him in the house at all. But what happens is that every time I leave, when I get back, Mr. Sebastian is inside."

"That's strange," he says with a quizzical look. "How does that happen?"

I have to chuckle again just seeing the puzzled look on his face. I don't think it occurs to Roland that Bobby would deliberately let the dog in. "It happens," I explain, "because his master opens the door and invites him in."

"Really? Did you tell him not to?"

"Yes, of course, but Bobby has no respect for my requests—and actually not even Bill's, because Billy has told him too. When Bobby brought Sebastian in on Christmas Day, Billy put him out and told Bobby we don't allow our big hunting dogs in the house. With a fenced-in yard and kennels, they're fine outside. As you know, Roland, Little-Bit is our only indoor dog."

"Sebastian is much bigger than your two hunting dogs. What does Bill say about him bringing the dog in?"

"Well, he hasn't said anything yet because Bobby makes sure that Billy doesn't catch Sebastian inside," I explain. "I keep hoping Billy will notice all the dog hair or mud or some evidence, but he just doesn't see it, probably because I'm cleaning hair and dirt constantly."

"What's going on here?" Roland asks. "You don't let Bill know that his brother is breaking the house rules?" I hear the disapproval in his voice.

"No, Roland, I gave up on that. Billy doesn't want to hear anything negative about his brother from me. If I report anything causing him to question Bobby, then Billy gets upset with me. I think he doesn't want to know about Bobby's infractions—that would require him to confront Bobby."

"This doesn't sound right."

I really don't want Roland disproving of Billy, so I hurry to explain: "You would have to know their history, Roland, to understand. The twins have always fought so violently with each other, verbally and physically, that Billy is determined not to let it happen this time. Billy told me that because he's the one who's found Christ since he and Bobby last met, it's his responsibility to be a good example to his brother. In light of his resolve, I just keep quiet."

"What's the good example?" Roland replies. "It's not a good example to let a guest in your home, even a brother, break the rules and have his way. Where's his respect? I'll have to see how they interact, but no wonder you're aggravated. Hey, wait a minute— surely Bill saw the broken window? You didn't have to point that out?"

"He saw it the next day, after Bobby had carefully taped it back together.

You should have seen how proud Bobby was, showing Billy his skill at broken window repair. It was funny; you would have thought he had done something wonderfully beneficial for us when he said, 'Look at this Billy, how clean I put your window back together. It's as good as new.'"

"Didn't Bill ask how it happened?"

"Not before he first acknowledged to Bobby that it was a great repair job. Then Billy turned to me and asked me how it got broken. Before I could answer, Bobby broke in with his own story: the dog must have snuck in through the sliding doors because he didn't know it was in the house. 'I was outside with Sheba,' he said, 'and when Sebastian saw me through the window, he just launched himself right on through.' It sounded so innocent that Billy's only comment was, 'I'm surprised he didn't hurt himself.'"

"You said *his story*. That's not how it happened?"

"I think he let the dog in himself; he's been doing it every day. But to be perfectly honest, Bobby keeps it so hot in the den sometimes they do have to open the doors—but that's a whole other irritating story. So maybe Sebastian did come in the sliding doors, but only when someone deliberately opened them. Anyway, when I got home from taking the children to school, Sebastian greeted me at the front door. I was trying to lead him out the kitchen door to the back, but when we passed the window, he did see or hear Bobby in the yard. Then that huge dog leaped, like a deer, onto the table and through the window before I knew what was happening. He's so big I couldn't have stopped him anyway. Everything on the table was knocked to the floor, but—and it's a thousand wonders—at least the table itself didn't break."

"Oh, come to think of it, let me tell you what else came in those doors."

"What?" Roland asks.

"This little fellow," I say, indicating the colt. "The day before the window-breaking, I came home around noontime and felt cool air throughout the downstairs. Looking in the den, which, as I mentioned before, is always hot as an oven, I saw the patio doors open and the colt inside the room. Bobby was sitting right there, in the lounge chair, while the little thing chewed and ripped my new curtains for all he was worth. They're actually not curtains but draw-drapes." Roland has a puzzled look, and I don't know if he understands. "You know, Roland, drapes that draw across the glass doors."

"I know what they are, Patsy," he says with a laugh. "Trish has totally domesticated me. I'm just trying to get this picture: Bill's brother allows his horse in your house, and then lets it wreck the place?"

"Yes, while he sat there in the room—I guess—watching. Kurina was there and should have seen it too, for that matter. But sometimes she's like one of the children; if Bobby doesn't correct something, she won't open her mouth."

Roland looks at me with uncertainty in his eyes. This story sounds so absurd I'm not sure he believes me. "Roland, I want to show you." I hurry to the patio doors and motion for him to come over. Sliding open the door, I point to the shredded drapery panels still hanging in tatters. "Do you know how long he had to sit there and watch that colt chew for it to have done this much damage?"

"So this was a deliberate job, and you saw it, and he's still staying here? Incredible!" I couldn't tell if Roland was skeptical or appalled.

"I can't expect you to understand this situation, Roland, but I explained it the best I know how. Billy isn't willing to cross Bobby, and by myself I have no clout. If I had my way, he probably wouldn't still be here."

"Oh, I understand the situation all right; you're dealing with identical twins, and that's not simple. But tell me, what did Bobby have to say for himself? Or did you even reproach him?"

"All Bobby did was drawl, 'I was fixin' to put him out.' But he didn't move, and I had to put the colt out myself. I guess that was the last straw because I couldn't hold back the tears."

"Is this sort of thing happening a lot?" he asks.

"Every day," I answer. "Every day it's something else. As I said, the drapes were the last straw. I had them custom made and installed not long before Christmas. They were brand-new and expensive! Oh! And that's another thing I don't dare mention around here anymore—the fact that something is expensive—because money is so very trivial, to hear Bobby tell it. Besides, it's only expensive if you replace it, which he would never do."

"From the sound of it, he has no respect for either of you. He might even scorn you—and Bill too, for that matter—for wanting nice things."

"Exactly! I confirm. "His attitude is: You must be stupid to waste your money on *things*. *Things* are so unimportant. The broken window is an example of his mindset; he thinks we would be foolish to buy a new custom window and go to all the trouble of putting it in when, duct-taped like that, it's 'as good as new.'"

"Patsy, I wish you had called me sooner," Roland says slowly, his eyes fixed on the floor. "I had no idea the situation here was this tense. I'm wondering how long he has been antagonistic toward you. I have a hunch this didn't just start." Before I can answer, he continues, "And I want to talk to you about that later, when we have more time. But you said the drapes were 'the last straw.' What did you do about it?"

"I put the colt out and went to my room and cried. He's so uncooperative, he makes me miserable. I don't know what to do anymore except put up with him."

"So weeping helplessly is your idea of 'the last straw'?" Roland shakes his head. "This is hard to believe. You're accomplished and strong in so many ways. I can see that his obstinate spirit is emotional abuse. No wonder your morale is low. Since this deliberate horse-in-the-house incident upset you so much, you at least told Bill about it?"

"No," I confess ashamedly. "I tell you, Billy protects Bobby. I feel safer letting him discover the truth of what's going on here for himself—if he would just discover it."

"This is wearing me out," Roland mumbles. "Let's get off this subject for a while." Then with more energy, he adds, "Hey, weren't we going to see a truck? Do we still have time?"

I glance at my watch; lunch is ready to put on the table, and we have another thirty minutes before Bill gets in. "Yes, we do," I answer. "Let's go."

As we approach the back of the truck, Roland walks right up the plank, and, looking over his shoulder, calls, "The door's open—come on in."

On the back of the truck is built a platform and box contrivance with three sides and a partial forth side. Inside it is a bale of hay, and Roland stops to investigate: "This built-on feeding device is pretty nice. Looks like the horses can nibble hay whenever they like, even when they're driving. And it's closed enough not to blow away." Attached beside the platform is an aluminum water can of probably ten to twelve gallons. "Guess this water is for family *and* horses?" he asks rhetorically.

"They probably cook with it. Let's ask him when he gets here, because I've wondered about their water supply too. Seems like this big metal container would get pretty germy."

Walking into the truck, Roland rolls up the tarp on one side to let daylight in. "This is not bad," he says. "Bobby's added a center post so they can stand up."

"Yes, his special custom design, intended to make this ugly contraption look even more outlandish driving down the road."

Roland laughs. "I wish you wouldn't say bad things about this nice military transport."

"Hey, would you look at this!" he exclaims, brushing hanging beads out of the way and climbing over things, heading straight for a big wooden box full of tools. He starts pulling out tools, some fairly clean and others rusty and antiquated looking, and exclaims with admiration, "This is a treasure trove. It looks like Bobby has every kind of hand tool imaginable." Roland carefully lifts and shifts them around like precious bounty.

It's a nice selection of tools, I'm sure. Funny I hadn't noticed them till Roland brought them to my attention. In a few minutes, his focus changes to the collection of kerosene lanterns, something else I hadn't really noticed.

I could not possibly have guessed that almost two decades later I would have reason to recall this very moment of Roland's discovery of the lanterns. These same

74

lanterns would sit burning and sparking on Bobby's "Judgment Table." Their hellish glow would radiate through the dark around my house, where, wracked with grief, I tried to hide on some of the saddest nights of my life.

Trying to divert his attention to something I'm interested in, I ask, "What do you think, Roland, about all these carved wooden pieces, and wicker images, and rabbits feet, and stuff?"

"He obviously collects these things too. I recognize most of them, and it appears they are almost all symbolic in one way or another." He looks over the various objects. "The thing I would ask is who are they important to—Bobby or Kurina? Do either of them believe the symbolism? Maybe neither of them do, or maybe they both do. What do you think, Patsy?"

"I really don't know what they believe. In spite of all the talking we've done, it's still not clear to me. But I think Billy will have a lot to say about Bobby's philosophy, if you want to call it that, when you two get a chance to talk."

"But," I continue, "now that I think about it, I will say this much—Bobby might think in terms of omens and voodoo. He must have attached some significance to the toy animals and dolls we gave his children for Christmas. His reaction was strange in that he ridiculed the little toys and shrank back from them and wouldn't touch them. I don't know what all that was about. Bobby acted like the toys were possessed and something to be afraid of. He didn't want his children playing with them. Maybe he got that idea from the gypsies or the natives he was with in South America."

"Yeah? Why do you say that?"

"Well, at night, when Bobby and Billy talk for hours, I've overheard some bizarre things, mainly about his experiences down there. I've heard him talk about images, and magic spells, and holy breath, and trees that sway and bow down—stuff like that."

"Some South American tribes have amazing hallucinogens. Sounds like Bobby helped himself."

"I'm sure he did, but even the little boy, Running Cub, who travels with him, tells things like that to my children. It upsets Ben and Katie."

"Not good." Roland seems lost in thought. "I can't believe, though, that even gypsies would give hallucinogens to a child. Running Cub would be telling those stories second-hand—surely. Well, I'll ask Bobby about all that later," he says, trying to dismiss whatever thoughts he has about the subject for now.

Turning to the collection under discussion, he continues, "But don't read too much into these things yet, Patsy. A lot of people collect religious symbols and folk charms and think nothing of them—except maybe that they are quaint or interesting. Let's hope that's the case here."

Roland rolls the tarp back down and says, "I want to see the cab before we run out of time," and he is running behind me down the plank and to the front of the truck.

As Roland climbs into the driver's seat, I go around to the passenger's side. "I've never been up here," I admit, opening the passenger door wide and climbing up to stand on the running board.

"Wow, this is a real blast from the past!" Roland says, acting silly, both hands on the steering wheel, making simulated truck noises with his mouth. "But what's this?" He leans forward to inspect the big mass of trinkets and junk hanging around the rear-view mirror. "How can he see to drive with all this stuff swinging around?"

He has the huge bunch of hanging things in his hand when I see a look of recognition and disgust claim his face. "Is this hair?" He seems to be talking to himself as he continues to stare in surprise at the offending stuff. Then he looks at me and says, grimacing, "There's a thick braid of human hair tangled in this mess! Is this some kind of charm?"

I see it. It looks like—no! I go limp; my knees feel like water. Hair? Tangled, hanging from the mirror. A girl's hair, maybe—long, chestnut color?

Roland is saying something to me; he's a million miles away. I step backward off the running board, away from the hair. I feel faint, cold. I'm going to be sick.

The doorbell rings; I answer it. It's Gloria! There stands Gloria. She looks horrible! She pushes past me and peers into the front rooms. I watch her, mystified. Satisfied that we are alone, she takes both my hands and pulls me to sit beside her. "Gloria, what?"

She holds her hands away from her face and stares at them. As if in a trance, she says, "I'll never get this feeling off."

"What feeling?" I ask with a sense of horror, waiting for her to continue— dreading what she will say.

"You won't believe what Bobby did."

"I knew it would be him!"

"Shhhh," she whispers. "Patsy, please, this is important. I've got to know something." She looks wild with fear. "Is Bobby dangerous?"

"What?" I gasp.

"You know he might be," she rasps. "Everyone wondered about Kathleen's death. They said it was an accident, but nobody knows."

"But it only looked suspicious because there were no fingerprints on the shotgun." None, I thought. Nobody's. Did someone say there was a wipe-down? Should I bring that up? Remind her?

"Patsy, we're supposed to be married in one week."

"I know, Gloria. Why are you saying all this? What happened?"

She becomes calmer now; more reflective. "He just did the most bizarre thing you can imagine."

"Tell me!"

"Bobby was acting strange this evening, quiet, really hushed, didn't want me to talk. Several times I caught him staring at me—just quietly staring. At one point he sat me on the sofa, gently, and watched me. Then he took my hands, placed them on my knees, and turned them both palm up. He told me to close my eyes. I thought, 'This is more like it—he's going to give me a gift.'"

"And?"

"I heard him place what was obviously a box, not too big and not too small, on the coffee table. And with no more sound or movement, something smooth and heavy was draped across my hands. It felt creepy. I opened my eyes instantly."

"Good grief. Go on; what was it?"

"Patsy, it was Kathleen's ponytail! He said so. I ran out and came straight here."

I couldn't think what to say to her. We just sat together in stunned silence.

"Why did he do that, Patsy? Right before our wedding."

I shook my head in dismay. "I'm sorry, Gloria. I'm so sorry it happened.

Stay here tonight."

Roland is kneeling over me.

"I know it, Roland, I know; I'm okay, though. The hair brought back a terrible memory—all of a sudden. Such a shock. I hadn't thought about the ponytail in years. Maybe it's not what I think. No! I don't want to see it. I can't explain—not now; later I will. I'll be fine, thank you. Could I have a coke?"

Before I know he has even gone, Roland returns and is handing me a cold ginger ale. "I found this in the fridge. Is it okay?" he asks, out of breath.

"It's the best thing I ever tasted," I say between gulps. As we walk toward the house, I gain strength with every step; so much so that when Billy, flashing his cheerful grin, comes out the back door and across the yard, I greet him, feeling a little shaky but otherwise as good as new.

I feel emotionally stronger than before, actually. I wonder why. Until now I've behaved like a dancing bee, frantically trying to give signals to Billy, while Billy, it seems, tries just as frantically to ignore them. Well before we go in the house, I'm going to *show and tell* instead of *dance and wave*. The chewed post will be the perfect vehicle to finally expose to him Bobby's disregard for us.

Billy and Roland carry on with friendly chitchat, mainly discussing the horses and truck—both of which I am sick and tired of by now.

When I reach the back porch, I "notice" the chewing damage to the support post. "Billy, look at this!" I call with feigned surprise.

He comes close, and fingering the damage, exclaims, "Good grief, I'm glad you saw this. It has to be the work of Goethe. Another minute of chewing and the porch will cave in."

"I think you're right," I answer, "in both cases."

"It's dangerous," he continues, assessing the damage. "One of the kids could push it in two with no problem. We'll have to fix this right away. Where's Bobby?"

"He took everybody to the store," I answer. "But they go out for hamburgers sometimes. They're probably at Kip's having lunch."

"And, Billy," I continue, "to keep this from happening again, the horses should be staked in the field, don't you think? There must be two acres of grazing back there. Bobby keeps them staked when they travel, so it would be nothing new."

This is much easier than I thought it would be—perhaps because Roland is here—but Billy agrees with me immediately. "You're right, Pat. I'll tie them out right now. If Goethe decides to chew, he could take the place down while we're having lunch."

Roland has been watching this exchange without comment, but he gives me a little glance of triumph, "I knew you had it in you," he seems to say.

I go inside, happy that Billy and Roland are leading the horse and colt outside the fence to their new grazing area. I like the idea of Bobby's horses and chickens out in the field—and away from the house—sort of a ranch-like effect.

I serve lunch in the dining room so we won't have to look at the jagged duct tape holding the bay window together. During the meal, Billy tells Roland about Bobby's family, including the two extra children traveling with them—and no, they are not orphans.

"Has he said why the parents want their children traveling with him and Kurina?"

"Lotus is the child of his present wife—the one he's legally married to and has two sons by. But Running Cub is not explained to my satisfaction, no," Billy answers. "But apparently Running Cub is a gypsy child. From our conversations, it seems gypsies have all sorts of reasons to leave their children in the care of others from time to time. Sometimes it's as simple as needing to earn extra money. For instance, the dad might hire on with a construction crew for a few weeks. Or maybe they need a rest from the kids. I told him this seems to be pretty slack family attachments, but Bobby disagrees. He says their family bonds are very strong. Running Cub was with Bobby in South America, but so was his mother. Apparently she's left him to the care of Bobby and Kurina. I'd be worried except the kids seem fine; they fit right in."

"No school, of course," I say. "But they are smart kids and they both read."

When we decide to have dessert and coffee at the more

comfortable breakfast nook, duct tape and all, Roland takes his former seat. "I like my seat with a view," he says, excitedly motioning for us to come quick. "What's the meaning of all this? Looks like we have a performance going on."

Billy and I, carrying dessert and coffee, hurry over to follow his gaze. The Morning Stars have returned, and in the very back part of the yard—to my chagrin, inside the fence—Bobby appears to be training his mare; and he has an audience. Kurina and the four children, including JaJa, are seated a few feet apart on the ground around and outside of what I can see in my mind's eye to be a large imaginary circle. Bobby is looking pretty cool in his blue jeans and suede shirt, with a red printed doo-rag tied around his head. He is standing, barefoot, on the other side of the make-believe circle facing his family. Sheba is in the middle of the circle on her back with all four legs straight up in the air. As we watch, she, with good control, rolls over and gets off the ground and into a beautiful standing position facing Bobby.

Roland says, "That's got to be Bobby. But let's not bother him. I want to watch this for a minute."

As we watch, the horse nods her head at Bobby and then rears high into the air. Bobby, as far as we can detect, has not moved a muscle, yet the mare kneels on the ground in front of him and rolls over again.

"I have never seen that," Roland declares. "It doesn't seem natural for a horse to do roll-over tricks."

"It's not customary, I'll say that," Bill comments. "And you'll notice the horse performs without Bobby moving so much as a finger."

"How does he do it?" Roland asks.

"He trains Sheba with his eyes," Bill explains. "Bobby and his animals have a certain communion with each other. Some trainers say not to look a horse hard in the eye, but Bobby said that is the way he selected Sheba—their eyes met, he said, and it was love at first sight for both of them."

"Just like in the movies," Roland jokes. "Interesting."

"Yeah, it is interesting," I agree. "And his stare works. It's exactly how he handles his family, even baby JaJa. He just looks them hard in the eye, and they are quiet as mice."

"My brother knows how to establish his dominance," Billy chuckles.

As we finish coffee and continue to watch Bobby, I wonder to myself: What is he up to? I know he's probably aware that I'm watching him from this window. Is this training session his ploy to bring both horses back into the yard? He naturally thinks I moved the horses out. He doesn't know Bill is home because Bobby drove down the side street and into the back field—like he does every time he drives my car, regardless of my inconvenience. No doubt he fully intends to leave the horses in the yard again. He needs to know Billy put them out. "Let's go out and join his audience," I say. "Bobby will love extra spectators."

"Let's do, Roland," Billy agrees. "I've got to get back to work, and I want to introduce you two."

When he notices us walking across the yard, Bobby, with ceremony and one last grand stunt, brings his performance to an end.

Billy introduces Roland and Bobby, then leaves through the side gate—but not before telling Bobby that the horses will have to be staked outside the fence. "And, Bobby," Billy calls, "we'll have to repair that support post on the porch tomorrow, before someone gets hurt." This may be the first time since *the unexpected arrival* that Billy has actually given Bobby direct orders!

"Yep" is the extent of Bobby's comment. From his lack of surprise, I get the distinct impression that he knows all about the support post, and that he fully intended to let the roof collapse; I say so to Roland too, as we watch Bobby sullenly lead the horses back through the gate. "I don't understand it. Why would he want to destroy our porch?"

"Anything to level the playing field" is all Roland replies as he turns away and walks toward the Morning Stars, leaving me to speculate about whether he really means that. Being *contrary* which is what I thought was going on, and *deliberately leveling the playing field* have different connotations.

Yes, I conclude, Roland does mean what he says. And in my

secret heart I've wondered about the same thing myself—though I hate to admit it. After all, I've loved and prayed for Bobby for years. Surely he wouldn't intentionally wreck my and Billy's hard work? But I'm left with the troubling question: if not, as Roland said, *to level the playing field*, then what motive does he have? Though I can't believe all this was premeditated, still there are too many destructive accidents to attribute them all to *accidental*. Even my girlfriends at church, who have been prayerfully supporting me, have suggested as much:

"Are you sure, Patsy, that all these deeds are not orchestrated to tear you and Bill down spiritually and financially?" Brenda, a close friend of mine, had asked me at our Mother's Lunch at church the other day. "I'm afraid the next time I see you, he will have wrecked your car."

Afraid he will wreck my car! An unexpectedly blunt statement from Brenda, but now it makes perfect sense if the intention is to "level the playing field."

The concern about my car might explain why, in no more than a month, one of our church members will donate a good-quality used car to Bobby. And, to tell the whole story, within three months Bobby will have sold it and spent the money.

"Excuse me for daydreaming," I call, running toward Roland, who is already laughing and chatting like an old friend with Kurina and the children. "Looks like you've already met Bobby's family."

"Unassuming people are easy to meet," Roland says as he beams at them and looks toward Bobby, who is strolling toward us. He must have heard that word because Bobby straightens his shoulders and smiles with approval at Roland's description of his family. This new Bobby likes to think of himself as being the earthiest of down-to-earth people, and Roland has said just the right thing. Good.

"It's getting chilly," I observe, pulling my jacket collar up. "I've got plenty of cookies and some hot chocolate if we want to go inside."

"We want to go inside!" Running Cub and Lotus jump and clap in unison. I take off toward the patio doors with the Morning Stars and Roland laughing and running close behind. As we tumble and spill into the den, Bobby says, "Roland, let's start a fire and sit in here; it's the most comfortable room in the house."

"I agree," Roland says, "this is my favorite room too, but could we do without the fire? It's pretty warm in here already."

I love Roland; he's so plain-spoken, and he remembers my complaint about the fire.

"We'll wait till it gets cool," Bobby concurs, and informs me that he wants coffee with whipping cream instead of hot chocolate. Then he plunks down on the sofa with Kurina. Since, in Bobby's book, Bobby is the most interesting topic of conversion possible, if Roland's goal is to get Bobby talking about himself, he will not be disappointed. Roland might, however, have to rely on more accurate information from other people for the deeper understanding he seeks. But we will see.

Before I have time to leave the room, a leading question from Roland has Bobby eager to talk.

As I go about serving the children in the kitchen and bringing drinks in to the adults and doing my various small chores, including cleaning up from lunch, I overhear Bobby being forthcoming. I hear snatches of: social protests; how he became a midwife, delivering babies in Haight-Ashbury; and involvement with lots of drugs there.

Finished with my chores, I quietly make myself comfortable in the den. I listen but don't break in, and they continue their conversation.

"Sounds like things in San Francisco weren't so bad," Roland comments.

"No, in fact I had a great time. We were a close community and always—"

"So why did you leave and go to South America?" Roland interrupts.

I look at the time and realize that Roland has less than an hour before his appointment, while Bobby would like to talk all afternoon.

"Well, Bobby answers, "I guess I'm a little restless. Maybe it was time to move on. And frankly, I've always been curious about the rainforest and Andes Mountains. I like to read about old native ways. In San Francisco I had heard a lot about native medicine and drugs and hoped to learn something."

"I understand that sentiment, Bobby. You're like Bill, a lot of curiosity. The indigenous peoples do have a lot of natural medicines and survival knowledge. They have powerful hallucinogens too, I understand."

"Yeah, man!" Bobby answered with feeling. "Let me describe—"

I have already heard his descriptions. And as to why he went to South America—he is telling only part of the story.

Bobby is not telling of his meeting a young woman who had been in an automobile accident: an accident that left her husband dead and her leg severed above the knee. The court found her husband to be the victim of vehicular homicide and awarded her a substantial judgment. In her diminished state, injured and still grieving, this woman was obviously helpless to resist the compassionate care and charm of Bobby Hale. And how could he, being the opportunist he is, resist her money and the opportunities it afforded him?

When I got the desperate telephone call from an anxious mother in California looking for a Bobby Hale and relating the story of her daughter's tragedy, my heart broke for her. "If my daughter's losing her husband and her own leg wasn't enough, she had the misfortune to meet your brother-in-law," she cried. Her daughter was about my age at the time, late twenties, and I could clearly understand her vulnerability. The caller said she and her husband had done some investigating around Haight-Ashbury and, given that Bobby was well known on the streets, they had no trouble finding the name and hometown of the man who had, in her words, "kidnapped my daughter and granddaughter."

Bobby's acquaintances had told the parents that he and their daughter had absconded with the child and the money to South America. "I am deeply troubled on several levels," the mother said on the phone, choking back tears. "First and foremost, I am sickened with concern for my seven-year-old granddaughter. I feel I can't live if she isn't returned safe. My husband and I have barely been able to eat or sleep for worrying. And my poor daughter, I am so afraid for her. If anything happens to her prosthesis, she will be unable to even walk! To add fuel to my fears, according to his friends, he is heading into the jungles to learn what they call 'the native ways.' And then her settlement—when she returns, she and her daughter will need that money."

This poor woman had tried to hire an attorney and had gone to the police, but they told her that because her daughter, an adult, left of her own accord from all reports, and because the child, and the money for that matter, were the daughter's, then she, the mother, had no valid legal complaint. All she had gotten from them was sorrowful headshakes and "I wish I could help." She was hoping against hope that Bobby's family could assist her with information. "Who is this Bobby?" she asked. "My daughter is a responsible young woman—not one who would wander off with a strange man; but he has totally mesmerized her."

When I told the caller that our family had not heard from Bobby in well over a year, had no knowledge of his whereabouts, not even that he was in South America, and did not know how to contact him, she broke down in hopeless sorrow.

"My husband and I will pray daily for your daughter and granddaughter's safe return," I promised. "If I hear anything, I will call." We exchanged addresses and phone numbers, and I hung up with a heavy heart.

That evening when I told Billy about the call, he was devastated. "What a trail of misery Bobby leaves—everywhere he goes. He's still married to Connie. I guess he just walked off and left her and their boys. Sometimes my burden for him is so heavy, I can hardly make sense of my own life. Do I need to leave here and go find him? See if I can talk to him? Make him put an end to this coldhearted selfishness? It seems he has no regard for the wrecked lives he leaves behind. And this woman he's run off with—you say her mother called her K.K.?"

"Yes," I confirmed, "and her name is Kathleen too. Just the same as Kathleen, you remember, before she and Bobby married and before her death— Kathleen's mother, and even us friends, called her K.K."

"If I believed in omens…" his voice trailed away, and his eyes had that empty stare of one who is lost in contemplation. "Maybe the name somehow drew him to her."

"She's unfortunate if that's the case," I said.

"You know, Patsy, it would be great if we heard of one good thing that Bobby has done!"

Almost three years later I got another call from the grandmother in California. Her daughter and granddaughter had returned—physically safe but penniless; and, according, to Kurina's later report, "That woman with one leg has mental issues."

"Patsy, I've got to run." It is Roland. I rouse from my reverie as he checks his watch and stands up.

"Roland, I'm sorry. I was lost in thought. Are you late?"

"No, but just about." He hands his card to Bobby and says, "I hope you and Kurina will drop by to see me. Keep your seat, Bobby, Patsy will see me out."

I walk him through the living room, and as I open the door he whispers, "Walk me to the car, Patsy." As we walk outside, he says, "We need to talk about your situation here—the sooner the better. What about breakfast tomorrow?"

Inside the house, I immediately call Billy. We frequently have breakfast with Roland and Trish, so this should be easy. "Roland feels we need to talk right away. He suggests breakfast tomorrow."

"Then let's meet at Denny's across from the clinic. It'll be easier for me."

8. BREAKFAST WITH ROLAND

"…be as wise as a serpent and as harmless as a dove."
~ Matthew 10:16

I enter the restaurant, and on first impression am disappointed that it is dimly lit and quiet. It is large, though, and will be good for our purpose. I spot Billy waving to me from a back booth and see that he and Roland already have coffee.

I wonder what approach Roland will take this morning. As he left the house yesterday, he was clearly troubled: *"We need to talk about your situation here—the sooner the better."* And how could he not be uneasy with all that he saw there and heard from me. Focused on Billy as I make my way across the floor, guilty thoughts start eating at me. I hope I didn't give Roland too harsh an impression of Bobby; Billy loves him so. Maybe I complained too much. Regardless of my own feelings, maybe I was too negative.

I have to remind myself that Billy wanted Roland to meet Bobby as much as I did. Our *immediate* motives are different, however; mine is for advice on how to wisely manage these complicated men before one of them wrecks my home and my nerves.

Billy's motive is for guidance in leading Bobby to Christ. With Bobby in our home, this is one of those "once in a lifetime" opportunities Billy feels he must take advantage of. Bobby is so restless he could vanish again any day, and that uncertainty adds to

Billy's urgency. He feels that Roland is his one close friend who has the background and moral authority to help him help Bobby.

When I reach the booth, we conduct our brief greetings and concur that time is short.

"At the risk of sounding clinical," Roland starts, "I'm going to get right to the point. I want to run through some of my observations and give you my thoughts.

"I do want you to know, Bill, that I enjoyed meeting your brother yesterday. He and his family exceeded my expectations in several ways. They are friendly, healthy, attractive, and charming—not what I would expect from people living out of a truck. Bobby is lively and curious and has considerable intelligence. He has charisma and good manners and, though he has his hippie way of dressing and grooming now, one can still detect that he was brought up in a home where etiquette and comportment were valued. It seems that a lot has gotten in his way since then—or maybe I should say it has come his way and influenced him—because he is stoutly embracing a way of life counter to the manner in which he grew up here in Fort Worth. I would like to have had more time with him to explore his belief system a little more, but he is a talker and he inadvertently managed to tell me a lot without my probing.

"From what I saw of him around your property, and from what you said about his ability to handle his animals and family, it's obvious he takes control of situations. My opinion is that he wants to exert control over those around him in every way he can, physically, philosophically, and even spiritually. I don't think this is idle speculation on my part because he freely told me of his leadership roles in Haight-Ashbury, including as a midwife. A man has to be pretty much known and respected for his skill to be called in to deliver babies, as high-risk as that is. He also seems pretty proud that he became leader of a band of gypsies in the Andes Mountains. Given Bobby's values, it's no wonder he's proud. It takes a lot of managerial skill and persuasion for an unknown man to come in and take over a large band of people like he did. He told me he took on the spiritual fatherhood of the children as well as delivered the babies. He said he learned about the native drugs and medicines and helped treat illnesses. To hear him tell it, he practically became a shaman. He got caught up in rituals and hallucinogens too. I wonder if a lot of it didn't wear off on him."

Billy and I both agree that we think he *was* influenced by his experiences in South America.

"It's plain these are some of the things he's proud of and wants me to know," Roland says. "No doubt he's told you all this and a lot more."

We confirm that Bobby has pretty much brought us up to date on his adventures, or more accurately, what we consider his misadventures. Billy adds, "But there's a lot he's not proud of and doesn't want you to know."

"Even so," Roland continues, "I'm sure you appreciate that what he's told us speaks to his ability to organize and influence people. He could, theoretically, be a force for good if he chose. I understand, Bill, you would like to influence him in that direction?"

"Yes, I would. You say he can lead and control—well, he can manipulate too. People who fall under Bobby's influence are often hurt. I feel that if God has a job for me in this world, it is to turn my brother around."

"What Billy says is true, Roland," I say. "Behind every story he tells you, you can figure there will be an underlying plot, typically a scheme of abandonment and manipulation. A perfect example is that big journey to South America. You can rest assured he will never tell you the full account, starting with the fact that he was married when he decided to go. He abandoned his wife, the mother of Lotus, and their two little boys and took up with another woman, a woman who had recently come into money. The poor thing had settlement money due to an accident in which her husband was killed and she was crippled. She lost one of her legs. Her money is what Bobby and she and her young daughter went to South America on. About three years later, the woman's mother called me from California. Bobby had sent her daughter and the little girl back home—penniless."

Roland frowns and just looks at us. What are his thoughts about this new bit of information, I wonder.

"What about the wife and boys he abandoned?"

Billy spoke up, "According to Bobby, they're still in California. Legally he's still married to her—not Kurina. But, Roland, that is a problem I have no control over! At this point I'm not even sure the wife is concerned about it. Kurina doesn't seem to be. The hippies see things different from us. I believe Bobby will take care of all this if he gets right with God. I don't know why you brought that up, Patsy; it just complicates matters."

Without hesitating, Roland said, "I think both of you want me to know there's a lot about Bobby I'm not likely to learn from him. But that's usually the way. Without a change of heart, people don't want to talk about things they're ashamed of. In that respect he's no different from the rest of us. But you're right, Bill; his reckless history does complicate matters. And I must tell you, I am very sorry he abandoned his children. I've been at this a long time, and from what I've experienced over the years, when children are abandoned by their fathers they are badly damaged. Making things right with the past, if it is even possible, will require a major and permanent change of heart. I know you've been talking to him about that at every opportunity, Bill. You mentioned these discussions usually last late into the night almost every night. I get the feeling the talks aren't going well. Is he receptive at all?"

"No, nothing's going very well right now. Bobby turns and twists everything I say till I don't even recognize my own words and thoughts—he is a master at doing that. He has his own take on every thing. I can't mention anything he won't argue about."

"Has he thought much about life and meaning, or does he just take what comes?"

"He's thought a lot about life, Roland, and accepted a bunch of stuff. You didn't know this, but he used to teach Transcendental Meditation...which I don't know if it was just a way to make a living or if he really got into it philosophically. Actually, he must have, because he rose pretty far with that practice. He even went to Spain and worked over there for the Maharishi. And, as you know, he did the flower child thing, taking drugs for enlightenment, he says. So he wanted to be enlightened—about life or something. And as we've just been talking about, he went on to that jungle voodoo and gypsy stuff. Yeah, he's probably mulled matters over too much. Most of his arguing is pure baloney. But, I'll tell you this, he has come to one firm conclusion, and that is that I am deluded and a slave to society. He tells me every day how we would all be happier living out of a truck, unemployed and tax free, and certainly not attached to some church."

"Yet he's living with us," I point out. "And, thanks to your employment, accepting our hospitality."

"How do you feel when he says you are deluded and a slave to society?" Roland asks.

"It makes me mad. Used to, it would have made me fighting mad. But, speaking of employment, let me say this, though he is unemployed, Bobby manages to have some source of income. Roland, I'm ashamed to tell you this, and wouldn't in front of Patsy except she already knows it, he is either living off California welfare or money he has managed to steal from the one-legged woman. He doesn't have much money, but he has some. Kurina is a seventeen-year-old runaway, and her family couldn't get money to her if they wanted to. So another of God's commandments he has no problem with is stealing. And to finally answer your question, no he is not receptive to much of anything I say."

"Yet," Roland says, "every evening you feel compelled to revisit that same hornet's nest he has waiting for you, and subject yourself again to all the painful haranguing back and forth; so far to no good end."

"Yeah, it sounds crazy to me too, but you're right. Though we are at variance on every issue; come evening I am ready to start up again. Every time I hope it will be different. Maybe this time I will say something that will touch him. Hours later I'm so tired that, like I told you earlier, I don't know my own thoughts and words from his. We usually reach an impasse and just start yelling at each other; usually I'm the one yelling loudest. It seems I'm further from reaching him now than when we started. And about his abandoned children being damaged, I'm sure that's true, Roland; it's a constant burden to me. I'm tired and need help. How can I bring Bobby around?"

Roland has listened to Bill with all the concern of a true friend.

"No wonder you're tired; all that contention… Contradicting everything you say! And don't think for a minute he's not enjoying himself. I bet he's not tired."

"No, he never is. He can go on all night. But, of course, he can sleep the next day. And, yes, he *is* enjoying himself; he loves to squabble. The only time he doesn't enjoy it is if I start getting the best of the argument—but he will never relent; his reasoning just gets more frantic and crazier. Like I told you, we wind up yelling."

"Well, let's step back and think about this predicament realistically," Roland replies, "and try to analyze it. The type behavior you describe presents a complicated problem, and you might not know this, but it could be dangerous."

"Oh, we're not going to hurt each other," Bill says. "We would have fought it out with fists at one time, but we're past that."

"I'm not thinking about you hurting each other physically. The most damage that can be inflicted on a person is not on his body. There is more profound damage to be inflicted on the mind. This is the complicated problem I'm talking about.

"But" Roland continues quickly, in his "clinical mode," "let's go on. Here we have twin brothers, each determined to change the other. Their late-night conversations become increasingly heated as they move from getting caught up with their six years' absence to discussing each other's philosophy of life. One brother is burdened because the other leads a life that is selfish, un-Christian, and hurtful to others. The other brother has integrated many experiences and practices into a mixed bag that suits him just fine. This brother is, or says he is—even told me that he is—'troubled because his twin is too hung up on things that don't matter.' By the way, he didn't give me any insights into what he thinks does matter, and I didn't have time to ask. Hopefully he and I will get around to that later. I could speculate here that Bobby's attitude about 'things that don't matter' might be the reason he has no respect for your house and your belongings, though I doubt it. As far as your home is concerned, I think his multiple infringements and destructive *accidents* have deeper roots. By the way, you both understand, don't you, that I'm trying to process this situation and lay it out for you as I see it? Can I go on?"

"Please do," we say in unison—though Billy squirms uncomfortably and bumps me under the table.

"We have already seen that Bobby is not only able to, but does, control people in his life. I would go a step further and say Bobby has a *need* to dominate those around him and, even further, that he has ideas about *how* to accomplish this. A man with the need to dominate uses different tactics depending on the person or group he encounters. Bobby not only wants to control you two, he wants to change you. The method he is using here is to tear you down to the point that you conduct yourselves to his liking."

Tear us down! I find myself remembering, for the second time in as many days, Brenda's pointed question: "*Patsy, are you sure all this is not orchestrated to tear you down, spiritually and financially?*" I want to relate this friend's insight to Roland because he knows her too; but how would Bill react? He would be furious if he knew I had complained to my friends about his brother's behavior. I will keep it to myself.

Roland is still talking, "He wants to change you, and it looks like he didn't waste any time. He is in the active process now. You do know that, don't you?"

Bill turns toward me with a quizzical frown. I am afraid I have missed something. "Roland, what did you say?"

"I said Bobby is trying to change and control you both, and the process has already begun. All you have to do is think about his actions and it is obvious how he's doing it. He is using argument and sleep deprivation on you, Bill, almost every night. Sleep deprivation is a powerful tool for confusing and breaking the will of a person; and with Bobby's cultish background, don't think he doesn't know how to use it."

"And Patsy, he's using random destructive accidents and intimidation to break your will. You have to stay on constant alert against his next aggravation. Think how stressful that is. From my experience in the military, I would say it's almost like being in combat."

I concur with Roland. "What you're saying sounds exactly right."

Bill disagrees. "Roland, it's not all that bad. I'll just make them leave if I get too fed up."

"It doesn't have to come to '*making*' them leave, Bill, but I'm afraid it might if these late-night yelling matches continue. It would be healthier for your family, and I think more productive for your purpose, if you find a nice motel for Bobby's family, where they can be comfortable and you can visit them there—as often as you like."

Bill did not react as strongly to that suggestion as I would have thought, but he did wrinkle up his face and say, "A motel doesn't sound right; I don't think I could do it."

It sounds like a great idea to me—but clumsy. How would we manage it? Just say, *We want our house back and we've found you another place.* I can't imagine being so bold and direct. In that regard, I agree with Bill. "Roland, I couldn't hurt their feelings like that," I say weakly. I don't look at him. I know he is disappointed in me. He must be thinking, 'Yeah, especially since Bobby is so concerned about your feelings.'

"It would be hard," Roland agrees. "Blood is thick. But in all truth, with Bobby and his family in your house, I am concerned for both of you and also for the children. We've pretty much agreed that Bobby hasn't come through all his many counterculture experiences unscathed. He has picked up and brought into your home beliefs and practices you probably aren't even aware of, things that haven't shown up yet but can be toxic to your way of life. And the children traveling with them have experienced many things at their young age that are misguided and wrong, and counter to the way you are trying to raise your own children. The stories these children tell are troubling—as you know, Patsy. I'm not blaming those innocent children, but that's the way it is. Your kids do not need to hear about drugs and rituals, or about stealing animals and food from peasant farmers, especially in view of the fact that these harmful things are seen by those children, thanks to the adults' attitudes, as harmless enjoyment."

I'm not sure Billy heard Roland's last statement about the children because in those couple of minutes he has hardened his view: "I can't put them out," he states firmly. "I don't care about the house. If he tears it apart, I can't put him out."

I reach over and take Billy's hand, hoping to soothe him, but he continues. "If Bobby leaves here unrepentant, I will never forgive myself. I'm telling you, if the house burns down, he has to stay."

"Okay, so that idea is not acceptable; let's just put it over here." Roland put his hand flat on the table and pushes the imaginary idea to the side. "There are several factors other than the house that concern me, Bill. One of them being you; I'm concerned about you. You have just recently started work with the hospital; if this late-night fighting keeps up, you could make a serious mistake. Has Bobby shown concern or mentioned, even once, that you need your rest?"

"No, he hasn't, but then he doesn't understand about being alert at work all day, because he doesn't work."

"Don't fool yourself, Bill. Your brother is your age; you seem to forget that. And he has worked part of his life at least. He told me he had been a crop-dusting pilot at one point and then a blackjack dealer in Las Vegas. He is intelligent and understands you have a demanding job that requires a night's sleep—he is deliberately keeping you from it. I'm telling you—in fact, I practically said the words a few minutes ago—Bobby is familiar with the practice of brainwashing. I think he has used it on people before, and I know he is using it on you now, every night. Not many people are able to resist this seduction. That's why he should be out of your house... But since that's not going to happen, we've got to come up with another plan. The first thing I want you to do is stop arguing with him in the evening. Just stop it. Do something else after dinner. What will that be?"

"But," Bill says, "it is impossible for me not to try to...to..."

"To what Bill?" Roland asks pointedly. "Convince him that you are right and he is wrong? I thought we established that doesn't work. In fact that method is almost always counterproductive. It often happens, especially with someone as stubborn as Bobby, that a person will become even more entrenched in his own ways. It's a protective mechanism we all have, and use, to some extent. He may harden his heart and become unreachable if you push too hard."

"My fear exactly," Billy says. "If I don't slow down, I might turn him off. But then I feel compelled—"

"Stop it, Bill," Roland interrupts. "Take some of that desperation out of your approach. What can you do in the evening, as two families to wind down for a reasonable bedtime? I say that when you put the children to bed, you end the evening with the Morning Stars and go to your own room. You can read, watch TV, or whatever, but don't be around Bobby. Patsy, what are your ideas? And don't include anything controversial that might set him arguing."

"Well, Bobby and Kurina both love to sing. Believe it or not, Bobby even has a favorite hymn. Billy could lead an evening devotional, very non-controversial; beatitudes or parables are always good. I could play the piano, Bobby could play his guitar, and we could all sing. We do that a lot anyway, and we all love it. Then, rather than leave you two to quarrel, Billy, we could call it a night. This new way would require some planning on my part because there's always the kitchen to clean and dishes to wash; I would have to do that early."

"Allison will help you, and so will Kurina if you ask," Roland says. "Stick to that plan instead of this late-night arguing. Bobby is enjoying it, but it's affecting both of your lives in negative ways. Cut that off and he will become bored. Just have your sing-alongs and light devotionals and stay involved with the church. Your church always has something going on; invite Bobby and Kurina to its activities. I think they'll go with you. I am sure they would like to do something other than stay at the house alone."

This proposed new plan takes a minute to sink in, and before we can answer, Roland continues, "How much influence does Kurina have over Bobby? Is she just one more girl he will dump, along with their children?"

"I can't possibly predict," Billy says.

"At any rate, if you will stick to that plan and not give another hour of your time to arguing with Bobby, he will get bored and go to church with you, and Kurina will go with him. I'm telling you this will happen; and when it does he will be much more receptive because he won't be fighting against you."

"Roland, I think you're right." Bill has a sound of relief in his voice. "I really want to do this. Patsy, you've got to help me stick with it. Bobby will try to engage me for sure, but you help me be firm about our evening family time and bedtime."

"I will absolutely help you, and it shouldn't be too hard. I will emphasize the fact that you aren't spending time with the children lately, and this will be a good way. And your duties demand you get proper rest. As for going to church, I'm with Roland; I think they'll go. You know how they both love to show off their hippie way of dressing and their different way of life."

"That's a point of pride," Roland states. "It differentiates them from *us*—this crowd of boring conformists."

"Exactly right," Billy agrees. "Why, they will have twelve hundred people to show off to! Roland, you know how you feel when, as they say, a weight has been lifted? That's how I feel. I've got a plan now that sounds reasonable and good." He slid from his seat. "You two go ahead and finish, but I've got to run."

We say our goodbyes, and Bill adds: "Roland, you never fail me; I love you, brother."

I had just accepted a cup of hot coffee, so Roland and I stay for a while. I can detect that he is not as lighthearted as Billy and me. "Patsy, I want a final word with you and then I have to go. There's one thing I want you to think about, and I want to talk about it later: How long has Bobby had this antagonism toward you? I have a hunch that, at least in his psyche, it didn't just start."

His words are so surprising that I am speechless.

"Just think about it, Patsy, and, like I said, we'll talk about it later: When did this adversarial relationship begin?" It could have been so long ago that you feel his behavior is normal—believe me, it's not."

He continues, "Now back to what we came here for. Not having Bill to himself, to argue with and manipulate, will be a blow to Bobby; it won't be as easy as you and Bill think. Neither of you had much reaction when I said the word 'brainwash.' You probably thought of this in the abstract or thought I was being excessive, but please believe me when I say the process has already begun. It has become a game with Bobby. If either of you start giving credence to any of his coaching, then he has won. Don't let them be alone at night when, as Bill said, 'I'm so tired I don't even recognize my own words and thoughts.' I want you to understand how risky that is. And I am telling you this, although I can't say it to Bill, Bobby is restless and dangerous—that's the reason I want him out of your house. Unfortunately, we've established that he will stay. With your help, I hope Bill can hold on. But please listen to my warning: If he ever does start listening to Bobby, it will be too late."

Over and over down the years, I will recall those words. They were spoken by a good man, a godly man, a man who loved our family and who saw things with a much broader scope than we did: "If he ever starts listening to Bobby, it will be too late." They proved to be wise words that for one excuse or another were forgotten—or ignored.

9. REMEMBERING THE FIRST DATE

"I will forgive your being young… Since time tricks all before he's done."
~ Mildred Greear

As we go our own ways after breakfast, Roland has left me with such dire warnings that I wonder if he is overly concerned. But I've always known him to be level-headed and able to get right to the heart of a problem. Maybe I don't fully grasp all he said, or—using his term—maybe I'm in denial. It's hard to accept the idea of my husband being "brainwashed" by his own brother. And I'm not even sure I know what that means.

Roland gave me a lot of things to think about, including the charged question he asked: "How long has Bobby had this antagonism toward you? Just think about it and we'll talk about it later." I must have time alone to think about all this.

Bobby and Kurina do not know about my and Bill's breakfast with Roland, so after opening the door I go straight to the den and announce to them, "I'm not feeling well. I think I'll rest in my room, maybe take a nap, till time to pick up the children. Kurina, please fix lunch for your family, I just can't."

"Of course," Bobby pipes up, "and we'll fix something for you too. What do you want?

"Thank you, Bobby, but no lunch for me. If this headache goes away, I'll come downstairs. Don't worry about me." I said all this while pouring coffee to take upstairs.

"Why are you drinking coffee? That won't make you sleep," Bobby observed.

"You're right," I reply, pouring the cup back into the pot and getting a ginger ale out of the fridge. "Don't know what I'm thinking."

Turning toward the stairs, I raise my voice, "If the phone rings, take a message. I'm shutting off the ringer in my room so it won't disturb me."

I lock the bedroom door, slip into loose jeans and shirt, and climb onto the bed with my notebook and a pen. Now I have two or three hours for my tumultuous thoughts, all vying for attention.

That last perceptive question Roland had asked me was a real bother: "Bobby's antagonism toward you, Patsy, how long has that been going on? I have a hunch that in Bobby's psyche this animosity didn't just start."

I feel immediately blameworthy. Bobby isn't the only one who withholds information.

No, Roland, it didn't just start. The truth is that I went out with Bobby first. The truth is that after warnings from my favorite teacher and disapproval from my mother, I didn't go out with him again. The truth is, with Bobby protesting, "I am a better man than my brother," I paid him the ultimate insult: I fell in love with Billy. Did the animosity start then—since Bobby always wanted what Billy had? Thinking about it, I realized he had always wanted to *prove himself*, whatever that means to the male ego, not only by winning any competition with other males but by taking from Billy.

Bobby was known at school as one of the biggest "skirt chasers" around. What a grievous shame that he married our wonderful friend Kathleen. We all loved K.K. After her death, Bobby dreamed up a phony "first date" seduction. He would tell his date that he was still grieving the death of his young wife... and now that he was dating again, she was his first date since his wife's death. He used that line to gain compassion from girls foolish enough to go out with him. I know because he used that disgusting line on my dorm mate—in front of me. What a day that turned out to be! We sure had a taste of his "animosity" that day. Bobby displayed not only animosity toward me but also, in my mind at least, rivalry and hostility toward his identical twin. That story might interest Roland:

Julia and I scurry around our rooms, getting packed for the beach, our surroundings fairly crackling with excitement. On this special weekend the North Texas State campus is nearly deserted; many students are on their way to Splash Day in Galveston. We, too, are going to Galveston, and we can hardly wait to be on our way. Oh, the giddy freedom of a fast car and no supervision!

Billy, my boyfriend, and Bobby, his twin, are driving Bobby's new blue Corvette up from Texas Christian University, where Billy is enrolled.

Bill and I have been planning this trip for weeks, not only for ourselves but more especially for Bobby, who has been grieving for months.

More than a year ago Bobby's young wife, Kathleen Connally, the daughter of our state senator, had been killed in a fatal accident only a few weeks after their marriage. The tragic death happened in Tallahassee, Florida.

The young couple had eloped to Ardmore, Oklahoma, and then promptly moved to Florida. Entering their apartment one afternoon, Bobby found K.K. sitting on the sofa, alone and crying and holding a gun—the shotgun Bobby's father had given him. Bobby tried to wrestle the shotgun from her hands but botched the effort. With both their hands griping the gun, it exploded, driving the hundred pieces of metal shot into K.K.'s head, entering from the back right side. Devastated, Bobby returned home to Fort Worth. Needing to finish high school but unable to cope with life as it had been, he finished his last two semesters at Polytech Vocational School, where he was not known—or, at least he thought he was, not known.

But he could not hide from the shooting death of a powerful politician's daughter. The story was in all the papers in Texas. I guess everyone in Fort Worth knew about Kathleen's death and its suspicious circumstances, and like people will, they gossiped and questioned. Perhaps this type of uncomfortable attention drove Bobby to stay out of sight.

At any rate, after finishing Polytech Vocational School, Bobby isolated himself at his parents home. During this time of grieving, the only company Bobby permitted was Billy. Billy was very closed about this tragedy. Rarely was he able to say his thoughts and feelings about Kathleen's death other than to me. Bobby's only consolation during his time of grief was Kathleen's terrier, Darlin. According to Billy, this little dog's slightest discomfort was cause for hysterical displays of anxiety and concern in Bobby. In my immature understanding, I felt Bobby's excessive attention to Darlin had something to do with Kathleen. His hands were on the gun, he was totally involved in the struggle, yet he failed to keep her from dying. When the police got to the couple's apartment, they found Bobby half out of his mind; so dazed and shaken that they were unable to get any clear communication from him. At some point he started trying to jump out of the two-story apartment's window and had to be restrained.

Bobby had a hard time trying to rid his memory of this catastrophe and, not long after her death, he returned to Tallahassee on two occasions to talk to the ambulance driver who had driven K.K. to the hospital that night. Two years later, on his return trip from another Florida city, he went to Tallahassee yet again to talk to the driver. I have no way of knowing what he hoped to gain by talking to the ambulance driver three times.

K.K. (this was an endearing pet name Kathleen's family called her and was picked up by all her friends and was the name Bobby called her) was my dear friend, and she had rushed me for her high school sorority. This sorority was a group of girls from families perhaps a social class above my own. Fort Worth in the late 1950s was less than egalitarian. But K.K. had taken a chance on me, and I loved her like a sister. She also took a chance on Bobby.

K.K. was only sixteen and hopelessly in love with the green-eyed, black-haired Bobby, a young man so handsome and charming that he, together with his identical twin, Billy, was well known throughout the region. At that time in Fort Worth, when mention was made of "the twins," it was understood by all that Bobby and Billy Hale were under discussion. Silence would fall in the room so that not a word would be missed. They were a favorite topic of conversation among old and young alike, as is still the case today so many years later.

"Yeah, Julia!" I call. "They're here." Three sharp buzzes of the hall phone signaled the arrival of the twins and the start of our adventure. The drive to Galveston is going to be fun and will give Julia and Bobby a chance to get acquainted.

Julia and I bounce downstairs, dragging our heavy overnight bags and giggling hysterically. Upon stumbling into the sitting room, I am surprised that only Bobby is at the desk to greet us. Billy stayed in the car, I think disapprovingly. Does he think sending Bobby inside is good enough? I feel it is obligatory for a "nice" boy to leave his car and come inside for his date. "Respectable" girls demand no less, but what am I to do? Teenage girls judge one another harshly, and I fear his bad manners will diminish Julia's opinion of me.

Though embarrassed, I cheerfully introduce Bobby to Julia. She is a pretty enough girl with blonde hair and a beautiful smile. They both seem happy to meet. Bobby grabs our bags and ushers us out to his car.

The blue Corvette convertible sits conspicuously at the curb. Billy is nowhere in sight.

The sickening feeling of something gone wrong starts moving in the pit of my stomach. "Bobby, where's Billy?" I ask, staring at the car to hide the confused hurt in my face.

Bobby seems almost surprised that I have noticed Billy's absence. He answers offhandedly, "Oh, I think he's coming later."

My throat tightens into a knot. "Coming later?" I croak. This may be the biggest disappointment of my life. The whole trip is Billy's big plan, and now he's not showing up?

From my overprotective parents I had finally been granted permission to go to Splash Day in Galveston with my girlfriends. I was very close to both my parents and had felt awful when I let Billy convince me that, instead of going with my girlfriends, he and I should go together and take his still-depressed twin. And, Billy had suggested that, to lift Bobby's spirits, perhaps I could persuade my friend Julia to go with us. The whole plan was actually easy to arrange, and soon excitement took the place of guilt; after all, I reasoned, I was doing a good deed. "I want my brother back," Billy had said. "I want to free him from the past. He can look at this trip as his first date, a double date with you and me." So this trip together was for Bobby. Though we had all grieved deeply at the death of Kathleen, Bobby had been inconsolable, according to Billy.

Well if it was true that he had indeed been inconsolable, then

Bobby has certainly unloaded his heavy burden in a hurry. Having left his secluded den of sorrow not more than an hour ago, here he is seeming quite his old self, not concerned about a thing, not even his missing brother.

Bobby helps Julia into the car and deftly motions her to slip over, leaving room for me on the front seat. Bobby grins up at me as he reaches down to hold the car door open. His amazing sea-green eyes reflect the hot Texas sky. Dazed, I grab at him as I almost lose my footing at the curb. "What's the matter, Patsy?" he chuckles softly. "Don't you think I can take care of you?" His good looks are absolutely unnerving, and he knows it. Flinching at his snide remark and suggestive stare, I struggle into the back seat, refusing to sit in front with him.

Alone in the back seat, I find this whole idea of Splash Day to be trite and wrong. I am disgusted with myself. Why did I betray my parents' trust and let myself be talked into this scheme? If it weren't for Julia, I would refuse to go another step. I want to run back to my dorm, show Bill that he can't exploit me into a horrible deception like this and then casually abandon me to his "sad and grieving brother." But I'm the one who invited Julia to Galveston; I've got to see this through.

The tires are soon singing as we gain speed leaving Denton, driving south on I-35. But that singing, the exhilarating "rubber meets the road" sound, only serves to make me more wretched.

In no time we are crossing Lake Dallas. Momentarily I feel the cooler air from the water and glumly watch the lake go by. Bill and I picnicked here just last week, lounging on our blanket and putting together final plans for this trip. How hollow it all seems now.

I slump miserably in the back seat and try to focus on the radio, but Bobby keeps up a constant barrage of loud talk. "Hey, Patsy," he calls, twisting the rear-view mirror so he can see me, crouched in the back corner as far away from him as I can get. "How would you like to eat at Giado's tonight? I know you love that place." He turns his talk to Julia. "Giado's is a great seafood place. It has this big old, huge plastic crab out front, so you can't miss it." Julia and Bobby break into laughter. "We can sit on the patio and watch the sunset," he says, "and they have this big Oriental gong that strikes the second the sun drops into the water. They have a contest too; whoever makes the closest guess to the exact time the sun disappears gets a free drink. What do you think, Patsy? Won't that be fun?"

Did he really ask me "Won't that be fun?" At this suggestion, the lump in my throat finally bursts. As Bobby glances back, tears are pouring down my face. To control them is out of the question. I can't, and don't, acknowledge him. A 7-Eleven store is coming up just ahead and Bobby, ever dramatic, whirls the car, tires screaming, into the parking lot and slams to a screeching stop.

"Patsy, get out of the car, please," he says softly and firmly. "I need to talk to you." He pulls me out of earshot of Julia. I stand defiantly, looking past him through my tears. "Patsy, look me in the eye. I can't believe you're acting this way. It's going to be okay. I told you I'll take care of you. Billy will probably come later."

"This is not the way it should be, Bobby," I practically scream. "What is Billy up to? What are you hiding from me?"

He twists his mouth in disgust. "Try not to let your imagination run wild. And don't ruin this trip for everyone else. How do you think you're making Julia feel?"

Julia and I look at each other as I walk back to the car. Poor girl, she seems miserable. "I'm sorry, Julia. I'm just so mad at Billy I don't know what to do. I may never speak to him again."

"Do you want a coke or anything while we're here?" Bobby offers brusquely as he puts the convertible top up. I do want a coke, terribly; maybe its coolness will wash away this stinging misery in my throat and chest. He comes back with three cokes and some cigarettes. Bobby slowly tears the pack open and lights his cigarette, cutting his eyes menacingly back at me.

With that last warning glance, Bobby spins the car into the road and the music grows louder. Bobby Darien croons, "I need a dream lover so I won't have to dream alone," my and Billy's favorite song. "Try not to let your imagination run wild," Bobby had snarled. Obviously I will learn nothing more from him.

As we approach the outskirts of Dallas, I want nothing more than to fall asleep and not wake up until we reach Galveston. Jana and

Wendell, my and Billy's good friends since junior high school, left early and are no doubt already in Galveston. I can't wait to tell them this story. What will they think? I wonder if Billy has been in touch with Wendell.

We navigate through Dallas and pick up I-45 South, the highway we'll stay on all the way through Houston and on to Galveston. I bunch up the pillow that I carry everywhere, and snuggle into it for a nap. Bobby turns down the radio, and he and Julia continue their small talk. Falling asleep is hopeless, so I keep quiet and listen.

Shortly Bobby must have decided to impress Julia with his knowledge of Galveston. He catches my attention too: "Did you know Galveston used to be one of the biggest cities in Texas?" he asked. "Actually, I read it was the most important city in Texas, and that's because of the coast and the port. There was so much business and money in Galveston, it was called the Wall Street of the South."

Oh brother, I thought. He's been locked up in that house and has read up on Galveston, probably just yesterday, so he can impress Julia.

"Like New York?" Julia tries to sound impressed, and probably is. "Didn't a terrible hurricane hit Galveston way back?" she asks.

"Oh yeah, a long time ago, Bobby answered. "It looks different now. There are places in town, hotels and restaurants mainly, where you can see old pictures. It tore up almost everything and killed a lot of people too. Anyway, they built a seawall along the beach. I think they're safe from hurricanes now."

"I can tell you something else about Galveston," Bobby continued. "My favorite explorer was shipwrecked and washed up on Galveston Island. That wasn't long after Columbus, and Indians were living on the islands then."

"Oh yeah?" Julia asked with a laugh. "And who, may I ask, is your favorite explorer?" Bobby throws his head back and they both burst out laughing.

"Julia, you think it's funny," Bobby teased. "But I really enjoyed reading about this guy, Cabeza de Vaca. Have you heard of him?"

"No, I don't think so."

"Well, like I said, his ship went down—probably in one of those

Galveston-type storms. Anyway he was captured by the Indians. What I really like about him is how he learned from them. He learned all about their secret ways and native drugs and became a better witch doctor than any of the Indian witch doctors."

"Huh," Julia mused.

"I guess I just admire the fact," Bobby goes on, "that he found himself in a terrible situation and really made the best of it. Old Cabeza was tough, the kind of guy my dad would call a survivor. Dad liked guys like that— survivors, and I do too."

Now I am finding this conversation pretty strange and pretty interesting. I have met Bobby and Billy's dad, and I know he had been an FBI agent—well known in Dallas and Fort Worth. I'm sure he taught the twins how to shoot and hunt and defend themselves— how to survive. Yes, I guess Mr. Hale would like survivors. I am kind of impressed, too, that Bobby has learned some history. Before Kathleen he was so notorious for chasing girls and fighting boys that I pretty much thought that's all he knew.

I guess they think I'm asleep back here because after a little more banter and laughter, I notice that Julia has moved much closer to Bobby. He leans toward her and purrs in a voice so low I can barely hear him, "Julia, I'm so glad you came with me."

"I'm glad I did too, Bobby," she says, gazing sweetly up at him.

He continues, "You know, you're my first date. I feel like a baby just learning to walk." He says this in a sad, faraway voice.

Oh, those words sound so familiar! Didn't Billy say, "He can look at this trip as his first date?" Is there no end to the twins' deviousness? And now he "Feels just like a baby learning to walk?" Sickening! He's going to use Kathleen's death as a way to come on to Julia. I want to throw up! What have I gotten my poor friend into?

Hey Bobby, I want to say, *Speaking of Kathleen, how was it that you and she both had your hands on the shotgun and yet it had no fingerprints on it? Why don't you explain that to Julia and me? Tell us about that wipe-down.* But of course I don't say any such thing—as far as I know, no one has ever asked him that question, not even the police. The lack of fingerprints was just missing evidence that, again as far as I know, was never accounted for.

We are well into the trip, and I don't want to see or hear Julia falling for any more of Bobby's talk. With my knees bent so that my feet rest against the far side of this small back area, and with a lot of effort, I do manage to fall asleep.

It seems like no time before Bobby announces, "Okay girls, here we are!

Julia must have fallen asleep too, because when I sit straight up, so does she. "We'll be going across the causeway in a minute; I'm going to take the top down," he says, pulling off the road. We all want the full impact of our getaway environment. The view of Galveston Bay and the familiar smell of the Gulf lift my mood and cause Julia and Bobby to become absolutely giddy.

"When we get off Highway 45," Bobby, acting and talking like a tour guide, says, "we'll be making a right turn up ahead and in minutes we're on Ocean Boulevard. It follows the sea wall for ten miles and is full of fun, food, and romance."

"The fun and food part sounds good," Julia says with a laugh and slides, teasing, away from Bobby.

Driving along the palm-lined boulevard, we squint into the sun, taking in the foam-capped waves as they roll in. The water, shining all the way to the horizon, the sound of gulls overhead, and the smell of salt water in the air is exhilarating to three kids from four hundred miles inland.

In no time we pull into the parking lot of our motel, The Sea Horse. "Patsy, this is groovy," Julia squeals. "Do all the rooms look out on the water? Let's find our room and freshen up."

Bobby walks ahead with our bags, and I whisper to Julia, "Let's see if we can find Jana and Wendell. They are here somewhere. Maybe they've heard from Billy."

Bobby opens a door up the hall and goes in—and comes out. "Okay, your stuff is in the room. Everything's all set. Let's hurry and get back out; I'm starving."

I already know Jana's room is #64, so I go straight there and knock. Wendell is with her, and I greet my dear friends with the breathless question, "Have you heard from Billy?"

Wendell answers, "Not me. What's up? Are you saying he's not here? Did you have a fight?"

"No, he's not. And no, we didn't. Yesterday on the phone we were both excited about this trip and couldn't wait till today. Then he didn't even show up at the dorm. I rode down here by myself with Bobby and Julia."

Jana joins in, "That's crazy. What did Bobby say?"

"Nothing! He won't tell me anything. Maybe you can get him to talk, Wendell."

Our conversation is interrupted by a loud knock on the door from Bobby. "I want food!" he yells. "Julia and I are going to Giado's."

Wendell jerks open the door. Good-looking with blue eyes and sandy hair, Wendell is the twins' age and a lifelong friend of them and me. The three boys were so close they had sealed their friendship forever in ink, long before tattoos were abundant. Each of them had a black flying bat with "HIH," tattooed under the bat, on the heel of his right foot. They were sixteen at the time, and to them the inscription stood for: Hale Iverson Hale, fly by night.

"Where the heck is Billy?" Wendell asks when he opens the door.

"I don't know what to tell you. I think he had something to do," Bobby says, shrugging his shoulders. "He'll be here, I'm sure. Hitchhiking is no problem for Billy. I expect him by dark."

Wendell narrows his eyes and frowns at Bobby. "Say what?"

Bobby just shrugs his shoulders again.

"So you're going to Giado's? We'll be there. Patsy will come with us."

My favorite, shrimp and crab cakes, are wonderful, but I am at battle with angry feelings. Everybody at the table wants to walk down to Stewart Beach and watch the sunset. Somehow, looking at the sunset by myself is not very appealing. Bobby playfully tries to charm me and make me laugh and feel part of everything, and he manages to coax me into going along with the group.

Walking along the beach, in the distance we can see the flickering tiki torches that are encircling the Beach Club's huge dance floor. This is one of Galveston's favorite entertainment spots, and the mood is certainly set for our first night of Splash Day. Bobby, walking ahead of us with Julia, catches the mood at once. "Let's go, gang!" he yells, waving his arm toward the tiki lights. We all pick up our pace and head straight there—then I have second thoughts. I know that Lonnie, an old boyfriend of mine, will be on the dance floor and will pursue me.

"Are you sure we don't want to go out toward the other pier, to my favorite club instead?" I ask. This club is where all the big entertainers perform, and Frank Sinatra was there the last time I was in Galveston. ZZ Top actually wrote a song about this favorite hot spot. I thought for sure Bobby would have preferred it. "I hear BB King is playing there tonight, Bobby," I try to convince him, to no avail. Now that he sees the lights and hears the music, he prefers to go to the Beach Club to dance. Bobby is a good dancer, as is Bill, and Jana and Wendell don't care either way, so, being outnumbered, I go along.

Outside, the dance floor is very romantic and alluring, and they are playing our favorite music. And here I am alone—and still don't know why. In only a moment I sense someone watching me. Turning around, I look right into Lonnie's face as he walks up. My relationship with him does not involve deep emotions, because my heart belongs to Billy. But he is fun and a fabulous dancer. Back at school we used to meet in the student union hall after classes and dance all afternoon. Lonnie was known to be the best dancer doing the "North Texas Push," a version of the popular "Push" that Lonnie himself probably devised, and I was his favorite partner. So in a split second I make what turns out to be a bad decision. Before the night is out, I come to believe Bobby had set me up.

Lonnie and I promptly move onto the dance floor, where they are playing the great 1960s songs that we love, starting with The Righteous Brothers' "You've Lost That Loving Feelin'" and the Four Seasons' "Bye, Bye Baby." By now I am hooked; the music and those smooth gliding movements are intoxicating, and I know I will dance till they close the place down. I am good at following Lonnie's lead and can spin like a top. We know we are the best couple on the floor and are really showing off. As we are "moving and grooving" to Bobby Darien's "Splish Splash," I feel a tap on my shoulder. Bobby whispers, "Bill is waiting for you out on the pier."

I move away from Lonnie and tell him I have to go. I glare at Bobby as he continues to dance with Julia. *You son of a gun*, I think. *You're at it again. You wanted Billy to see me with Lonnie. You want him to be mad at me.* I leave the dance floor at a run.

The moon is wonderfully bright and I spot Billy right away, looking at me, forlorn and unhappy. As I approach him, I realize it is not just the hurt in his eyes that is different. To my huge surprise, the whole lower part of his face is wired. He lifts his beer to his chest, and I see him sip it through a straw. I stare speechless, but my mind is racing with a thousand questions. Finally Billy speaks in a voice so low and so muffled I can barely understand him, "Patsy, why did you leave me? Do you know I had to hitchhike all the way from TCU?"

"What are you talking about—why did I leave you? When you didn't show up at the dorm, your brother told me to come in the car with him and Julia. All he would tell me was that you would probably be along later."

"He didn't tell you he broke my jaws?"

"He broke both your jaws? No, he didn't tell me, and it makes me want to scream. How can he be so stupid and mean? Billy, I was so miserable without you that I was crying. I thought you had stood me up, and your brother let me think that."

"I was in the emergency room, for God's sake," he rasps.

"And he abandoned you," I say incredulously.

Billy's sad eyes take on a whole different level of hurt at this realization.

I continue, "Bobby totally misrepresented you. He had all of us, especially me, thinking that you didn't care if you were with us or not. If we had known your predicament, anyone, Wendell or Ray, would have waited for you. And anything that was needed I would have done. Were you two fighting again?"

"We…had an accident at school, in phys ed," Bill hisses through clinched teeth. "He threw a discus and broke my jaws."

This is too much for me to comprehend. Now I doubt Bill's story. A discus weighs a lot, probably six or eight pounds. I say, "I don't know why it didn't knock out all your teeth too—or worse."

"Loosened some teeth, but I got lucky. The doctor says they'll tighten up. I'm wired together. Can't eat for weeks. I have to drink through this straw."

"Billy, I'm so sorry you had to go through all this," I say. "Do you know it's one o'clock in the morning?"

"It's been hell. Then I find you hugging up to Lonnie."

"I wasn't hugging up to him; he and I have always danced. Besides, if I had known you were coming, I'd have waited for you. Bobby set me up. I know he did. He wants us to fight."

Billy gives me a look that tells me he believes it too.

I know he is hurt when he says, his muffled voice barely audible, "This is crazy; he's my brother, but look at what he did: He breaks my jaws, abandons me at the hospital, and lets my girl think I've stood her up. Does Bobby want to hurt me? Why does he want to break us up? I don't know what to think."

All that talk is a big effort for him through clinched teeth, and I start to give him a comforting embrace. Over my shoulder, he spots Wendell. Bill mumbles through his wires, "Is that Wendell? I've got to talk to him about all this."

"Uh-oh," I say. "He's by himself, which means Jana has run off— so typical of her."

Wendell approaches with the most comical, questioning look on his face. "Hey, Billy, old bud, glad to see you alive. He comes close, scrutinizing Bill's wiring. "I didn't expect to see you like this. You and Bobby fighting again?"

"I'll tell you about it, Wendell. Let's talk in private. Patsy, you understand."

"I'm going to find Jana," I answer.

In the early-morning hours, after Wendell and Bill's conservation, the gist of which I was never privy to, Billy and I walk hand in hand on the beach. It feels so good to be with him and feel the sand between our toes and know that things are all right between us. A twinge of conscience tugs at me, however. My parents know where I am, and they probably guess that Billy will meet me here, but they do not know the depth of my love for him. It is with firm resolve that I determine I must and will be strong in my convictions and not betray their trust.

The next day, Billy and I are at the Beach Hut, both of us drinking milkshakes for breakfast and watching the sea gulls. This early rising is in spite of Bill's ordeal yesterday.

I think I am much more troubled about Billy's horrible accident than he seems to be. I keep visualizing Bobby, whose aim is sure: those cold pale eyes, leveling the heavy discus, sending it silently, flawlessly, at just the right part of Billy's face. Oh, my God! Surely I am wrong! But that vision alarms me; and it continued to haunt me for years.

What is incredible to me now, is that I never questioned that "accident" further, either to Billy or to Bobby or to Wendell. As a result, I don't know to this day what really happened. Nor do I understand how we all just overlooked Bobby's behavior.

It isn't long before our friends Marty and Ray show up at the top of the sea wall. I have known Marty since junior high, and Ray is her boyfriend. Bill tells me what the boys have planned: "We're all going for a Jeep ride on the beach after lunch."

We girls want to sunbathe before the ride, so we run across the road to our room. I put on my purple two-piece bathing suit and Julia her polka-dot bikini, and we run back down to the beach. Jana has our homemade suntan lotion, which is baby oil spiked with iodine. We all slather it on, believing it will prevent sunburn, and we laugh at how we think Marty, in spite of the lotion and her long t-shirt, will look like a lobster in no time.

Billy, with his wired-together jaws, joins us for a tan while Wendell and Ray go after the Jeeps.

Billy lies in the sun for about five minutes with me before he says, "Patsy, let's jump some waves."

"Do you remember, Billy," I say, laughing as we bounce in the shallow waves, being careful not to wet his face, "how traumatic yesterday was?"

"Naw," he mumbles. "I don't remember." This causes me to break up laughing.

Down the beach, it looks like Bobby is having a good time with Julia. He's probably thinking the little polka-dot girl is pretty cute.

"Hey, the Jeeps are here," I holler to the girls basking in the sun.

"This is going to be a blast." Since Billy can barely talk, I suggest, "Billy let's hop in the Jeep with Wendell and Jana and let Ray and Marty go with Bobby."

The boys turn the Jeeps around, and we head a little farther west down to Stewart Beach. There won't be any interference there because it is very private. What an adventure it is to ride the Jeeps in the sand. Even though we are going pretty slow because of Billy's injury, we are hollering and yelling like wild things. Our friends are so much fun, but we are already painfully aware that we will be leaving in the morning and must make the most of our last night. "It's time to turn the Jeeps in," Wendell says. "Let's make plans for tonight."

"Well, here is the plan," says Bobby, holding up both hands: "We are going to have a big cookout and Ray is going to play his guitar."

We all cheer and confirm that the plan is just exactly what we all want.

That night we grill up some pretty mean fish and drink plenty of Land O' Lakes beer. As Ray plays the guitar, Marty and I harmonize with him to a song his friend from Amarillo wrote: "Once I lived the life of a millionaire, spending my money, Lord I didn't' care… Oh Lord, without a doubt, nobody wants you when you're down and out." So we sing and laugh and tell stories and take great pleasure in one another's company. All too soon, our evening—one of those treasured, carefree moments of youth—is gone, slipping into our memories like a good dream.

The morning sun slams through the window and hits my eyes like a blazing hammer. Julia has opened the blackout curtains and says urgently, "Get up, Patsy. We barely have time to gather our things before checkout. I'm not sure everybody's even awake." She goes into the hall to start knocking on doors. What groans and moans up and down the hall as we prepare to get on the road. Our three-car caravan will shortly be headed for TCU and North Texas State. As Julia said, we barely have time to dress and grab our things before checkout time.

Forget about packing—we throw everything into suitcases and

bags. The boys start blowing the car horns as we head out of town—their way of saying goodbye to Galveston. There is something so joyous and funny about the boys making all this racket, my girlfriends and I laugh hysterically.

As soon as I can stop laughing for a minute, I ask Bobby to pull over at the next service station. We drive the palm-lined boulevard, and he signals to the other cars, pulling into the first Gulf station. "Julia, I'm going to the restroom," I say, and she follows me.

When we are out of ear shot, I ask, "Julia, what do you think of Bobby?"

"Oh, Patsy, he's gorgeous," she says, gripping my arm with both hands. But some things about him are strange, like the way he didn't tell you about Billy. That's weird. He's gorgeous and fun to be with, but a little sketchy."

"Well, I don't want to influence you either way," I tell her, "because he is Bill's twin brother. But as a friend, I will advise you to be careful."

When we reach the ladies room, we find the door locked. Marty has followed us and sees that the men's door is wide open. "Let's have one of the guys guard the door for a minute while we run in here," she says.

In what seems like only a minute or two, we hear loud voices outside the door. "What's all that racket?" asks Marty.

"I don't know," I say, "but the bad news is, one of those voices is Bobby."

We are on guard and look at one another with dread. Everyone in our group, except Julia, knows that loud voices and Bobby mean a fight.

We three girls carefully open the door—to a barrage of cursing like I have never heard. This big oaf of a guy is cursing like a madman and calling us girls unspeakable names.

In the South at that time, a gentleman—actually forget about "gentleman"; let's say a male of the species—didn't curse in front of a female. It was considered a huge offense. "Holy smoke" was pretty strong language for our crowd.

Hearing this man curse us, Bobby, our door guard, is having none of it. In a second he is throwing punches and connecting with a right hook to the stomach of this maniac.

Around the corner of the station comes a large cop. In the near distance we hear two more police sirens closing in on the Gulf station.

Ray and Wendell are holding onto poor Billy with his broken jaws. Apparently he wants to get in on this fracas.

You've never heard such a commotion with all the screaming and yelling. I think our eyes must be as big as plates as we gawk in amazement at the next move:

Bobby is on the ground pounding the vulgar-talking man when the cop comes up from behind and raises his billy club to, unbelievably, strike Bobby in the back of the head. Instinct must have played a strong part in this drama, for I have never witnessed anything as perfectly timed: Bobby turns, almost like a dance move, and grabs the descending club in his right hand, stopping the hit in midair—as if a "sixth sense" has guided him. We all gasp with relief.

The next scene is almost comical. All of us friends stare spellbound as Bobby stands up holding the blackjack aloft. Then, with polite ceremony, he hands the club back to the stupefied officer.

We all immediately take up a defense of Bobby, trying to reason with the policeman, telling him that Bobby was only protecting us girls from this drunken, cursing wild man—who is no longer wild but lying dazed on the ground.

The cop hears our explanation but is also telling us, in no uncertain terms, that there was a better way to handle this incident than to beat the man up. Then the other two squad cars shriek into the station, the policemen jumping out and heading toward us.

This is the first time in a long time that my knees turn to jelly. I can picture Bobby looking out through the bars of a South Texas jail, and I can hear my parents' troubling verdict as to my truth-telling about this trip.

The first policeman tells the other two—only after they have intimidated us to the point of begging—that everything is under control.

You never saw eight shaken teenagers pile into their cars any quicker. We headed North on Highway 45, thanking our lucky stars. We didn't part until the Dallas turnoff, when, with hands waving and horns blowing, we sped away in our different directions.

For a long time after that, whenever we friends got together, this particular Splash Day was a favorite topic of conversation. We would recount the day's and evening's events, and I loved how Ray would sum it all up: "You know that morning at the Gulf station in Galveston?" he would say, shaking his head back and forth. "I said to myself then: Don't ever mess with one of the Hale boys." Then he would whisper and give a secret wink, "That one being Bobby."

Yes, Roland, I thought, the enmity goes way back. And though I didn't realize it until now—as evidenced by Bobby's behavior and your astute observation—it must still run deep.

10. THE STAKEOUT

"Oh what a tangled web we weave, when first we practice to deceive."
~ Sir Walter Scott

With the Morning Stars in the house, Billy and I have little privacy to talk…, so I wait until we retire for the night and tell him: "I think we are being staked out."

"Staked out? As in under surveillance? Why would we be staked out, and by who?"

"By the police for one, and by the sheriff's department for another," I answer.

Billy gives a long sigh. "Why would they be interested in us?"

"The children maybe?"

"Huh?"

"You are aware," I remind him, "that we have two children in our home who are basically unaccounted for."

"That's not so. Bobby accounted for them. Lotus is his third wife's child, and Running Cub is a gypsy kid.

"Well, there is a big blue car that's been parked on the street across from our house for two days. I pretend not to notice it, but it's like, maybe, a Ford Fairlane from the '60s. There's a woman and a man who sit inside the car, and I have seen them watching our house. Today, when I left to pick the children up from school, there was a sheriff's car parked behind the blue car and a deputy was talking to the man and woman inside. For some reason the occupants of the blue car had called the sheriff's department; at least it appeared that way to me. I tried not to look at them—thinking that if some of our neighbors are in trouble, I don't want to stare. But truthfully I was only pretending, because like I said, I had seen them looking at *our* house. When the kids and I got back from school, both cars were gone. What do you make of that?"

"Nothing," Billy says, "unless something further develops."

At about four o'clock in the afternoon on the day after this stakeout conversation, I climb the stairs to the solitude of our bedroom and call Billy at the clinic. "Do you have a minute?" I ask.

"One minute. What's happening?"

"You said last night that you weren't going to make anything of my stakeout story unless something further develops. Remember?"

"Yes... And?"

"Something further developed. The same deputy sheriff I told you about yesterday came here today."

"To the house? What did he want?"

"He came to serve papers on Bobby from Running Cub's mother. She wants her son back."

As he often does when he is mulling over a problem, Billy hesitates a long minute. Then he says, "This reminds me of that case in Hawaii. Do you remember?"

"Yes, I do."

"Running Cub's mother didn't file kidnapping charges against Bobby, did she?"

"It didn't turn out that way in the end—but there was something else."

"What else?"

"There was yet another complaint against Bobby. You see, Running Cub's mother and her boyfriend found out where you live, and they have been watching our house to see if Bobby came out. And you know how irritated I get that Bobby always parks my car way in the back, outside the fence? Well, he's actually had his reasons for doing that. When the mother and boyfriend saw him through the fence in the backyard, she called the sheriff's department. Ironically, when Running Cub's mother called the sheriff's department they found another complaint against a Robert Allen Hale. That complaint was filed months ago by Bobby's wife—the one he is still married to and who is the mother of his two boys."

Billy says, "The same wife and little boys we tried to get some financial help for? That's been a year or two ago. We didn't know where Bobby was."

"Yes! You're right. And you can probably guess the complaint against Bobby as well; it was nonpayment of child support."

"Uh-oh. Was Bobby there?"

"Well, it got very interesting. Running Cub's little mother and her boyfriend barged right into the house and confronted Bobby."

"Really! What did Bobby do?"

"He was shocked, and he got a little excited but, considering that the deputy was with them, Bobby controlled himself pretty well. You know your brother's gift for argument. He can talk his way out of anything, and that's what he did today."

"Go on," Billy says eagerly.

"Bobby told the deputy that he would never have taken the boy without the mother's approval. Bobby said, 'At the Rainbow Festival in Arizona a few months ago, this woman agreed to let her boy travel with me and my wife'—meaning Kurina. 'We have taken far better care of this child than his mother ever has. She was letting him run unsupervised at that festival; anything could have happened to him.' I watched Running Cub, as he was there in the room with us, and he didn't seem to favor his mother.

"The mother got really mad and said she had plainly told Bobby that Manuel could stay with him and Kurina only during the festival. She never meant for them to take Manuel away. She screamed, 'Did you really think I was giving my child to you? Are you crazy?'

"Then Bobby turned to the deputy sheriff and asked, 'Officer, who is this man here with Manuel's mother?'

"By the way, Billy, Manuel is Running Cub's given name. It was the first time I've heard Bobby say it."

"It was bound to be something besides Running Cub. What

then?"

"Bobby repeated, 'Who is this man? Has he taken care of Manuel? Is he Manuel's father? Is he your husband?'

"I felt the deputy should be asking those questions, but he turned to the mother and said, 'Answer the question. Who is this man with you?'

"'He is my boyfriend,' she said. 'His name is Eddie Bledsoe.'

"'Not Manuel's father?' the deputy asked. 'How well do you know Eddie Bledsoe? Do you trust him with your son?' And so on it went with Bobby and the deputy registering plenty of disapproval of her lifestyle. But the deputy reminded Bobby, 'In the end, this woman is still the boy's mother.'

"They had had the poor little mother in tears. I felt sorry for her. She is a cute, petite woman with a head full of curly black hair. She seemed very vulnerable and sad. She hugged and kissed Manuel, and you could tell he loved his mother. But in the end, on his way to her car, he stopped—hesitated in the driveway—and looked back at Bobby. He was obviously torn between them. He loves Bobby too."

"Are you telling me Running Cub is gone?" Billy asks.

"Yes, and not only Running Cub but Lotus too."

"What?"

"I know it sounds confusing, but just listen to me," I say, when Billy tries to interrupt. "Lotus's mother is actually Bobby's current legal wife, Connie, and Connie is also the mother of his two boys, that we were just talking about. Anyway, somehow she knows Running Cub's mother. The deputy had the complaint filed by Lotus's mother, Bobby's wife, with him and he called her on the telephone. Lotus's mother told the deputy that she wanted her daughter back. She did not approve of her young daughter traveling with her faithless husband and his new, teenage girlfriend. She asked the deputy to please send Lotus with Running Cub's mother."

"So both those children are gone?" Billy asks incredulously. "Just like that?"

"Just like that. When the officer moved in, it went fast. I think Bobby barely knew what happened. In less than an hour, it was all over. Bobby was lucky too; in another place there might have been a huge court trial in this situation—and it would have been valid. In fact, I wonder if your dad's being good friends with the sheriff had anything to do with this deputy's leniency."

"No telling, but that could be the case."

"At any rate, Billy, I thought you should know that today Bobby has lost his two—I guess you would say foster—children, and he is grieving."

* *

"Laughter is the sun that drives winter from the human face."
~ Victor Hugo

Billy is smiling and squirming in his chair, and I can tell by his body language that he has a funny story to tell. Bobby is despondent, what with the children being taken from him this afternoon, and Billy would like to cheer him up.

The fact is, we are all sad that Running Cub and Lotus are gone. I had felt a great pang of sympathy when the beautiful little Lotus ran out to the old truck to retrieve her few belongings. She had held her little things in both arms and looked around at us grown-ups, bewilderment in her eyes. Then, with no choice, she followed Running Cub's mother and boyfriend, complete strangers to her, into their car. She seemed to me the poster child for innocent children—children who are dragged around from one home to another by thoughtless adults.

In light of what has happened today, I would like to get my children to bed early so I can sit and talk with the men tonight. I tell them, "Well, kids, you've got your old sleeping arrangements now," trying to be cheerful while helping them rearrange their bedrooms. They are non-committal as they position their toys and dolls back into place. I am almost as subdued as they are, but I try to brighten their spirits before turning out the lights: "Do you know how happy I would be to see you if one of you had been away for three months? I would be jubilant. That's how happy Lotus's and Running Cub's mothers are to see them."

When I walk into the den I recognize a ridiculously funny episode from St. Andrew's Academy that the twins are recalling with each other. It involves the "restaurant" they set up in their dorm room there:

At about age sixteen, Bobby was at odds with his parents on several levels; one in particular was the almost constant trouble he was in with girls. Bobby actually volunteered to his parents that, due to the fact he seemed unable to stay out of trouble, and since they were so unhappy with him, they could send him to another school, a private school, if they liked, and he would go without protest. I.B. and Virginia jumped at Bobby's offer and found another school that would accept him. That school turned out to be an Episcopal academy in Tennessee. Virginia, being an Episcopalian, was infinitely relieved. With any luck, her son would improve his attitude and morals under the tutelage of the Episcopal Church.

It happened that not long after Bobby was enrolled in the academy, Father Stephen, the headmaster, called I.B. "Mr. Hale, your son Bobby seems to miss his twin brother. He tends to be pretty sulky, but I think he might settle down if you sent your other boy to join him."

Many of us girls at the high school were broken-hearted when Billy was shipped off too—to "some dumb school in Tennessee." How could we stand it with both the Hale twins gone? They were the guys who drove us crazy wearing the James Dean look: white T-shirt, Levi's, and penny loafers.

As it turned out, Billy did not like a number of things in this new school: Number one, there were no girls. Number two, the food was bad. Maybe he could at least do something about the food. "Bobby, I'm going to cook our food in the room," he announced in disgust one day in the dinning hall. Several of the boys at the table heard him, and every one of them liked the idea. They bombarded Billy with questions: "Can you cook? What are you going to cook on? What kind of food can you cook?"

With all the interest generated, it was only a matter of days until the twins were in business. One of their friends, Clink, became their partner in crime. He had a car and a permit to drive, so Billy sent him out with an equipment and grocery list and the money they had pooled. Clink came back with a two-burner hot plate, a toaster oven for the French bread, a small fan to blow the smells out the window (fortunately, the bathroom, which would serve as the kitchen and galley, faced away from the quadrangle and was near the school cafeteria so smells weren't that big a problem), and all the ingredients for Billy's famous Texas-Hungarian goulash.

The business was arranged thusly: chef, Billy; sales rep, Bobby; buyer, Clink.

In no time, the academy's cook was complaining to Father Stephen that the students had stopped eating in the dinning hall. "They've stopped eating dinner. Here lately there are no more than twenty or thirty boys who come to dinner, and they come so late I have to shut down the dinning hall behind schedule every evening. This is costing us a of money…and we're wasting a lot of food."

The truth was that just about the only students to show up in the dining hall were the ones who were last in line at the "Texas Café," after the big pots of spaghetti or Hungarian goulash had run out. A couple of these tardy boys had overheard the cook complaining to Father Stephen, and they laughingly reported the conversation and the men's bafflement to the Texas Café crowd. This private joke was great fun and caused a huge surge in good humor among the students.

Bobby, being the sales representative for the Texas Café, felt obligated to find as many customers as possible. When most of the boys were sold, he decided to expand the business across the river…to the private girls' school!

The truth was that from the time Billy arrived, the twins had been plotting to infiltrate the girls' campus. Now, all these years later, they are nearly bent double laughing at the memories. "How in the world did we think we could get away with involving the girls in our scheme?" Billy says with a laugh.

"I don't know what we were thinking," Bobby says. "We were sneaking goulash down to the riverbank, and the girls were rowing over in rowboats. We were bound to get caught!"

"Especially since we had less food for the guys, and they got mad. They wanted Texas goulash."

"I think it was one of those hungry students that squealed on us," Bobby says.

"Are you kidding? Nobody squealed on us; we were caught redhanded. You remember all that drama! Father Stephen caught us sneaking down the river path and called Dad."

"Yeah, and all of a sudden the Texas Café was closed down, after all my hard work building the business."

"Nope, we didn't last very long at that school," Billy said.

"It was a shame. We were doing really good on the wrestling team. I even got a wrestling team letter jacket," Bobby said.

"You? We both earned letter jackets, in case you don't remember."

"But Father Stephen never trusted us after the café. He kept complaining about us to Dad," Bobby says. "I think it had something to do with the girls. I think he imagined they were still sneaking across the river."

"And soon here comes Dad to pick up his bad boys."

"He wasn't happy," Bobby says. "I remember how I was so ashamed."

"Well, I didn't care," Billy says. "I was glad. I wanted to get back to friends, high school, and waterskiing."

"Waterskiing." This word reminds me of another story I haven't thought about in a long time. The twins and Kurina talk on, but I relax in my chair and remember the time when Billy, just sixteen, was...

PRONOUNCED DEAD

"What a tragedy this is," Dr. Fields commented to the emergency room staff as they all ran down the hospital hallway toward the operating room, where the ambulance had just arrived.

This accident had been called in to the hospital by the two very competent teenage friends who were in the boat with Billy at the time of the accident.

The surgeon had been briefed on the ambulance phone by Richard, one of the friends with Billy, and was already prepared to begin whatever lifesaving procedures were necessary. "Dear God," the surgeon gasped as he pulled the blood- and water-soaked towel out of Billy's back. "The motor's blades have sliced into his back and side…sliced between his ribs like a butcher's knife." The surgery team began to flood his body cavity with sterile, saline water, and blood was already hooked up and running into his arm.

Dr. Fields left the operating room looking shaken. "I'm afraid he's as good as dead," he mumbled to the staff as they walked down the hall. "His body cavity is full of polluted lake water—and I mean polluted. I've heard from reliable sources that Carswell Air Force Base is dumping untreated waste into Lake Worth. No telling what all is in that water: oil, sewage, chemicals? We can't give this boy enough antibiotics to kill an infection like he'll be experiencing in a couple of hours. This is going to be very hard—you know my wife and I play bridge with his parents, I.B. and Virginia Hale. It's going to kill them." There was a reporter who overheard this conversation and called the local radio station. (We actually had important local stations in every city and just about every town in the United States at that time which announced all the local news, even the obituaries.) That evening the 5 o'clock news announced: THE SON OF I.B. HALE DIES IN BOATING ACCIDENT ON LAKE WORTH.

There were lots of lakes around Dallas and Fort Worth, so for those who loved the water and had access to boats, boating and waterskiing were favorite pastimes. The Hales had a speedboat for skiing, and Billy was an excellent waterskier. He loved to show all the tricks he could do on one ski. Plenty of Billy and Bobby's friends also had boats, and the twins spent many happy days skiing and picnicking at various lakes.

It was well into the summer of 1957, and school would be starting back in two weeks—the day after Labor Day. Most families would be having their private "last weekend of school vacation" on that Labor Day week-end. That being the case, Billy and a couple of his friends, Richard and Johnny, decided they had better claim a boat and have their own private all-day-and-night boating and camping trip before school started. Bobby was not with them.

Johnny wanted to take his family's boat. It had just been outfitted—especially *for Labor Day—with a new motor with lots of horsepower, more than enough to pull two people up at one time with accelerating speed. That fast, new motor made the decision very easy for Billy and Richard.*

Johnny's dad kept his family's boat at Eagle Mountain Boat Club, and usually they hauled it the short distance to Lake Worth. This would work out perfectly as Lake Worth was the boys' favorite lake for waterskiing and it had an island, Goat Island, where they loved to camp.

Johnny launched the boat, and Billy and Richard climbed in carrying a heavy cooler filled with beer—which, of course, they told themselves, they would not drink until they finished skiing and got to Goat Island.

With lots of energy spent skiing, and the sun beginning to fade in the western sky, Johnny turned the boat toward Goat Island. There they would listen to the radio blasting Elvis Presley singing "Jail House Rock" and other favorites, roast hot dogs, open cans of pork and beans, and drink beer.

Then—at the last minute—Johnny decided to check out just one last bend in the lake before closing out the day: Billy was sitting on the back of the boat and had just opened a beer. He was balancing himself, trying to light a cigarette. Richard, looking at Billy, started to yell, "Don't keep those beers to yourself; throw me one!" when he saw a horrifying sight—Johnny turned the boat in a graceful curve, and Billy fell over the back, right into the blades of the powerful new motor.

Instead of a friendly call to Billy, Richard screamed, "He fell into the motor, Johnny! Billy fell into the motor! Turn around!"

Billy later described these few minutes as surreal: He was conscious, but things seemed to slow down and expand outward, then narrowed. In what seemed like slow motion, he reached around his side and his hand entered his rib cage. "I felt my own ribs, and my hand got hung up for just a second in them. I knew exactly what they were and what had happened. I didn't feel any pain," he said.

Richard lifted Billy out of the lake, under his arms as; the bleeding was so bad they couldn't see where the cuts were or how deep. When the boys pulled him into the boat, Johnny saw the injuries and said, "He's cut deep all the way around his side—his ribs are showing." He threw a towel at Richard and told him to stuff it into Billy's body to slow the bleeding—then headed full throttle for the shore.

"There's a new emergency station on the lake somewhere," Richard yelled.

"I know, Dad showed it to us right after it went in; they keep an ambulance

there. I know exactly where it is. As soon as we reach it, jump out and tell them to get down to the boat. Tell them what happened—we need a stretcher."

In what seemed like hours but was really only minutes, Richard jumped into the ambulance with Billy; and as the trip was under way, the attendant let Richard, as the eyewitness, speak with the hospital.

With the help of horror-struck bystanders, Johnny pulled his dad's boat onto its trailer and drove to the hospital.

Days later, Johnny and Richard received many grateful thanks from Billy's family. The doctors and other professionals involved in Billy's treatment agreed, "Those two young friends were amazing; they did everything just right."

When he was recovering, Billy related, "I don't think I lost consciousness until I got to the operating room. I heard it all clear. I remember, in the ambulance, Richard was doing something to me with a towel and he said, I guess into the phone, 'He's got eight slices so deep his ribs are laid open.'"

Back at school, weeks later, Billy had to carry a soft pillow to lean against to protect his side from touching the desks and tables. Oh how the girls loved to carry that pillow and his books for him. He just ate up all that attention and, in my opinion, dragged his recovery out as long as possible.

On one of Billy's follow-up visits to the doctor's office, Dr. Fields told him earnestly: "Son, when they brought you to the hospital, I just happened to be there. I saw the shape you were in, and I knew for sure you were as good as dead. I told the staff around me exactly that: He's as good as dead because we won't be able to treat an infection like he'll have. I was already grieving for your parents. But the infection I had predicted didn't happen. God must have spared you for a reason. He must have a purpose for your life."

That story reminds me of the beautiful passage from Psalms 121. It is meant to be reassuring and seems perfect for this drama: *"He who keeps you will not slumber or sleep."*

11. THE CONVERSION

"Come, let us reason together. Though your sins are as scarlet, they shall be white as snow."
~ Isaiah 1:18

I've just dismissed Sunday school, and church service will start in twenty minutes. I teach this class, so I straighten up the room a bit. Just as I pull the door shut, I feel a slight tap on my shoulder. It is Phil, our music director. He says in a lighthearted voice, "Patsy, have you seen the leftover nativity scene out in the front parking lot?"

"Nativity scene in February? No, I haven't." I walk with him down the hall toward the sanctuary.

Phil continues with good humor about the small colt tied to an old truck. The truck is filled with hay, chickens, a dried-up Christmas tree, and a small doll that is swaddled in a blanket and lying in a realistic, homemade-looking manger. He goes on to say that the truck is interesting. It's an old, open-sided Army truck probably left over from the second World War. He is inclined to think this setup is a joke, but a benevolent one, and he wants to be sure that Billy and I show it to our children before we leave for home.

I know full well that what he describes is Bobby's truck, but I answer innocently, "Thanks for telling me about it, Phil. I'll be sure they see it." I believe Phil already knows our story and just wants to hear it from me; if so, I don't have time to tell it. Of course he may not know about the truck.

Bobby and Kurina have already been to church with us a couple of times, just as Roland had predicted they would, Bobby proudly introducing himself and his family by their gypsy names. But they had not come in the truck. If they are indeed here today, Billy needs to go ahead and introduce Bobby and Kurina to Phil.

But what is behind his bringing the truck to church, I wonder. They have the use of my Suburban. Oh well, I thought, Bobby obviously is not getting enough attention. He enjoys flaunting how different he is from us and the rest of our community, and the truck is one more way to draw attention to himself—as if showing up barefoot and ragged with long beard and hair is not enough. But if my sweet church members were ever shocked at his counterculture appearance, not a single one ever showed it; and they respected Bobby's wish that he and Kurina be called by their gypsy names. (Billy and I never went along with that gypsy name weirdness, even at church. I never called Kurina anything other than Kurina, from the night of their arrival. Their children had no other except gypsy names, so there was no choice with them.)

I see Billy walking with the children into the sanctuary, and I join them in the pew where we usually sit. Although I have the voice, the training, and the will to sing in the choir, Billy prefers that I sit with him in church. I look around for Bobby and Kurina and spot them over my left shoulder, near the back. From that glimpse I see that Bobby is wearing the beautiful leather shirt that Billy had made by hand and given to him. Before we left the house, Billy had found the shirt and laid it out on the sofa, along with socks and shoes, hoping that Bobby would wear them since the weather is cold. I had also put out a thick shawl for Kurina. She has it around her shoulders now as well as her Christmas shawl, and I am glad that she is warm.

Our church has a wonderful choir, and the music program Phil has put together for this cold February morning is exceptionally inspiring. Right before the sermon, the entire church is hushed with reverence as Stan, our fabulous tenor, holds us spellbound with his solo. Brother Miles, our pastor, delivers an especially compassionate and moving sermon, and I think to myself that I am glad Bobby and

Kurina have decided to come today.

During the service, however, I can't help noticing the activity slightly behind me as Bobby goes out the front door and then returns to his seat—more than one or two times. Kurina even follows him out once. We will later learn the significance of this pattern.

When the pastor closes his sermon for the altar call, Phil starts leading us in the beautiful old hymn "Just as I Am": *Just as I am and waiting not, to rid my soul of one dark blot...*

Out of the corner of my eye I see someone literally running down the aisle toward the altar. It is Bobby, running barefoot—I can tell by the sound. Bobby is answering the altar call. He is extremely emotional and sobbing rather loudly. He puts his arms around Brother Miles and begins poring out his heart. From what he is hearing, the pastor feels Bobby needs to be saying these things in private. He glances at a couple of deacons, who come forward, and with tender care, ushers Bobby into the counseling room.

I have been so intent on watching Bobby that I have forgotten about Billy. Turning to him now, I see his eyes are closed, hands supporting his bowed head. Billy has missed the very thing he is praying for. I take his hand and whisper, "Darling, your prayers are answered." I am fighting tears myself.

He looks at me, not comprehending my words. "What are you saying? What is it, Patsy?"

"Your brother has come forward."

"Are you sure? I didn't see. Where is he?"

"The deacons are with him," I answer. "He seems to be under serious conviction."

At that point, Billy's attention becomes riveted on the counseling room door. I know he is waiting, as I am, for the deacons to bring Bobby out and for Brother Miles, as is customary in our church, to introduce him before the congregation as a new brother in Christ. However, the pastor only walks to the pulpit, prays his dismissal prayer, and we are free to go. It is apparent that he feels this may take a while.

At this point I whisper to Billy that Katie and I are going to get the children from the nursery. I glance back at Kurina and can see that she is glued to her seat, waiting for Bobby to reappear. As I make my way toward her, several of the church members are pausing to greet her and express their hope for Bobby.

I motion to Kurina that I will bring her babies. I hurry to the nursery, anxious to return and not miss any of this wondrous experience.

By the time my girls and I return with JaJa and Spring Flower, Bobby is coming out with the deacons to join us and our friends. These friends have all been praying for the Morning Star family since their arrival at our house and are very encouraging to Kurina and Billy, expressing their happiness and support.

Kurina is a little apprehensive about all this, I can tell, but she does not want to appear in any way ignorant of what is going on, even though she has no prior experience with the Baptist Church and its doctrine. Kurina, however, with her cultic background, is experienced in spiritual happenings—so much so that when she sees Bobby, she recognizes a change in him, and her face shows surprise.

When he approaches us, Bobby, the former Morning Star to all except our family, introduces himself: "My name is Robert Allen Hale, and I am contrite before God. Please pray for me." He turns to Starlight: "And this is Kurina, my wife."

Figuratively speaking, we are bathed in the glow coming from Bobby. His countenance, though still unkempt, is radiant. Billy holds Bobby in his arms, and they weep until we are all weeping for joy.

Finally there are only five or six of our closest friends left with us; and Harold, wanting to prolong the afternoon of our miracle, says, "I need to check through the church and lock it up. Why don't we all go out to eat? Maybe we could meet up at Luby's."

We agree that the cafeteria is perfect. The lunch crowd will be dwindling, so we can linger awhile and talk if we want to. This will be our little celebration.

My good friends, Zoe and Susanne, twins themselves and known to Bobby, Billy, and myself since junior high, are with us today. During lunch, Zoe turns to Bobby and asks: "Bobby, I was sitting behind you and noticed that you couldn't sit still. You kept getting up and going outside and coming back in. Why did you do that?"

His answer makes me glad that we have a back, corner table and that the children are occupied with taking care of Bobby's babies in a booth several feet away.

"I wanted to kill myself," he blurts out.

A chorus of "What?" is heard around the table.

"I just didn't feel fit to live," he says. "I felt like I should leave and not come back. I didn't think it was fair for anyone to have to live with, or be associated with, such a sinner as me; and maybe worse, how can I live with myself? I was running my life through my mind and seeing my sins with fresh eyes—and I couldn't stand it. I was in pain."

Kurina speaks up and confirms his statements: "The third time he got up, I went outside myself to see what was going on. He was headed toward the truck and said he was not coming back. I told him I was going to go inside and get help. That stopped that."

"Well," Bobby continues, "Most of you have known me most of my life; and when I said, back at the church, that I am contrite before God, let me say now that I am contrite before God *and* man. I need to ask forgiveness from a lot of people."

After we finish our late lunch and return home, we have many things to talk about, not the least of which is the obligation Bobby feels to rename his children. They will have Christian names in the very near future, he tells us.

The day seems to fly by, and soon it is time to get ready for evening church service.

Bobby is already changing his taste in clothes. Tonight he is wearing lots of Bill's clothing, even a jacket and shoes.

I feel sorry that I don't have anything to offer Kurina to wear. I watch helplessly as she goes outside to the old truck to look through her clothes. She came back in the house with a pair of old sandals. I pretend to ignore her as I comb my girl's hair. Kurina sits on the ottoman and places the sandals on the floor. Staring down at them, she looks completely lost. Like in a dream, she starts to put the poor things on her bare feet.

I wish I were an artist and could paint that poignant scene with the tenderness it deserves. The pathos of Kurina's effort with the shoes breaks my heart. My emotions well up so that I have to leave the room. I go in the powder room and look in the mirror. My makeup is already in ruins. Just dare cry, I warn myself, and you'll have to put mascara on for the third time today. With that, the tears start to pour.

Kurina is larger and taller than I am and, probably because of neglecting herself, looks almost as old; but in truth, she is just a girl, a teenager. The sight of her trying to dress with that old pair of sandals brought the fact of her youth home to me. Her "husband," a man almost twice her age, has changed completely within a matter of hours. What will he expect of her, she must wonder. Bobby and Billy have been together all afternoon going through Billy's clothes. If Bobby has been alone with Kurina for one minute today, to discuss anything, I don't know when it could have been. If my clothes and shoes only fit her, I felt at that moment, I would give Kurina anything I owned.

Billy finds me in the powder room crying. He slips in, closing the door behind him. "Mama," he whispers. "What in the world?" He looks so baffled that I start to laugh. Then I explain that Kurina was so sweet and pitiful that she was breaking my heart.

"Hurry! Get ready." He hugs me tight. "You started crying this morning and now you can't stop." I kiss him, wash my eyes, and in nothing flat we are out the door.

Following Bobby's example, Kurina goes forward to the altar this evening. Brother Miles calls Bobby to the front and introduces both of them to the congregation. "We have two new followers of Christ," he says, and asks them if that expressed the desires of their hearts. They both confirm that it does.

Bobby can speak with eloquence and feeling when he wants to, and I am impressed with what he says to those present tonight: "At the church service this morning, it was revealed to me that my sins were crimson; like the song said, 'a dark blot.' Everything the music said and everything the preacher said was directed right at me. I had to rid my soul of that dark blot or die. I'm confessing to all of you that I was so deep in sin and darkness that I knew for sure I couldn't live. But I begged God, and he has forgiven me; I know that he has. And I no longer need to hide behind a gypsy name. At one time I thought that name gave me a new identity. Well, I don't need that anymore. I am Robert Allen Hale and I am, and will always be, a true follower of Jesus Christ. From this day forward, I want to live for Him."

Now it is Kurina's turn to convince the congregation of her intentions.

Standing alone before this crowd of expectant strangers, in her gypsy clothes and big strappy sandals, Kurina is the picture of innocence and humility. She seems very fragile, and I feel so tender toward her that I almost choke up again.

Then, in a voice that doesn't waver, Kurina tells us that until Bobby brought her to his brother's house in Fort Worth, she had never concerned herself much with Christianity and knew very little about Jesus. Now, she says, the desire of her heart is to join her husband in his faith so they can be a Christian family.

After their testimonies, the entire congregation goes down to the front and welcomes Bobby and Kurina, shaking their hands and congratulating them on their newfound faith.

When we arrive back home, I am drained of energy and ready to give Billy and Bobby their space. They are still going nonstop, revisiting the day and planning the future. I tell Kurina, who seems exhausted herself, and Spring Flower goodnight, and I go upstairs to see my own children to bed.

With that chore finished, I am alone at last, free to place a phone call—the call I have wanted to make all day.

"Roland, I've got such wonderful news…" I rehearse my greeting and message to Roland… "Normally I don't make phone calls so late in the evening, but this is Sunday and I knew you would still be up. I know you will welcome my good news about Bobby. Because of your warnings at breakfast last month, and your urging us to find somewhere else for the Morning Stars to stay, I just wanted to let you know that things are going to be fine with Bobby and Kurina after all..."

I reach Roland on the phone, but his point of view regarding Bobby's conversion surprises me. What Billy and I took for granted as true conviction in Bobby, and a permanently changed heart and mind, Roland seems to question...or at least he is cautious.

"I'm not worried about Kurina," Roland says. "She is pretty keen on doing her husband's will. But knowing what I know about Bobby, he will soon begin to think all this over; he will have questions, and he will begin to doubt. He is going to need solid counseling to keep him moving in the right direction. I would like to be there for him, as it may take a while until he is strong in his new faith. Christianity stems from our rebirth and change in our heart, and has got to become a way of life for him. In spite of our wishes, that doesn't always happen overnight... Patsy, are you there?"

"Yes, I'm here, but I am speechless. This isn't what I expected to hear. I thought you might rejoice with us."

"I'm sorry," he answers, "but speaking from past experience, this is a critical time in Bobby's spiritual growth. The forces of evil will be trying to confuse and destroy so fragile a new Christian, especially one as damaged as Bobby.

"I know you don't want to hear this," Roland goes on—and he is right, I don't want to hear it; I want to be assured that everything will be fine—"but it is more important now than ever, believe me, that you get Bobby out of your house. I repeat, he will be questioning his conversion in a few days and, like I said, I want, and need, to talk with him. Bobby can come to my office anytime, and of course I won't charge him a dime. I'm going to call him tomorrow."

He pauses, I don't know for how long, then says, "Patsy, you are so quiet. I would like to call Bobby tomorrow, let him know that you phoned me; are you okay with that?"

I've got to focus. I wish I hadn't made this call. Roland is not responding like I expected. He is repeating what he said at breakfast nearly a month ago. What a drama that caused! It was then that I came to understand that Bill's devotion to his twin surpassed any *trite* concerns that I, or even he, might have about our home or belongings. "I don't care about the house. If he tears it apart, I can't put him out. If it falls down or burns to the ground, I don't care," Billy had said. Doesn't Roland remember that? If Billy wouldn't put him out then, he certainly won't put him out now. "He won't put him out," I whisper.

"What? I didn't hear… Oh. No, I suppose not."

"I guess I am quiet, Roland; I'm a little tired. But go on, I'm listening."

"I'm going to let you go, but don't be surprised if Bobby starts to use his faith as just another tool to gain control; I've seen it happen, and it's not rare, particularly with men like Bobby who like to have the upper hand. If he is so inclined, and I suspect he is, it won't be long before he tries to put his own spin on the Bible. He will have it mean what he wants it to mean."

"Maybe he won't do that, Roland."

"Maybe he won't, Patsy. But if he does, he now has a new tool— the Bible. He has had a lot of exposure to this world, and he likes to do the thinking, teaching, and controlling. If he does have a new take on the Scripture, he will try to change his brother. That's why it is important that he be away from Bill for the next few weeks. But you say it won't happen; I know that, and it worries me."

I've lost the thread of this conversation. I love and trust Roland, but I don't want to believe he is right this time. I want to believe that Bobby is a new child of God. "You're going to call him for an appointment tomorrow—didn't you say that?"

"Yes, I'll call him. And in spite of all my warnings, I'm proud of you and Bill. You have done good. And I'm hopeful for Bobby—but be wary. When he does start questioning, as I think he will, don't let him get hold of Bill and try to confuse him, especially late at night, like he did before. It could be dangerous for Bill if he does. Patsy, do you understand what I'm saying?"

"Yes." I answer. Truth is, I *don't* understand, but I am tired and ready to drop the subject. I know I will not mention any of this to Billy.

In time—in fact in only a few weeks—I do come to understand Roland's counsel. By then it is too late.

After Roland called him, instead of keeping the appointment at Roland's office, Bobby went to his house. Roland was cordial but did not let him in. Roland told me later that he felt Bobby wanted a relationship with him that was too casual for comfort. Roland was well acquainted with people who manipulate, and he had recognized Bobby as one of those people from the first time they met at my house. Roland said something like, "Bobby, I make it a practice not to counsel in my home. I am leaving for my office very soon; I will meet you there."

Roland is plain-spoken, and most people aren't that blunt with Bobby; but, unlike Billy, who has always suffered feelings of rejection, and who would have been hurt that Roland didn't let him into his home, Bobby did not have his feelings hurt or feel any ill will toward Roland. Bobby was different from Billy in that he was very bold in his approach to people and assumed everybody liked him. I will say this, however: Bobby never visited Roland's office. Roland felt, and so did I, that Bobby did not feel he needed—and was not likely to accept—counseling or information from someone he considered "a professional." And Roland was not ready to become his "friend."

In spite of Roland's reservations, I must admit I am drawn to helping Bobby and Kurina, and instead of wanting them out of our home, I am glad they are here. I have known Billy and Bobby since I was twelve years old. We have practically grown up together, and Billy and I have grieved and fretted through many stages of Bobby's life. Now that Bobby is throwing off his old ways, along with his and his family's gypsy customs and names, I want to believe that we can all face the rest of our lives with some degree of normalcy.

Bobby and Kurina are constantly trying to help out around the house now, which in all truth is usually more of a hindrance than a help, but they are at least trying, and I never say a discouraging word.

The surest indicator of Bobby's true change, in my opinion, is the fact that he apologized to me. He and I were alone one afternoon when Billy had taken all the children and Kurina out for ice cream. I was practicing a song on the piano that Billy had requested. I got the feeling that Bobby wanted to say something to me, and maybe had even been waiting for a chance to talk with me alone. His exact words were: "Patsy, I have not even been a good friend to you. I know I have caused trouble between you and Billy, and before you and God I am repentant." When he said that, sincerity was written on his face—a look I seldom saw from him. I accepted what I felt was as close to an apology as anyone would ever get from Bobby, and gave him my forgiveness, though he had not asked for it, with love and gratitude.

Though Bobby was not amenable to counseling from Roland, he did meet with Brother Miles, who pretty much insisted that new converts either attend a weekly class for one month or meet with him personally. Bobby had so much previous disorder in his life, it was felt he needed to go the personal route. After interviewing Bobby, Brother Miles said to Billy, "Trying to right Bobby's entanglements with the women and children in his life is like trying to unscramble eggs."

Bobby had never helped financially with any of the five children he had abandoned, plus he was still married to Connie, the mother of Lotus and two of those children. At Brother Miles's behest, Bobby found Connie and apologized to her for abandoning her and their boys and reminded her that they were still legally married.

Brother Miles and the deacon who was with him when he made the call told Bill that the conversation, after Bobby asked about Lotus, went something like this: "Maybe you have lost affection for me, Connie, but I have found God and am a new person. What would you like to do about our situation? You know, us being legally married and all."

Connie said something to the effect, "I would like for you to pay child support for these children, who you've never helped me with, and I would like a divorce. Not long thereafter, with the legal help and advice of one of our church members, Connie and Bobby were granted the divorce.

As it turned out, though Bobby was soon making good money, he paid exactly one child support payment to Connie for their two boys.

12. THE MARLBORO MAN

"Man's sin is his flight from responsibility."
~ Dietrich Bonhoeffer

In the days to come, the polishing of Bobby's appearance is exciting for our family and the community.

As Bobby throws off his old ways, he shaves his beard—leaving only a tasteful mustache. A friend of mine, and of the twins since high school, offers to give the family hairstyles at her salon. Susanne tells me in private, "What better person than me to cut and style that long, graying hair? I know what Bobby is supposed to look like." And she is right—what a difference! Billy gives Bobby several outfits of good-looking clothes and...voila! He looks like my husband's twin, the grown-up version of *Mr. Neiman Marcus*. Contributing to his healthy good looks, both face and physique, is the fact that he has gained a few pounds since coming to our house.

Some of my friends and I were having a little hen session recently and discussing the dramatic change in Bobby. "He looks like that poster of the Marlboro Man," they decide.

Kurina's visit to the salon, however, is a different story. She draws in her neck and cringes when the scissors come near her hair, permitting only a couple of inches to come off. She resists looking in the mirror, turning her eyes first to Susanne and then to me. I think she doesn't know what to expect.

"Do you feel naked?" Susanne teases her. "That's what some of the girls tell me."

"Yes, I do," she answers.

"I can't tell any difference at all, Kurina," I reassure her.

After Kurina dismisses our few suggestions regarding her clothes, we say nothing more about her clothing. Though just a teenager, she is not a shy girl. She gives her opinion without hesitation and can be quite argumentative—to all but Bobby.

Having rejected her mother's Hollywood ideas of grooming and beauty, Kurina really doesn't know how, in my and Susanne's opinion, to dress and groom herself like a modern woman; nor does she care to learn. Though it's a huge enhancement to her natural beauty, the slightest touch of makeup is out of the question. This girl has a lot of pride and is determined to maintain the outward identity she has become comfortable with. Suzanne whispers to me, "She is very resistant to change. I see it all the time, usually when mothers bring their daughters in. At this point, since she will take no advice, there will be a lot of difference between her and Bobby—and we both know Bobby."

"Yes, we do," I agree. Let's hope his faith will help him ignore other women, because they are going to be gawking."

Susanne takes one of Kurina's rough young hands in her hands and starts massaging it with lotion; the lavender aroma is intoxicating. Susanne is talking with her about taking care of her hands and skin. What must it be like for Kurina, I wonder, an unmarried teenage mother traveling the back roads with an older man. Practically overnight she is surrounded by people who want her to change. I doubt she has received so much attention from grown women since she was a young child, all of us wanting her to feel good about herself and her appearance. Kurina is eager to make a getaway from this salon, but before she drags me out, Susanne mentions that her skin is looking older than her eighteen years. "Kurina, darling," she says, "I've just put my favorite lotion on your hands... Let me give it to you. Use it every day—and this," she says, handing her a jar of emollient face cream. "Use these, Kurina; they will nourish your face and hands." As the lotions are very soothing, I think Kurina will at least use the skin care.

Now that Kurina and Bobby belong to our church family at Birchman, many of the members want to have a part in their well-being. Generous donations of clothing and food regularly show up at our house. Sometimes the doorbell rings and upon opening the door, we will find no one in sight—but sitting on the front stoop will be one or more bags of groceries.

An abundance of clothes, for each of Bobby's family members, also find their way to our home. And, a blessing for me as well as Bobby (he won't have to use my car now), one of the church members gives him a nice used car.

Bobby needs and in fact wants a job. With no end in sight of his being here, Billy is eager to teach him the new trade of upholstering walls, which he mastered by doing the bedroom and den in our home. "It's the brand-new home improvement craze," Billy says, encouraging Bobby. "Everybody who can afford it wants it. You'll learn in a snap."

I know that Billy is right because their dexterity and mental aptitude are practically identical. Geneva, the designer friend who helped me with our den furniture, was amazed at Billy's exceptional talent after he upholstered our walls. She told me, "If Billy trains Bobby, I can keep him busy. I can send him as many jobs as he wants for interior designers in Dallas and Fort Worth."

Her confidence was added encouragement for Billy, and as he predicted, Bobby easily mastered the craft. He is soon doing excellent work with more referrals than he can handle. Billy likes to tease him, "Man, you've got yourself a bona fide trade."

What a relief to us that Bobby is earning money. It should lessen our financial burden to have him contributing to groceries and other household expenses; or even better, I hint to Billy, "With any luck, now that he has income, maybe they will find their own place." I'm surprised when he agrees with me.

Considering the damage to our home, we will need a lot of repairs to the house if and when Bobby's family moves out. We need to save for that eventuality, and in the meantime, a little monetary help from him will be nice.

In retrospect I'm not sure Billy ever expected Bobby to contribute to his own upkeep. Nor, truthfully, in my heart of hearts, did I. Neither of us asked him to. I had just assumed that he might want to toss in at least a little, and he did, just a little, and just for groceries. But for cleaning and repairs—it never happened.

So I continue to do the major cleaning myself. On more than one occasion, I tackle the huge sectional sofa with a toothbrush. In fact, I have a sweet story:

Remember that in the 1970s, people almost never locked their doors. Friends would just give a "yoo-hoo" call and walk right in. One afternoon, as I am on my hands and knees cleaning the sofa with a toothbrush, I turn around to the laughter of Gaye Lynn, Brother Miles's daughter. "Has it come to this?" she asks with a giggle.

"Well, Gaye Lynn, what can I say? I'm sure you have totally noticed the small runny noses swiped; wet soggy diapers changed; peanut butter from small, precious hands smeared on this suede couch. And don't even look at the chair and ottomans. What else can I do but crawl around and try to scrub it off?" I am laughing with her now.

"It's a sight to see, Patsy; pardon my laughter. I just wanted to drop by and see if you are maintaining your sanity. We are all thinking about you and praying for you.

"My darling church family; what would I do without you all?" I give this remarkable teenager a hug and she leaves, saying she will see me soon.

Two days later, Gaye Lynn walks in again. She is still smiling and in a good mood. To my complete surprise, she hands me a $500 check and says, "Patsy, this is out of love. Please do what you want with it: cleaning, repairs, or maybe you need new drapes." She glances over at the rags I left hanging after Bobby's colt chewed and ripped the drapes.

By the time she finishes her remark, we are hugging, giggling, and crying at the same time.

Basically, the two Hale families are doing well. Kurina tries to help me the best she can, but she is inexperienced. It pays me to stand by, ready to clean up any accidental spills. When Spring Flower or JaJa— oops, I'm still using their gypsy names—I mean when Naomi or James spills chocolate milk or food, for instance, I quickly snatch an old towel that I keep close at hand. Otherwise Kurina will grab anything within reach, the tablecloth or my best decorative linen, and ruin it with the spill. I try to give her chores, but it often doesn't go well. One evening I had her put away some ground beef left over from fixing dinner. Next morning I found the raw meat in the fridge, unwrapped and bleeding onto the shelf below. She has a lot to learn, and I try to be a patient teacher.

When ten people live in a house, it takes almost constant work to maintain order. Kurina and I cook and clean a lot, and while we work we talk a lot, mainly about family and often about Bobby's dad. I get the impression that she wonders about the truth of Bobby's stories— especially about I.B. I pretty much confirm the stories as true and not exaggerated like she suspected. Yes, he was All-American in football and baseball. Yes, he was an FBI agent. Yes, he did bring the Golden Gloves to our city. And on and on with I.B.'s many accomplishments. Yes, he was a sharpshooter, probably the best in the world. "And Kurina," I continue, "I.B. was hired to go on European cruises to demonstrate his skill at sharpshooting exhibitions overseas. And speaking of exhibitions, he was also well known for his 'making salads in the sky' exhibits when he was training the Security Force at General Dynamics."

We hear baby James crying in the den, and Kurina leaves to take care of him. But her questioning has started me thinking about an incident that made me wonder at the time. Since I never got any answers, I still wonder:

After Billy and I married, I took a semester off from college, at my dad's suggestion, to get used to married life. We were living in an apartment we had rented before we got married. Even back then, Billy wanted to paint the walls and renovate; not only that, but he insisted we have new drapes, custom-made, that covered an entire wall. Bobby made us a beautiful upholstered headboard for a wedding present. He had learned that skill when he lived in California, for a short while, and upholstered restaurant booths. This, our first home, was in the Hickory Arms apartment house in Denton, Texas. When we got married, Billy's buddies had wrecked this apartment—in fun of course, and when we arrived after our honeymoon, the light bulbs had been removed, the toilet seat greased and rocks were under the mattress, to mention a few pranks.

Billy continued his education at North Texas State University while, it appears, I cooked for every person in the whole Hickory Arms Apartments. I must say, because my Mother had taught me, I excelled in the art of cooking, but not cooking with gas. On one hurried occasion, I was fixing dinner for a big group but left the gas on—forgetting that I wasn't using electricity and needed a match. I came close to blowing the place up. I wound up with burned hair, no eyelashes, hurt pride, and a lot of teasing. Bobby was also enrolled at NTSU, and he and his new wife were living upstairs in the same building.

About midday one Friday, I hear Bobby calling in a loud and urgent voice for Billy. "Connally's been shot! Billy, Connally has been shot!" and he runs through the front door looking like he's seen a ghost. He is as white as a sheet and shaking all over. I've never seen him so rattled and am astonished to see him grip the back of a chair, obviously to steady himself, and I notice that his knuckles are white. He says, "Patsy, I've got to tell Billy that John Connally has been shot."

"Billy's at school," I tell him. Trying to make sense of his claim about Connally, I ask, "Where did this happen? Who shot—?" But he is far too disturbed to answer my questions.

Without hesitation, he shouts, "I've got to find Dad!" With that statement, he bolts out the door. I stand speechless and watch him jump in his car and spin away, tires screeching.

I guess because he married the governor's daughter, Bobby has a fanciful idea that he and Governor John Connally have some sort of special relationship. That is a ridiculous assumption, for, though the governor got through Kathleen's funeral with all the graciousness of a true gentleman, since that funeral the governor won't even speak to Bobby—by phone or otherwise.

I rush inside and turn on the television, hoping to get a station saying something about Connally's shooting. Within a minute, as soon as the TV warms up and the sound and picture come on, I am bombarded with the news that President Kennedy has been shot in his motorcade at Dealey Plaza in Dallas. Governor Connally and his wife, Nellie, were in the car with JFK and Jacquelyn Kennedy. Connally was also shot.

In another minute, Billy opens the door. He has already run up the stairs to Bobby's apartment and is breathless. "Where is Bobby?" He pauses for breath.

"He just left to find your dad."

"Was he berserk?"

"He was totally berserk. He didn't have a drop of blood in his face, and he was shaking all over. He wanted to tell you Connally had been shot. Not a word about the president."

"I've got to find Dad before Bobby does," Billy says and runs to the bedroom for the telephone. But he does not find I.B., who is not at home, and I.B.'s wife does not know where he is or when he will be back. Billy says she was as vague as could be, as usual. "Please! Have Dad call me the minute you hear from him," Billy pleads. "It's very important that I talk to him."

On the third day, we still can't contact I.B. and have not heard a word from Bobby. We call his wife in Midland, where she went to be with her parents after a heated argument with Bobby, and she, too, has heard nothing from him. Billy is studying for a major trigonometry test, but he cannot get Bobby out of his mind. On Sunday afternoon we drive to Fort Worth, straight to I.B.'s home. His wife has no idea where he is. "Maybe at work," she says; and she hasn't seen Bobby. Accomplishing nothing, we drive back to Denton.

We have no sooner parked the car before Bobby drives up. From the time I saw him on Friday, when he was half wild, there is a complete change in his demeanor. He is calm, subdued, and doesn't want to talk. Billy asks him, "Well, how is the governor? Have you been at the hospital?" These questions are tongue-in-cheek because we both know that Bobby would not have been welcomed nor would he have been allowed in to see the injured Connally. We are sure that Bobby's deflated manner is out of the rejection he received when his usual "I was married to the governor's daughter" spiel didn't work for him.

"Yeah, I went to the hospital. I think he's going to be okay." He turned and climbed the stairs to his apartment, and that's all we got out of Bobby. He never said anything about the presidential assassination or where he spent those two days and nights or if he found I.B.

When Kurina returns to the room, we continue our conversation. Bobby has not told her as much about his mother as he has about his dad, so I proceed to tell her a lot about Virginia: about her intelligence; her language arts degree, majoring in French; her many talents, most of them passed on to her boys; her master's in bridge; her gracious personality; her being well acquainted with all the social graces; her family background, and the rich heritage that the family traces all the way back to the Mayflower and William Bradford. Kurina is quite interested in Bobby's background, and I think that is to her credit. I just wish I had more time to talk with her alone, without all the constant distractions.

As I see it, Kurina is in many ways, a typical California/Hollywood teenager: She came from a broken home; left her mother, who would have probably been more of a disciplinarian than her father; went to live with her father; and experienced drugs. But that is pretty much where "typical" ends. I would say the past three years of her life have been out of the ordinary.

Kurina left her dad's home at fifteen and ran into Bobby, a man seventeen years her senior, and with a *history*. He was charming but carried a great deal of baggage: He already had five children by four women and three marriages. One of his babies had died unborn, with its mother, his first wife Kathleen, when she received a shotgun blast to the head.

However, the young Kurina was seeking adventure, and certainly found it when she met Bobby.

According to Bobby's story, he and Kurina met when he was lounging in a park. It was a beautiful setting, he said, near a waterfall in the San Bernardino Mountains. I guess to this young girl the whole scene was irresistibly romantic. Physically she is very well developed: tall and shapely, pretty tan skin, pretty blue eyes, and long blond hair. To give Bobby a little credit, she no doubt looked more like a young woman than a fifteen-year-old child.

Kurina does not make friends easily. She told me she was lonely and trying to find any excuse to break away. She wanted to be free of the responsibility of school and having to fit in. Rules and authority did not appeal to Kurina any more than it did to Bobby. His gypsy lifestyle and philosophy were exciting to her and easy for her to adapt to. So, though she disliked control and authority, Kurina headed straight toward being totally controlled by a thirty-three-year old man who is a master of control.

I sympathize with Kurina's parents. I know they must worry about their daughter. In fact, Kurina told me her mother was troubled about Bobby being so old.

Except for the few words they spoke outside Roland's home—when Bobby went there instead of to his office—Roland has not talked to Bobby since his conversion, and Trish has not met him. So when Roland calls on Sunday afternoon and says he and Trish would like to stop by the house, we are delighted.

Bobby scurries around making the den, everyone's favorite room, presentable. Bill puts on fresh coffee, and I get out my good china cups and dessert plates. I'm always ready for drop-in guests since Billy wants a dessert with every meal. Because of that, I usually have a cake or pies baked and a half-gallon or two of Blue Bell ice cream in the freezer.

I have not seen Trish in weeks and am thrilled when they walk through the door. I introduce Bobby to Trish, and Roland says, "Bobby, it's amazing how much you look like my good friend Bill."

Bobby is pleasant and welcoming, "You mean I look like my brother now? Come on in and let's get comfortable."

Relaxing in the den with coffee and dessert is the perfect setting for a cordial afternoon visit. Roland wants to hear all about Bobby: "I've been hoping you would come by my office, but Bill says you are really busy these days. Tell me how you're doing—and we could start with your accepting Christ."

In the spotlight, where he loves to be, Bobby dominates the conversation. After telling the details of his conviction at that fateful Sunday morning service, he says, "Roland, I am a changed man. My eyes have been opened. My conscience bothers me now, and it's clear to me how much I've sinned. I understand my responsibilities now…for my children. I know I must, in God's eyes and for my own peace of mind, do the right thing by them." Then he adds, "Of course doing the right thing will be tough; it will cost me a lot, personally and financially."

Roland broke in for a question, "How do you feel about that? The tough parts, I mean. Do you have a plan?"

"I've got a trade now, mainly upholstering walls, and about all the jobs I can handle. I am doing pretty well. Now I'm trying to figure out when I can afford to send a support payment to Connie and her two boys. She has Lotus too, and I don't think she gets anything from Lotus's father."

"You said, 'her two boys.' Are those your two boys?"

"Yes. Oh, I forgot to tell you, I'm getting a divorce from Connie—you know we are still married."

"By the way," Roland says, "I'm missing Kurina."

"Her mother sent her and the kids plane tickets to visit her in California. Brother Miles thought it would be a good idea for us to be apart while I decide what to do—about my marriage to Connie, I mean—so Kurina agreed to go out there for a while."

"You mean you weren't sure what path you wanted to take, whether with your wife or Kurina?"

"I really did not. I didn't know which woman I should be with. As I said, Brother Miles and I both thought it would be good for Kurina to go to her mother until something is worked out. Of course I understand now that I need to be supporting Connie, Kurina, and their children… I've got three other children too: Teddy, who lives with his mother; Jessie, who also lives with his mother; and another child who was born in Midland, Texas who I've lost track of. But there's just one of me.

We are all staring at Bobby—except Billy, who has fidgeted and twisted and turned until I'm sure he's going to fall out of his chair.

"Yeah?" Roland finally says.

"You see I didn't know if Connie would want a divorce. She is a Catholic."

"And if she hadn't?

"I would have had to take her back."

"Were you prepared for that?"

"I told God I would do his will. 'Lord, this is all too confusing for me to sort out,' I told him. 'God you're going to have to figure it out for me.'"

"And I trust he did," Roland says, "to your satisfaction? You said you're getting a divorce."

"Yes, I'm okay with that; it's God's decision. It's as simple as that, God has taken charge of my life and that's his decision."

I am thinking: Roland says he has *seen it all*; I wonder if he's seen one like this.

"And what about Kurina?" Roland asks. "Have you and...uh... Have you decided her fate yet?"

"We've been writing almost every day, and she wants to come back. And I want her to come back. I will be glad to see her."

"So you are satisfied with the way things turned out—with Kurina coming back to you?"

"Yes, I am. I'm glad. I love Kurina."

"And the children? I know you miss those babies and will be glad to see them."

"I do miss them, Roland. I love all my children."

"We can see ourselves out," Roland says when he and Trish prepare to leave. It has become obvious that Billy, barely looking up, and Bobby, are going to talk right through their departure.

This is not like Billy, to practically ignore his good friend. I think the truth is that he is embarrassed.

As I see them to their car, Roland says, "Patsy, be careful and pray earnestly; he is like a chameleon. He could change again any time. Of course he likes all the attention he's getting here of late, but like I told you weeks ago, now he has a new tool to use. He's already saying, 'God shows me, and God told me.' This is a newfound power for him. He hasn't been able to say before that "God told me" such and such; it must be pretty heady for him. Not many of us, after a lifetime of service to God and his church, would make such claims other than in the abstract. There's no telling what he might say God has told him or showed him—and believe me, he will try to drag you two along. I keep repeating this, but I'll say it again, Bill must not believe or give credence to Bobby's claims. If he does, then it will be hard if not impossible to turn back. Being his twin, Bill will find it tough to resist the influence Bobby will exert over him. Bill thought he was tested before Bobby's conversion—I have a feeling that now comes the real test."

As we stroll to their car, I listen carefully and look innocently at them. What I do not tell Roland, because I am ashamed, is that what he had warned me against in that first phone call after Bobby's conversion, and is still warning me about right now, has already come to pass. It goes like this:

In less than two weeks after his conversion, Bobby is inspired to teach both families, including Billy and me, about the Bible!

Now, I have a lot of things to do and really doubt that I have much to learn from Bobby. Nevertheless, to encourage the new converts, our families, me included, sit all evening talking and listening to Bobby read the Bible and teach. Bobby and Billy never seem to tire of rehashing things that I learned as a child and heard all my life. Nevertheless, I try to remember that, though this "teaching" is tiresome to me and to my children, the twins were not exposed to much Sunday school and church as children and a lot of what they read in the Bible is new and exciting to them, particularly to Bobby.

Still I do not understand why it is so gratifying to Bobby, or necessary for him, a new Christian, to have all of us *old Christians*, if you will, gathered around while he teaches us. "Is the tail wagging the dog?" I asked Billy one night, feeling that if any teaching is done, outside of the church, we should be the ones teaching Bobby.

Oh boy did Billy let me have it: "Why can't you just be glad my brother is becoming a strong Christian? You can't accept that God has changed his life! Bobby is growing in knowledge every day. I celebrate his understanding. What is holding you back, for crying out loud?"

Calmly, I try to explain, "Billy, of course I accept that Bobby has changed, and I didn't mean to complain."

What has happened to Billy and me? It used to be that we could at least discuss our opinions, but not anymore. He can't handle the slightest questioning of Bobby. "Please excuse me, darling," I said. "We've been staying up late every night. Guess I'm just tired."

One night after Billy finally came to bed, he tells me, "I have never heard anyone with so deep an insight into the Bible as Bobby. He even sees some things that Brother Miles hasn't seen." I listen and think it wise, at the time, not to touch that statement with a response.

But hadn't Roland told me repeatedly that Bobby might see the Bible his own way and try to teach us new things? And hadn't he said that this phase would be dangerous for Billy? To paraphrase Roland, 'Bill trusts Bobby now and will have his guard down.'

Later, with Roland's help, I recognize that at this very time, his change in attitude and his early acceptance of Bobby's heresy were the early seeds of Billy's destruction.

13. IDLE TALK

"What lies behind us and what lies before us are tiny matters compared to what lies within us."
~ Ralph Waldo Emerson

Billy and Bobby get along so well these days they are together nearly all the time. Gladly sacrificing his rest for his twin, today Billy went out with Bobby to help him finish an upholstering job with a deadline.

After nine hours, the twins walk in with huge appetites. Accordingly, we have an early supper and send Billy, who has already been working with Bobby all day, off to do night duty at the hospital. Though I feel bad for Billy, for myself I am thrilled…this gives me a chance to get caught up on my own sleep. I don't have to listen to his and Bobby's long-winded discussions tonight.

Since Bobby and Kurina are trying to help me around the house, I leave the kitchen cleanup to them tonight.

I turn to the children. "Allison, I've got to get some rest. I want you kids to finish your homework and be in bed with lights out at nine o'clock." So it is that I, miraculously, crawl into bed at a decent hour.

I haven't been asleep long; it couldn't be more than a couple of hours, and here I am propped up on one elbow listening to voices—adult voices, and noises: what sounds like drawers being opened and closed and hangers being pushed around in my closet and bathroom.

My walk-in closet and bathroom are side by side next to my and Billy's bedroom and can be entered from the hall or from our bedroom. Because I am always the one in my own closet, I never realized how clear the sound from it passes through the bedroom wall.

Tiptoeing over to the wall, I can hear Bobby's voice as plain as if he were standing beside me; in fact he is just inches away. What is he doing? Where he seems to be standing is near the shelf, where I keep the jewelry my dad made for me.

Bobby has had the run of our house for a while now, coming and going and getting into anything he pleases. He is liable to appear anywhere. He even walks into our bedroom unless I lock the door. But his being in my closet is unacceptable.

"Can you believe all this stuff poor Patsy is burdened with?" he asks—I guess he is talking to Kurina. "So much jewelry and clothes. Such vanity. And Billy is not much better. I blame Patsy for his materialism."

I can hear another box slide out from under my jewelry boxes, and I know exactly what he has found—Virginia's antique doll. It was passed down from Belle, her mother, to her, and now to Allison. I have it carefully stored there in my closet until Allison is a little older. I can hear the paper rustle as he takes the tissue off to expose the doll. He's not taking it out of the box, thank goodness, and he quickly shoves it back into place. I remember, again, Bobby shirking from dolls and stuffed toys at Christmas.

As he continues snooping, he carries on with his materialism spiel:

"I say Patsy is responsible for all this worldly vanity and materialism. I remember when Goethe chewed those *de-sign-er* (dragging the word out in contempt) curtains. She nearly went into mourning. I thought then, what on earth are you doing to my poor brother—you do know, Kurina, that he helped her with all that designing stuff? That's not like Billy. He likes rugged living: boating and camping and hunting."

Yes, I think, he *is* rugged Bobby, more rugged than you are, and he also likes a beautiful home, and he works for perfection. With all his cabinetry and upholstering and painting, he worked harder on this house than I did.

"Yes, Kurina," Bobby continues, "life is about so much more than those stupid curtains, and, if you remember, I said so when it happened. Now the time has come that they really need to get over this materialism. There are a lot of things in this house that need to go. I think we will just have a good old-fashioned cleansing purge."

Cleansing purge? He wants to throw my things away? How can he be so unfair? I've welcomed this man and his family into my home, and here he is in my private quarters, my closet, plotting against me. He is unappreciative and cruel. I wish I had the courage to speak up, to yell through the wall that I hear his scheming, and run him out of my closet. But as usual, I keep silent.

He closes the closet door, and I hear the splash of water in the tub as he, from the sound of it, climbs back in. Kurina laughs…a little too loud. The tub is on the other side of the wall just a couple of feet away from the closet. I put my ear to the wall as he continues his despicable ranting. "I'm serious, Kurina. God has shown me that there are things in this house that are evil. All those dolls and stuffed animals they gave their children for Christmas need to be purged. The children have those idols all over their rooms—it's pure evil."

Evil? Has he lost his mind? I do remember that he recoiled from the toys we gave his children at Christmas, but how could I even dream it would come to this—him wanting to throw them away? How much voodoo influence has he had anyway? As a Christian he should already be over those superstitions. Hearing Bobby say all this irrational stuff is not only disgusting to me, it is threatening.

If I hadn't already lost my confidence in Bobby, I have now. I had come to trust him as a fellow Christian; Jesus is on his lips every breath. And compared to the "old Bobby," he has been wonderful since his conversion, rather obsessed with all his reading and teaching but truly changed: He became caring and sincere in wanting to help around the house; in wanting to learn a trade and work; in at last showing a little thought for the women and children in his life; and, wonder of wonders, he apologized to me. That apology—or was it just an acknowledgment—meant everything to me. Shh, he's still talking.

"I'm going to approach my brother about getting rid of a lot of things in this house. And I want that TV destroyed while we're at it."

Kurina finally speaks up, "I don't think Patsy will let that happen."

"God wants it stoned, and she can't stop it," he says with a knowing voice. "Oh I'm not going to say anything yet, but when I do, Billy will go along with me. God is speaking through me and Billy will listen."

They start splashing and making noises I don't want to hear. They're supposed to be using the guest bathroom. I feel violated. I go back across the room and crawl onto my bed. I've got to think about all this. I am definitely back at square one with Bobby; how else can I put it? He's in my closet and wanting to destroy things in my house—like before his conversion. Except then I don't think he actually *planned* his destruction… or did he? "*…to level the playing field,*" *Roland had said. And Brenda had asked, "Is all this orchestrated to bring you down spiritually and financially?"*

Now he says "Jesus" fifty times a day, but what does it mean? *Roland had reminded me, "Words are cheap."* I wonder if Jesus is just another word to Bobby…another tool, like Roland said, to gain our confidence and manipulate us. *He said, more than once, that Bobby might use his religion and the Bible as a tool to confuse and manipulate.*

I lift the telephone off the nightstand and pull the cord into the far corner of my room. I sit on the floor and face the wall—Bobby must not hear me! Why am I trembling? I dial the hospital. "Billy," I am whispering and sobbing, "I want you to come home."

"What are you talking about? Come home? What has happened? Where's Bobby?"

"Bobby is what's happened, Billy. He is in my bathroom and he's in my closet—rummaging through my jewelry and clothes. He's wanting to throw our things away—he said so. He said there are evil things in our home that he wants to get rid of—purge, he said."

"You are hysterical! He did not tell you that, and you know it!"

"No, not me; he told it to Kurina, and I overheard him! Billy, I'm telling you the truth, he was in my closet. I could hear every word he said. He was going through my jewelry. He wants to throw our 'materialistic things' away. He's going to approach you about it, about getting rid of a lot of our stuff, and the children's things and about stoning the TV."

"Patsy"—Bill is smiling, almost laughing; I can hear it through the phone—"don't you recognize Bobby's idle talk? This is not an emergency, and I cannot come home."

"Billy," I say, trying to sound calm, "what are you going to do when he approaches you— about this cleansing purge, as he calls it? He told Kurina that you will go along with him."

"He won't approach me. It's just idle talk. And if he ever does, I'll deal with it then. Forget it."

Not one word does Billy utter about his brother being in my bathroom and searching through my closet. He just conveniently ignores what I consider burglary.

Bobby has robbed me before, before Billy and I married:

It is summer and I am living in Hollywood for the season. I have come to Hollywood with a girlfriend, Mary Beth, from North Texas State. Her older sister, Eva, is a movie and television star. Eva is the Batgirl on Batman *and a regular on* Dobie Gillis *as well as several other series. She has also played in several movies, including two with Elvis Presley. Eva phoned Mary Beth before school was out, and Mary Beth related the conversation to me. 'Patsy, Eva told me, 'I have a beautiful condo on Hollywood Boulevard. I want you to come see me. You can stay the whole summer, and bring a girlfriend.' Patsy, you are the girlfriend I want to take. Go with me!'*

My parents are very approving of this trip because I will be away from Billy. They are hoping that a three-months' absence will spell the end of the Billy Hale/Patsy Dorris relationship.

As it turns out, I may be free of Billy, but in only two or three days Bobby shows up on our doorstep—the movie star's doorstep—at one o'clock in the morning, with an old buddy of his from Texas! I am appalled. He is the last person on earth I want to see. I don't know how Bobby tracked me to this house in Los Angeles, because, though my parents had the address, I didn't even know the address until we got here.

Once Bobby found me it seems impossible for me to avoid him. What an opportunist he is. Everywhere I go in Hollywood, he shows up. He wants me to introduce him to my friends, especially anyone to do with movies. He has a special obsession with Marilyn Monroe. "I bet your friend could get me an introduction to Marilyn—or knows someone who could. You've got to help me with this, Patsy. Look at it this way: I'm all the way out here from Texas, and it may be my only opportunity. She is a goddess—I just want to be in her presence."

That favor was not hard to arrange. In Hollywood, where fakery was rampant in the early 1960s and extravagant good looks respected above all else, people took Bobby seriously. It was hard not to take Bobby seriously; he had everything Hollywood required. He had the extravagant good looks, the vocabulary, the taste to dress just right, and he presented himself flawlessly. Also I should add that Bobby was persistent. If he ran into any objections or hesitancy on anyone's part, he would begin his persuasion and he usually got his way. I refused to even ask Eva for an introduction on Bobby's behalf, but my cousin in Fort Worth had a friend in LA who introduced Bobby to one of his friends who knew Marilyn Monroe very well. The friend had an invitation to attend a Hollywood party in the fall where Marilyn Monroe was scheduled to be a guest of honor. That friend promised the excited Bobby an introduction at that time.

Bobby's great anticipation, however, came to naught. Before the party could take place, his goddess was dead. All of Hollywood was heartbroken, and rumors were flying about the why of Marilyn's death. Was it suicide or foul play? Many people speculated that, if it was foul play, her connection with President Kennedy might have been a factor.

Bobby's attempts to meet people in the movie industry or people with influence governed his every plan. He made friends readily and had one of them introduce him to an heiress to the McDonald-Douglas fortune. A couple of weeks after he started dating the heiress, I learned that Bobby had been invited for an audition and tryout for a movie that was to be made in the South. He wasn't hired, but the producer did tell him to come back—as soon as he dropped the Texas twang. I guess Bobby wasn't that interested after all because he never took an acting lesson and never changed his accent. I think the truth was, and is, that Bobby is too stubborn, and in his own eyes, much too perfect, to take anyone's suggestions about self-improvement.

We girls are soon invited to a Hollywood party at Ricky Nelson's house. He is a heartthrob, and we are very excited. I don't know how it has happened, but somehow Bobby, in his Hollywood guise and looking like a movie star himself, shows up at the party—completely ruining everything for me but quite a hit otherwise.

As the party is breaking up that evening, and we start preparing to leave, someone discovers there has been a robbery. Most of us women had piled our purses together on one of the beds—a common enough practice at parties. One of the attendees discovered, upon leaving early, that her keys were not in the usual pocket in her purse where she left them and her money was gone. When she yelled, "Robbery!" we immediately rushed to the bedroom and went through our purses. We had all been robbed! Missing from my purse was: $200; my return airline ticket; and most important, a beautiful charm with a gold tiger-shaped body and head. It was intriguing to look at and was my favorite piece. The mouth was open and contained a diamond held in place with sharp, gold teeth; two red rubies were the eyes. My dad had designed and crafted the charm for my gold bracelet. I was not wearing the bracelet because we girls had spent the morning at the beach and I had slipped it into my purse. The thief had jerked the charm off and left the gold bracelet. Why only the charm, I wondered? I couldn't help remembering how fascinated Bobby had been with that bangle. He told me, as soon as Daddy gave me the bracelet, "You need to take that tiger off and give it to me." Had he committed the robbery? It seemed a lot like him—to leave the gold bracelet and snatch the charm out of pure spite.

The robbery, along with Bobby always lurking around, trying to make connections with my friends and their friends' friends, sours the trip for me and I almost called Dad for another ticket home. Before I could do that, however, Bobby, all of a sudden, left California for Texas. I don't know if the heiress dumped him or if he had another reason.

All too soon, the time to register for classes at NTSU was upon me. Dad sent me another ticket to replace the one I told him I had lost. I did not want to worry him, so I did not tell him of the robbery. I flew out of Los Angeles the day Marilyn Monroe was found dead.

Several months later, after Bobby marries, I am in the couple's apartment and see something catch the light…a sparkle, coming from a dish of odds and ends sitting on the kitchen windowsill. I am drawn to that sparkle. The thing has an odd shape and looks familiar. It is my charm! In Bobby's house.

So it is true—Bobby is the one who stole my charm! Also my money and my ticket… In fact, he committed the robbery! I remember it clearly now; he and his Texas buddy had left the party early, before the crime was discovered.

I am sickened but not surprised. The way the charm was snatched off the bracelet had made me think of Bobby at the time. I wonder: Is he still stealing? Somehow he has given some amazing gifts lately, mainly to his wife. They include multi-carat diamonds and a mink coat. And he is taking her to the most expensive restaurants and clubs in Dallas and Fort Worth. We all just thought he had made a lot of money in Las Vegas, where he got a job dealing the blackjack tables at Harrah's. Now that I know for sure he stole from me, I wonder if he stole his wife's gifts too.

Billy knows I was robbed in California. That was two years ago, before Bobby somehow "came into money." Shouldn't I tell Billy that his brother committed the robbery at Ricky Nelson's house? I pick up my charm and slip it into my jeans pocket. After that, I wear my bracelet and charm often—especially flaunting it whenever Bobby is around. He never lets his eyes rest on the charm, the charm that he had been so intrigued with, and had asked me for and had stolen from me—not a single time, like he didn't even see it.

Oh, and by the way, I never told Billy anything—neither that I had proof that Bobby had committed the robbery in California nor that I strongly suspected his activity didn't stop there.

Speaking of California—the very day I returned to Fort Worth, the following incident happened:

My parents meet me at Love Field, the Dallas airport, and take me straight home, where, much to their displeasure, I immediately call Billy. We were arguing when I left for California in May, but as soon as he answers the phone, it is as if we had never parted.

"I've missed you a lot, Patsy. How about we go to Kip's for a coke and burger?"

When we finish eating, Billy is ready to take me home. "I don't have to be home so early," I tell him. "Let's go to the show."

Billy's surprising reply is, "A movie would be great, Patsy, but not tonight. I have to head for California in the morning. Early."

I guess I looked at him like his head just fell off. Billy had never been to California. If he was going to go, why didn't he come out while I was there?

"Well, why didn't you say something?" I ask.

"I was going to tell you," he answers. "And I just did."

"I can't believe it. I just got back from California today! And now you're going out there? All of a big sudden?"

"Afraid so."

Sitting across the table from him, I continue my questioning stare.

"Believe me, it's a surprise to me too, Patsy. Bobby only told me right before you called. In fact, I bet we leave tonight. I need to call him from your house and find out for sure."

"What's his big hurry? It can't be to meet Marilyn Monroe, like he wanted to, because she was found dead this morning."

"No. He's going to Los Angeles to sell his blue Corvette, and he wants me to go with him."

"That's crazy, Billy. He could sell that thing on the TCU campus in thirty minutes. Why go all the way to California?"

"Exactly what I told him. But he can get more money in L.A. That's what he thinks, anyway. Bobby says we need to be there pronto—like tomorrow, to meet Dad. Dad is already in Los Angeles waiting for us.

Waiting for them? I thought. I guess he's lined up a buyer.

When we get to my house, Billy calls Bobby and, as he predicted, Bobby's ready to go. So it is that the twins leave, before midnight, August 6, driving to California.

A few days later, I get a call from Billy. He has hitchhiked back to Texas and is waiting for me outside Fort Worth. When I pick him up, of course I quiz him about the drive to California. He tells me that driving across the desert, they never got the Corvette below 110–120 mph and stopped only for gas and food.

"That's the way to take care of a car you're going to sell!" I scold in jest.

"Yeah, we thought so too," he says, laughing. "We blew out that carburetor."

"And did you get there in time?"

He spins his head to glare at me. "For what?" he snaps.

For whatever it was you had to be there for, in such a big rush. To sell the car, to meet the buyer—I don't know."

"Oh. Yes, but barely."

"Well, what did you do?"

"We sold the car."

"And you hitchhiked back here by yourself? Where is Bobby?"

"Still out there; with some friend, I think. He'll fly back."

Billy's statement annoys me, but I say nothing. I just think: Bobby insists on Billy driving fast and dangerous all that distance so he can sell his car, then dumps Billy to find his way home as best he can. Of course Bobby will fly home, probably first-class. Hitchhiking is okay for his brother but way beneath Mr. Neiman Marcus.

We found out later that Bobby had stayed in California to attend the funeral of Marilyn Monroe. It was no doubt shocking to his infinite ego to be turned away as an unknown.

In 1995, more than three decades after the twins made their trip to Los Angeles, I receive a phone call from the investigative journalist Seymour Hersh. He is researching material for a book he's writing, The Dark Side of Camelot, *and asks me if I have any idea how to get in touch with a Bill Hale, or Bobby Hale. He wants to question them regarding an incident he is investigating. He thinks they may have information that will shed light on the story.*

At the time of his call, Billy had left home and was in Waco, but I did not know how to get in touch with him. Bobby was in the wilds of New Mexico with no telephone. This little bit of information was vague, and I didn't tell Mr. Hersh much of anything. His investigation came at such a bad time in my life that I could not think about it. I did refer him to other people.

Two years later, while reading Seymour Hersh's newly published book, I realized why he had been interested in talking to Billy and Bobby about their activities the month of August 1962:

At that time we were in the early stages of the Vietnam War, and it seems there was a drama playing out between two large military contracting companies, General Dynamics, where I.B. was head of security, and Boeing. At stake was a multibillion-dollar contract, the largest military contract until that time, for a fighter jet produced by one or the other of the two companies. The Air Force and Navy favored the plane offered by Boeing.

In future interpretations of the circumstances that follow, the huge military contract was key—enough money on the table to, perhaps, risk blackmailing a president:

Living in Los Angeles at this time was a lady, Judith Campbell Exner, who had three very powerful friends: two crime bosses, Sam Giancana and Johnny Rosselli, and the president of the United States, John F. Kennedy. For reasons I guess obvious, the FBI had had Exner's apartment under surveillance for six months. Late at night on August 7, 1962, the agents spotted two young men climbing onto the balcony of Exner's apartment. One of the young men stood watch as the other opened the sliding-glass doors. The agents watched in amazement as the men entered the apartment. After fifteen minutes or so, enough time to place a wiretap or listening device, according to later speculation, the pair fled, one of them in the getaway car—a rental car registered to I.B. Hale, a former FBI agent.

The FBI did not report the breaking and entering of Judith Exner's apartment to the local police. Fear of blowing their cover was later the accepted excuse for not reporting this crime.

Shortly after the break-in, and probable wire tap, Robert McNamara, secretary of defense, overruled the recommendations of both the Air Force and Navy, and persuaded the Pentagon to award the $7 billion contract to General Dynamics for their experimental, and highly controversial, TFX (F-111) bomber to be built in Fort Worth, Texas.

Yes, Mr. Hersh, to answer the purpose of your call, I do remember a trip, unexpected and quick, to California on August 6 and 7, 1962. The twins drove out to meet their dad to sell a Blue Corvette.

14. THE GOOSE HUNT

College Station, Texas, winter 1967

This is a real privilege. Billy and his close group of guy-friends have invited me, the only wife to be invited, to join them on their big annual snow goose hunt. The hunt will take place in the middle of the seemingly endless rice fields east of Houston, near El Maton, the birthplace of Billy's father, I.B. As I listen to the excited conversation, it doesn't take me long to realize that if I ever want to get a word in edgewise while these five old buddies lay out strategies for the hunt—well, it just isn't going to happen.

The goose hunt crew, seven of us in all, consists of: Ray, husband of my lifelong friend and college roommate, Marty, and life of the party because Ray always has tales to tell and, while he is playing the guitar, songs to sing; Danny, another childhood friend, who has a beautiful head of blond hair, round boyish face, and is always looking for a laugh; Milton, a friend of ours since junior high, who already owns a real estate company and loves getting away for a hunt, and who is tall and has the same blue eyes as his adorable nine-year-old-son, Donny, also along for this trip; Wendell, who is now married to my wonderful friend Janna and is employed in the oil trade as "a land man"; and finally, Billy and me, make seven of us goose hunters in all.

Unable to break in with even a simple question, I go about cleaning up the kitchen after our early lunch of hot links with white loaf-bread and mustard, washed down with RC colas. Given that I am having no input, obviously my most important contribution to the hunt will be chief cook and dishwasher for the well-prepared hunters. And well prepared they are—anyone participating in anything with Billy Hale has to be prepared. To him, the planning of an event is as much fun as the event itself—and he can make anything fun. Therefore, by association with Billy, everybody participating enjoys the planning and gets caught up in the excitement he generates.

From the time of our graduations from colleges in Fort Worth and Denton, we friends had all scattered to different towns in Texas for either graduate studies or jobs. But for the past two weekends, the guys who were able to make this hunt have converged on our little house in College Station (Billy is in school at nearby Texas A&M) to plan; Wendell even drove in from faraway Lubbock. Finally, this third weekend is the big date.

Billy calls me to join him and his friends in the living room, where they have laid out equipment, guns, and every possible gadget known to man for a goose hunt.

"Patsy, take a seat and give me your closest attention. I want to tell you about hunting snow geese: The snow geese appear in the very early morning hours. As you know, we've hired a guide and he will call the geese in to us with a goose call. As they get closer to us, you will hear the ha-ha-honking of wild geese. They will fly in a V-shaped formation and will be flying low and going South."

"Now listen to me," Billy continues (he has my rapt attention anyway), "the geese are very watchful and wary. They will not come near any cover in which you, the foe, may be lurking. We want to make sure that you don't give us away to the—"

With that remark, I leap up, put my hands on my hips and look the guys straight in the eyes. "You know this isn't my first hunt—with you guys or without you! And I know how, believe it or not, to be attentive to the geese."

Wendell and Billy start their contagious laughter, and they all roll with laughter at my expense. Billy has just been kidding with me to see if I would get riled. Little Donny, eager to be a part of this joke, speaks up and reveals, "Aunt Patsy, we are planning to give you the best gift ever; you will get the first shot."

"That's right," Wendell says. "The best shot gets the first shot."

I know they are still teasing me, but I jump for joy. I'll show them—this will give me a chance to bring down the first goose, and by George I'll do it!

"I'm going to pack right now," I announce as I run into my bedroom.

With renewed excitement, I begin to check out my clothes situation. You always get wet and muddy on a duck hunt, so I figure goose hunting will be the same. I throw in a couple of changes of clothes and socks and my camouflage clothes and boots. I will wear my camouflage hat; it's kind of cute on me, and I certainly won't be able to fix my hair on this camping trip.

Now I need to do a quick check of the twenty-gauge I am going to use. Billy is keen on all the guns being clean, a practice I.B. instilled in both his sons, and this one is gleaming. I.B. gave Billy and Bobby identical twenty-gauge Ithaca Blu shotguns for their fourteenth birthday. He made the boys take the guns apart and reassemble and clean them over and over. For one year I.B. would only let the twins "dry fire" the guns. Being probably the most renowned sharpshooter in the world, I.B. wanted his boys to respect guns and their destructive capability. He was exceedingly careful with firearms, especially around people, and taught his boys likewise. I've heard this story about I.B. more than once: When he was a young agent, and already one of J. Edgar Hoover's favorites, Hoover nevertheless suspended I.B. for three months to reprimand him for firing over the head of a robbery escapee. The lesson being, do not fire your gun unless you have to kill.

Dear God! The realization dawns on me that the gun I am holding is one of those birthday guns—one not used carefully around people, as I.B. had taught. I cautiously lay it across the bed and look at it with revulsion:

This is Bobby's twenty-gauge, given to him by his dad; the gun that killed Kathleen. This is the very gun that was found in their Tallahassee apartment, the scene of her death—bare, without fingerprints, neither Kathleen's nor Bobby's. It is this gun, without prints, that caused so much speculation about Bobby's role in Kathleen's death. When Kathleen's dad, future governor of Texas, had questioned I.B. about the lack of fingerprints, I.B. said he would have an FBI investigation to clear his son. Other than idle gossip, that ended the questioning.

I pick up the gun and hold it, feel its coolness and its weight, try to imagine Kathleen's hopeless frame of mind when she last held it.

My poor friend. We did all we could do, K.K.—attend your funeral. Hundreds of stunned high-schoolers crowded into the beautiful old First Methodist Church in disbelief. All of the Hale family was there; I was with them. They were devastated—your husband, Bobby, most of all.

And your darling "Uncle Lindy," almost a brother to your dad, who had doted on you all your life—he too did all he could do. He canceled his busy Washington schedule, including a lunch date with former President Truman, and flew to be with your parents at your funeral. So it happened that future President Lyndon Johnson was pallbearer for his precious Kathleen.

Little Donny is calling through my bedroom door, "Aunt Patsy, Daddy says they're loaded up, and it's almost time to leave—I can't wait!" Donny is an intense little hunter and loves every minute of being with us adults.

"Oh boy, Donny, I can't wait either! Come in and help me carry my stuff." I like this child and, although no one knows but Billy, my being two months pregnant probably makes me feel even closer to him.

We take both Milton's van and Wendell's car on this trip, so we have plenty of room—making the ride into the Houston area comfortable and pleasant. The constant drone of the guys talking is lulling me to sleep. Billy had informed me that we are all going to a well-frequented hunter's cafe for breakfast early in the morning. That's wonderful. I can relax now and dream of the first shot instead of planning to cook.

The cars come to a stop, and the guys start scrambling out. I peer through bleary eyes at our campsite and see the Eagle's Lake sign.

"We've got to hurry and set up this camp," Billy says, "so we can get some sleep. And by the way, Patsy, breakfast at the cafe is at four-thirty in the morning! We'll be meeting our guide there and we can't be late."

My heart sinks at the thought of four-thirty a.m. This pregnancy seems to make me want to sleep a lot. "Hurry with the setup then," I reply. "I'm staying out of your way."

Wendell and Billy both have Camp'otels, which are tents that open on top of the car and sleep four people per tent. I like these nifty contraptions because we have to climb a ladder to get on top of the car and into the tent, putting us up off the ground and away from any bugs and spiders crawling around. There are several amenities that come with the Camp'otels, including awnings to sit under and kitchen attachments that include two propane burners and a grill. The guys start putting these together so that I will have a bountiful kitchen arrangement at my fingertips along with two sets of pots and pans. As chief cook, I can't complain. After all, I will get my reward—the first shot.

The guys have the camp set up in no time. Tonight we eat the sandwiches and fruit I brought from home, and climb the ladders to bed. As I fall asleep, I realize that I haven't even seen the lake or our surroundings; I'll see it all tomorrow.

The wake-up call, at four a.m., comes almost immediately, it seems. Sleep refuses to let go of me. Do I really want to do this, I wonder miserably. "Billy, we've just this minute gone to sleep," I complain. "Snooze that clock."

"Girl, I thought you were tough," Billy says. "If you don't get up, you're going to miss the first shot."

With that reminder, and with all the groggy vigor I can muster, I spring out of bed and crawl down the steps in my camouflage clothes. I greet the guys with my best "I'm ready to go!" I have on my cute camouflage hat and what I hope is a sunny face.

We load everything into Milton's van, including ourselves, and head for the rendezvous with our guide at the cafe. This predawn breakfast is tasty enough, but the strong coffee is absolutely the best I've ever had.

We get back in the van and follow the guide in his pickup truck to the rice fields. He has already spread numerous white sheets over the ground (I'm thinking the man must have been up all night), and now he is putting out even more sheets, surrounding us with them. He explains these sheets to me: "When I call the geese to us, they will see the white sheets and think the sheets are other snow geese. That will encourage them to come our way."

The guide has us lie down and covers us with big white hoodies. He says to me, "Don't look up till I tell you to fire!"

From under my white cover, I detect just the faintest glow of sunrise when I remember Billy saying, "The geese must not see your eyes. Hide your eyes." I am so cozy all scrunched down and relaxed, eyes closed, warm in my insulated clothes... I vaguely hear the distant honking of the snow geese.

The guide, having been fully instructed that I was to get the first shot, calls my name, trying not to make too much commotion rousing me.

I rally, get to my feet, see the lead goose, aim my gun, and fire. To my astonishment and the guide's horror, the barrel of my shotgun mushroomed into a near explosion—sending shot, close range, in every direction. Even in shock and pain, I manage somehow not to scream as I am thrown backward, staggering almost to the ground. Dazed, I look around at the guys. All of them are looking at me with saucer eyes and mouths agape. "Patsy," Billy whispers loudly, "you could have been killed."

"I'm not hurt." "She's not hurt," the guide and I say almost in unison as he helps me to the ground, where I will gladly stay until this experience is over.

I know I have put quite a damper on our hunt, for even though the guide calls and calls, we do not have another good formation come our way. Little Donny does manage to get one goose, and he receives many congratulations. And someone—we don't know who—does wound a goose. Billy names the wounded goose Lucie

Goosie and scoops it up to carry home to be nursed back to health. Billy has a way with animals, and we watch as the injured, struggling goose relaxes into his arms, its instinct letting it know that it is safe with this human.

The guide cannot understand this care and attention for one goose. "Don't worry about that goose," he says. "We've got lots of snow geese. They forage in the rice and wheat fields, and there's lots of them. Don't worry about one."

"Well, I am worried about this injured one," Billy says. Billy told Donny later, "If you see an animal is dying, don't let it die in pain. If you can't help it, then humanely kill it." As it turns out, Lucie Goosie becomes famous. My cousin at the *Fort Worth Star-Telegram* features Lucie in a cute half-page write-up before the goose is properly returned to the wild.

Anyway, back to the rice field and the end of the hunt. Billy and all the guys want to inspect my gun with its splintered barrel to try to determine what went wrong. They all comment on our good fortune—that no one, especially myself, was hurt.

Only Billy and I know that this is the gun that killed Kathleen. His look is sober as our eyes meet over the barrel, and I know we are both thinking: This could have been the second tragedy linked to this gun.

Many years later, I decided that both the twins' guns, because of the memories they evoked, would be better off in the hands of unknowing new owners. Before the mood left me, I pawned them. So much of my past had been destroyed by that time; I might as well do away with this part myself.

Pawn ticket for Billy's and Bobby's first guns, given by father I.B. Hale.

In the evening, back at camp, I try to redeem my carelessness by preparing a gourmet feast. I fix fresh corn in the husks, baked in the ground; my famous baked beans with a pound of crisp bacon; jalapeno peppers stuffed with cheese; and shrimp from the nearby Gulf. Since we don't have geese to cook—Donny wants to carry his home to his mother—Ray, who has a reputation for grilling, grills our steaks to perfection. The supper's crowning touch is my camp-skillet peach cobbler.

After this meal, I feel my hard-won pardon is forthcoming when Billy says, "You know, we will always remember this as an outstanding hunting trip. It will be the day Patsy mushroomed her gun and missed her best shot ever."

"You know," I say sheepishly, "I think I know what happened. I've been embarrassed to mention it, but I might as well confess. I must have got mud in the barrel when I fell asleep under those warm sheets."

15. THE CLEANSING

"Woe to you, teachers of the law and Pharisees, you hypocrites! You clean the outside of the cup and dish, but inside they are full of greed and self-indulgence."
~ Matthew 23:25

Our busy lives surge on. I cannot mention the closet incident to Billy again and dare not confront Bobby. If only I had the nerve to confront him and tell him I overheard his plans. Could the two of us talk rationally, just between ourselves, and come to a different conclusion other than his selfish idea of a "cleansing purge"? I know better. Mention of it would only bring on a conflict, and Billy, in all likelihood, would take Bobby's side. Actually, there's no telling what would happen. These two brothers with their strong-minded, often unpredictable personalities are more than I can handle right now. So I leave it alone and hope that, like Billy said, the conversation I overheard was only idle talk. The incident soon becomes a memory—another disturbing *Bobby* memory.

Bobby is working regularly now, and eighteen-year-old Kurina is still trying to help out around our house and tend to her own two children. I am forever busy with my children and their school and the church and cooking.

Bobby continues to want all of us gathered around him after supper so he can "teach" us. I am tired of it. When he starts reading strange things into the Scripture I even fear it. I don't want our children to hear some of what he is saying. But I have to pacify Billy, who thinks it's all wonderful.

I think of Roland often and remember that he cautioned that this might happen. I dare not tell Roland all this, not after his clear warnings. It's too late now and would only reveal my helplessness and naiveté.

Then comes a weekend when both of the Hale brothers are off work. They are in a good mood, and I decide to pamper them with their favorite breakfast, including homemade biscuits and sausage gravy.

Soon after we finish this late breakfast, as I am cleaning the kitchen and dining room, I sense a difference in the atmosphere. It is way too quiet in the house. Billy and Bobby are not talking nonstop as usual. Billy is antsy, preoccupied, and pacing the living room with his thoughts a million miles away.

Bobby ambles into the kitchen to refill his coffee cup. There is an air of mystery about him and an intense presence in his eyes. "Patsy," he says, "I need to call a family meeting in our den."

I bristle when I hear that verbal slip—"our den"—or was it a slip? I am uneasy, and I almost know for sure what this meeting is going to be about. I want to look into those intense eyes and shock the daylights out of Bobby. I want to say, 'So you're finally going to carry out the plot you hatched in my closet a while back!' But I only say, "Fine."

Maybe I'm wrong. Maybe he won't bring that subject up. Maybe my prayer has been answered and he has found another place to live and wants to talk about that. So... "Fine" is all I muster.

Billy is calling the children into the den and pulls my arm to join him. Shortly we are all sitting in a circle around Bobby. He is training us—I think to myself, like he does his animals. So humiliating! I almost become sick. I can easily lose my breakfast right here in this circle. He starts to speak and I feel my head will burst. My fear is coming true—Billy has betrayed me.

"Many of these Christmas gifts you kids have received," Bobby says in a singsong manner—calculated, no doubt, to sound harmless to the children—"are going to have to be done away with. We must destroy them in a certain manner."

Bobby's little children sit and stare innocently, not comprehending this crazy jargon. But my children are all looking at me with various expressions of questioning and dismay. But even though I must be pale with nausea, giving my true feelings away, I maintain a posture as stoic as Gandhi.

Bobby continues, "Kids, I want you to understand that God has led me to this decision. It has been revealed to me that the dolls and stuffed animals are a significant source of evil."

He sees their looks of incredulous disbelief and his voice is a little shrill now. "This has been revealed to me, children—and I am glad, that with my help, your father has seen this through my eyes."

This is crazy—sitting right here in front of me, our *Mr. Neiman Marcus/Marlboro Man*, has come to this: destroying children's toys.

Billy, who has been sitting surprisingly still and intent, starts shaking his foot and fidgeting around at the reference to him. I cut my eyes at him, but he will not look at me. He knows he should have told me this was about to happen. I turn my eyes on Bobby, but he too looks at other family members, ignoring me. If he goes for my jewelry, my dad's gifts to me, that will be it—I will let loose.

"Your Daddy is in total accord with me, and today is the day. So go now and gather them all up, all the dolls and animals."

"I would like for you to show me, biblically, how these children's toys are sinful," I blurted out, surprising even myself. "The toys aren't graven images! They're just toys."

Billy whips his head around and glares at me, like he wants to say, "How dare you." I fall silent.

I'm just glad that none of our children have strong attachments to any of their dolls and stuffed animals. The grandparents and myself usually buy those things because we think they are cute and cuddly, not because the kids have asked for them. Even so, the children look dejected. Tears are gathering in Katie's eyes, but I think it's more anger than sadness.

Bobby ignores my request for biblical proof of his actions and croons, "Children stop. Don't be sad. We are doing the right thing. It is a dreadful sin for you to love and cherish these idols. That's the reason I am glad that God has enlightened me and that I can help you overcome this wrongful attachment. When you gather those idols together, we are all going to have a special service. Then we will go and find a good place to burn them."

"And boys," he brightens his voice and leans forward, "you are going to have fun stoning the TV."

The mood of the children does not match that of Bobby's pretense—nor does mine.

Billy steps into the conversation at this point. "I want you all to be reasonable," he says, trying to convince us. "The TV really doesn't offer anything wholesome for us to watch."

The children sit scowling in dismay. This is much worse to them than burning the toys.

I've got to stand up for the kids. "We don't watch the television a lot, and when we do we are always careful about what we watch. And Bobby," I said boldly, "we have already set strict guidelines; we did that before you ever came here."

"There is nothing of value in it," Billy says firmly.

"That's not always the case," I continue, as bravely as I can, trying to reason with them. "Sometimes the programs are educational. I think if we continue to use discernment about our choices…surely it will be fine."

I've got to leave this alone. You don't confront these men! I feel faint from the effort. I remember Bobby as a young man, full of fight and ready to challenge the biggest male in any crowd. I am no match. They are glaring at me now, identical pairs of green eyes, burning into me as cold as ice.

I try to pull Billy aside, my voice and my body starting to tremble. "Let me stay at home. You can go about stoning the TV. Get rid of whatever Bobby deems necessary. Please don't make me go."

Billy turns away from me and tells Bobby, "We need to get the children busy."

"Kids, gather all those things up," Bobby says loudly. "And get every one of them."

"We can hurry this up," Billy says to Bobby, "if we help them."

With that suggestion, these two grown men try to make this

horror scene seem fun, running with the children upstairs and throwing stuffed animals down and acting stupid and laughing pretentiously...like it's some kind of new game. When they have gathered all the toys into the den, I see the doll I was praying Bobby would forget.

"Bobby, that porcelain doll was stored in *my* closet! What are you doing with it? It was your grandmother's doll...and your mother's."

"Patsy, Patsy," he purrs condescendingly, "don't you see? That is all the more reason to get rid of it."

"No," I said weakly, "I don't see." A lump the size of a grapefruit is choking me. I manage to mumble, "Your mother wanted it in the family."

Billy spoke up, "Patsy is not going with us. She will stay here and fix dinner instead. Her heart is really not in it.

**

"What is done is done, what is not done is not done; Let it be."
~ New Zealand Book of Prayer, 1800s

I live now with conflicted thoughts and feelings. Had Billy taken part in Bobby's *cleansing purge* just to placate him, thinking it's no big deal, just let Bobby have his way? Probably. Why not? He has let Bobby have his way from the time he walked in, on Christmas Eve. I try to understand what is happening around me—in this household since Bobby arrived. From the very beginning I believe he has tried to cause trouble—to pry a widening gap between Billy and me, a gap he can step into and more easily influence us both. From Bobby's disagreeing with me on every issue, starting the first hour he got here, and refusing every request I made—especially upon seeing that Billy would not, and will not, stand up for me, I can't help concluding that he aims to diminish my husband in my eyes. The why of it all is hard to understand—but here it is, in our home, and we are living the confusion.

Bobby's actions I can understand better than Billy's. Bobby lived for several years among people who practiced voodoo and black magic. Was he really scared of dolls, though, or did he want to show me he could have his way with Billy? It's not even that I care about the things that were destroyed; those particular items meant little to me—except for his mother's doll. But the fact that it happened at all is an insane act, as well as a defeat for me. And I feel that his compliance with Bobby further weakens Billy.

Another thing I wonder about: Did Bobby rifle through Billy's closet? Billy has far more expensive clothing than I do. To my dismay (though I never complain), Billy spends top dollar on everything he buys, including his apparel. Bobby had to know they were in Billy's closet because after the conversion they both went through Billy's clothes in order to outfit Bobby. Did Bobby find things belonging to his brother, smacking of vanity, that he wanted to burn?

At any rate, the ridding us of toys and television is just one more frightening example of Bobby's ability to control us; and it has caused a stain to spread in my mind. No one knows about this but me—I know; I feel the difference. I can no longer look at Bobby with an innocent heart. Though I felt at peace with him after his conversion, that peace is gone. He is an impostor. An imposter who snoops in my jewelry and lingerie, and burns my children's toys. The most bitter pill I must swallow is that my husband is his accomplice. Billy doesn't understand. There is a blockage between us now. I can't talk to him about my feelings or anything of substance.

If anything good has come from this episode, it would be that I am no longer expected to sit and listen to Bobby go on and on every night misrepresenting God's word. I do join them occasionally anyway—to keep the peace.

There's a lot about Bobby that Billy doesn't know—things I've never told him and can never tell him now. Sometimes I feel I'm a prisoner of these secrets. Would it have made a difference if I had spoken up—told him about some things? "I'm a better man than my brother!" Bobby had spat at me one day. Would Billy be less willing to follow Bobby if he knew that Bobby thinks he's "the better man"? Bobby has certainly not changed his mind about that.

Why didn't I tell Billy about the theft at Ricky Nelson's party? I had proof that Bobby was the thief—but I kept quiet. I would like to know if it would have made a difference to Billy or if he would have brushed it off. That's something else I will never know.

Another incident I still wonder about is the accident—when Bobby broke Billy's jaws. What was that all about? How could Bobby bear to abandon his injured brother at the emergency room, lie about his whereabouts, and drive carefree, all the way to Galveston? If Billy ever held him accountable for that incident, I saw no evidence of it.

I've known from the time we were teenagers that Bobby is controlling and manipulative. If I describe him now, I will say he tries to control from the *dark side*—he always has. Bobby would lie to anyone, especially girls, and he would steal and fight, often unprovoked and with strangers. Billy, on the other hand, would not steal, and though he could be tough, he never got into a fight other than with Bobby.

Yes, I believe Bobby's motives are always to intimidate and control. He is intimidating me with the threat of damaging my house and destroying my belongings. Bobby is not finished. I think it will happen again; the 'cleansing purge' I mean. There are things, like my jewelry, that Bobby would like to rid me of. I can't doubt it—I heard him say so: "Can you believe all this stuff poor Patsy is burdened with? So much jewelry and clothes. Such vanity." Yes, he wants to unburden me of all my possessions, I'm quite sure of it, and he will try it again. He will wait, though, until he has made Billy ready. And I can't change it. I have to live with Billy regardless—live with Bobby too, it seems.

Unlike those of Bobby, Billy's motives—as far as I know, and most likely as far as he knows—were and are benign. Motives aside, his tactics can be hurtful. He is an idealist, a perfectionist, and at this time in his life he wants his family to be the most perfect Christians on earth. I say "family" meaning not only the children and me but also his brother. I will say this: He is extremely proud that Bobby has, in Billy's eyes, *taken to the faith* (if you could call it that) with such commitment. At this point it could be that Billy and Bobby are feeding off each other.

So, as we say, life happens, and the weeks continue as before; they fly by, thankfully, with relatively few incidents. The memories of our burning and stoning grow dim for me, and the children seem to have forgotten altogether.

I'm not sure Kurina ever thought of that event as anything out of the ordinary. She treated me as if nothing had happened, and I'm sure for her, little had. At fifteen, Kurina had left her broken home and probably has little family experience to base her judgments on. Living with Bobby, a man who is certainly out of the ordinary and seventeen years her senior, has ensured that most of her experiences have been pretty bizarre. From the beginning of this unexpected visit in our home, Bobby has had a lot of power over Kurina, but since she got back from visiting her mother in California, that power seems to have intensified in a way that does not seem natural. She seems even more submissive to him at this time, maybe because he divorced his wife and now she is the only woman in his life.

For every uneventful day I am grateful.

A skilled marksman, I.B. Hale
was famous for trick shots.

I.B. with future NFL star
Davey O'Brien.

A photo from I.B.'s playing days at TCU (1936-39), where he was
an All-American.

More shooting demonstrations from I.B.

I.B. Hale in Boston, where the twins were born, where he'd gone on assignment for the FBI.

Bobby, Billy, and their high
school buddies.

Patsy, Billy, and their first two
children in 1969

Billy and Patsy Hale at a Southwest football conference ceremony
celebrating I.B. Hale.

Bobby Hale's corral at his home in Mora County, New Mexico.

Billy at his second veterinary clinic in Fort Worth, 1980-81.

Billy on horseback visting the New Mexico homestead.

Billy in South Carolina while traveling and preaching.

A drawing of Billy in Guyana; the last image Patsy ever received.

The Hale family's army truck.

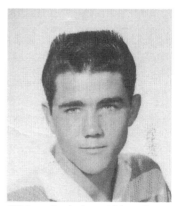

Billy's yearbook photo, 10th grade.

Billy and Patsy Hale's Weatherford, Texas home.

Billy Hale's final home, in Nicaragua.

16. FIVE ACRES AND A BARN

"The work of your heart, the work of your taking time to listen,
to help, is also your gift to the whole world."
~ Jack Kornfield

Finally good news. Bobby tells us the whole story at dinner. Today he, Kurina, and the babies went driving around just to get out. On the way back to our house, Bobby decided to show Kurina the area where a friend of his, Stanley Tallent, had lived when he was young. "I was getting all nostalgic thinking about playing on these same streets with Stan, when I made a wrong turn. It was a lucky turn too. In a few blocks we were in an area that is still undeveloped. I saw a sign on this corner lot—really a corner field—that read: 'For Sale, 5 acres and a Barn.' On the bottom of the sign was scribbled a phone number."

"You got that much money already?" Billy interrupts.

"Let me finish. We got out and walked to the horse barn, the only structure to speak of on the place…and there you have it. We both loved it. There is running water and the structure is sound. We could fix it up with no problem."

"Fix it up for what?" Billy roars excitedly, grinning his big grin and starting to shift around.

"To live in, brother," Bobby yells back, happily.

I put my hand on Billy's arm to calm him down and keep him in his seat. "Kurina, did you like it? I ask. Without waiting for her answer, I continue, "Go on and tell us everything, Bobby. Do you really want to buy it?"

"Well, let me talk and I'll tell you. I wrote down the phone number and started asking around the locality. One of the neighbors let me use the telephone to call that number, and we went to see the owner. I told him I want to keep my horses in the barn and see how I like it before buying. I worked out a rent amount, and we are going to start fixing it up right away. We want to live in it, you know. It will be a good place to have people visit. That's the main reason I want a big place. That barn and land will be perfect."

"What people are you talking about?" Billy asks.

"You know, people from church. Or just people who want to know about the Lord. He laughs and adds, "Don't worry, I'll invite you, brother."

"You know, Bobby," I said, "this is a real happening. People everywhere are fixing up old barns to live in. I read about this trend in the magazines all the time now. Is this really a done deal? The man agreed to rent it just like that?" I think I must be giddy—I'm out-talking Billy.

"Yes," Bobby said grinning ear to ear, "it's a done deal. It's going to happen."

"Kurina, I'm thrilled for you. Some of these barns turn out to be beautiful—and always charming. Bobby, Geneva is going to be very interested in your new project... By the way, is she still sending you work?" *I am so excited! Bobby may soon be out of my house!*

"This will take a long time," Billy says. "Months, if not years, depending on how much you work and what you want to do." He has already left the room and is walking back in with paper and pencils, rulers and a calculator. I know my husband; he wants to plan the whole renovation tonight. In no time he will know all about this job: how many pounds of nails are needed, how many bags of concrete, how much paint...

I am snatching dishes off the table as Billy lays out drafting paper left over from our renovation. "Here, Bobby, draw that floor plan and let's figure this thing out."

I notice that Bobby is taken aback. He had probably rather preach to us tonight than work on plans for his barn. But with Billy looking expectantly over his shoulder, Bobby stares at the table, slowly takes up a pencil and adjusts the lead.

I see Bobby is unsure of himself. To avoid witnessing his embarrassment, I head for the kitchen to clean up. Bobby says there will be plenty of room in the barn and he wants to have people over. "People from church," he said, "or just people who want to know about the Lord." Yes, I think, that will be wonderful. And it will keep him and Kurina moving forward in their faith. When the time comes for them to have people over, I will help Kurina. She is young and has not been a hostess on her own. I have only one reservation: I hope he doesn't expect our church people to sit at his feet and stare worshipfully into his "all-knowing" face. Other people are not his twin brother and his accommodating family.

And so it happened that the Bobby Hales moved out of our house and into a barn on five acres of land—in the city limits.

As it turns out, Bobby's barn project is not nearly as ambitious as Billy had thought. When Bobby knocked out two horse stalls and swept the floor, he and Kurina were ready to move in.

Billy was a little disappointed, but I understood completely—they had been living in a truck for three years. The barn, with running water was a big step up. People from the church picked up things from yard sales to give them: a couch, La-Z-Boy chair, kitchen table and chairs, bed, and some sort of freestanding cabinet. Someone even brought in a big, pretty throw rug. Those furnishings allow Kurina to take a few of their things from the truck, like dishes, pots and pans, and my still-stained quilts, and set up a living quarters.

Bobby is already building cabinets for a kitchen sink and storage.

Sheba and Goethe have plenty of room to graze, and the chickens are scratching all over the barnyard with Sebastian to protect them.

Billy and I have been over to visit a couple of times, and all is well. Bobby loves the place and asked Virginia to buy it for him. He thinks she might if they get a fair price.

A few days later, my good friend Geneva calls the house, and she is excited. "Patsy, I've just got a contract on the most fabulous job I have ever had. It is for the Dobsons in Garland."

"Geneva, that's great," I say almost matching her excitement. A contract with the Dobsons is good news for Geneva. The Dobsons practically own the whole county, and everybody knows them. What a great boost for my friend's reputation.

"Patsy, this will give my business the boost I need desperately."

"That's exactly what I'm thinking! It's just what you need, but how did you get such a job—way over in Garland?"

"Well, hang onto your seat, and listen to me with an open mind because I might need your help. Mrs. Dobson is completely redoing and updating their beautiful old home. She chose three designers in the Dallas–Fort Worth area to interview, and I was one of them. And why did she choose me, you ask? Because I told her all about my incredible contractors. 'Mrs. Dobson, I told her, they can install the upholstered walls and pleated trim that you have your heart set on more perfectly professional than anyone south of New York City.'"

"You really have a lot of confidence in Bobby," I say, ignoring her allusion to "they."

"Patsy, I said "they." This is where you might have to help me. Billy must be with Bobby. This job is just too important. If I call Billy, will he agree to help Bobby? He can totally set the schedule...but it will be a two- or three-day job. I know I had no right to promise this...but Mrs. Dobson was right there and I got carried away."

"I know, and you were seeing dollar-signs in front of your eyeballs like Uncle Scrooge," I tease her. "But seriously, Geneva, we do owe you a favor. How much money did you save us on our furniture? And that's not the last time I'll call on you, believe me. Billy is in the next room—I'm handing him the phone."

"What did you tell her?" I ask when Billy comes in to hang up the phone.

"I told her I will help her. What else?"

"Good. She was afraid you might not be able to schedule two or more days away."

"Not a problem. Actually, I'm glad. This will give me a chance to teach Bobby another technique. I've done what Geneva described when I was learning to do our rooms."

Billy should have been cautious, knowing how prideful Bobby has become of his new skill. He has received a lot of flattering comments on his work, and now, from what Billy told me, Bobby thinks he has a monopoly on the craft. Billy explained: "My brother, once he learns a thing, he thinks he owns it—you can't teach him another thing; he thinks he should to do the teaching."

"He's like that about his religion too," I was anxious to point out. I didn't get a comment from Billy.

From what I learned later, on the job in Garland, it became obvious that Bobby was jealous of Billy.

Bobby, now beyond being taught anything by anybody—especially by

"Doc-ter Hale," is primed to cause havoc when Mrs. Dobson addresses Billy as being the person in authority. That bit of recognition seriously bruised Bobby's manly ego. After that, he fought and argued with Billy every step of the way: mocking his authority, questioning his skill, and yelling at him abusively. When I heard about it, I thought he must have lost his mind. To risk his reputation as well as Geneva's? In spite of the embarrassment, Billy would not let Bobby do anything less than perfect. He even tore out some shoddy work that Bobby was going to pass off as finished and threw it at him.

Mrs. Dobson told them to get out of her house before she called the sheriff. "And," she said as she tore up Geneva's contract in front of Billy, "tell your boss the deal's off."

Billy and I grieved with Geneva. I can't remember when he was more furious with Bobby. "I taught my brother a skill so he can make a living, and this is what comes of it. I'm sorry, Geneva, that your trying to help him has caused you this trouble. He is out of my house now, and I'm glad. It's going to take a lot of effort on his part to mend the riff he's caused between us, not to mention the damage he's caused you."

I welcomed all those strong words from Billy—venting his anger with Bobby—they were long overdue.

Mrs. Dobson made sure that everyone she had the opportunity to talk to (even the employees in a high-end furniture store in Fort Worth, where two other friends of mine worked and heard the tale) knew the story of the twin men who came to her house and fought until she threatened to call the sheriff. "Don't ever use those clowns," she warned.

Bobby's truck is parked on the street outside our house. I see him sitting in the front seat with his family even before I turn the corner. It was only last week, seven days ago, that he made such a fool of himself on poor Geneva's job in Garland and alienated Billy. What could he possibly want? Billy is not here; he should know that from living with us so long. I've just returned from driving the children to school—he or maybe Kurina must want to see me alone. Do they want to come inside, or do I get in the truck? It's misting rain, so I pull nose to nose with the truck and wave and point to the house. Kurina gets out of the truck, and I open my door at the same time. "Why don't you all come in the house," I call.

She nods. "Okay, if it's all right."

"Give me a minute to open the front door." I back up and pull into the garage. A minute later I'm waving from the door for them to come in.

Watching the family come across the yard and up the steps, I can tell that Bobby is unbowed. He is still clean-shaven and in dressy casual attire—Billy's attire. He looks wonderful as usual. He has not come here to acknowledge to anyone any wrongdoing on his part. He enters first, carrying both babies, then waits for Kurina.

Kurina is a different matter. She looks pale and is walking like an older woman, not a teenager. But when she looks at me, there's an excitement in her eyes.

"Patsy, I just had to see you—we're leaving."

"Kurina, what are you saying?" I ask. "Come in the den and tell me what's happening."

I wish I could have five minutes to talk to her in private, but Bobby sticks to us like glue. "Kurina," I say, "come with me to the kitchen while I make coffee." Bobby traipses right behind her. I can forget privacy. I want to ask her about her pregnancy. She had told me she was pregnant when they left our house and moved into the barn; but does he know that I know? He must, because even though Kurina is tall, she is beginning to show. Billy was disappointed when I told him they were expecting again. He said Brother Miles had told Bobby he should take care not to have more children until he gets his life sorted out.

"Kurina, you look pale to me. Are you feeling okay?"

"Not really. I'm having a lot of trouble. It's not like before. That's why I wanted to talk to you."

And so we have to talk with Bobby right there in the room. He reminds us that he has delivered more babies than both of us combined, which equals exactly zero, and I remind him—rather bold for me—that the times he has been pregnant equal exactly zero.

"Let's go in the den with our coffee, and I've got almost a whole loaf of banana bread in the fridge…if you'll bring it, Bobby."

"Kurina, you said you all are leaving. Why?" I ask. "With this pregnancy, you should stay here. And where are you going? You've just moved into your barn. You've got five acres and a barn. Why would you leave?" I'm discovering I really don't want them to go. I'm worried about Kurina.

Kurina leans into the sofa, her back in an arch, unable to drink coffee or eat sweets. She turns weakly to Bobby for help in explaining. It looks like an act of surrender.

"I know what's best for us, Patsy," he says. "We are going to head for the mountains. You know that Kurina's mother and stepdad are big into Hollywood and movies—him being a movie producer. They know Jack Nicholson. He owns a huge amount of property in the mountains of New Mexico. We are hoping Nicholson will rent us that land, along with its cabins and outbuildings. He could charge us ten dollars a month and get a big tax write-off. And if he does or doesn't, we are still moving to New Mexico. We like it there. I feel I can have an influence on the ranchers in the mountains around

Taos." He turns to Kurina and holds her hand. "We can have our own following again."

Her only response is a feeble smile. I realize I'm missing Kurina's laugh. They have been here an hour, and I haven't heard a single hearty laugh.

"That barn is not working out, Patsy," Bobby continues.

"I'm so disappointed. It seemed like the perfect place. I thought you loved it."

"Too many problems. Mother is hesitant about buying the property, for one thing. And Kurina doesn't feel up to us holding prayer meetings as I had hoped. Personally, I don't think she will ever fit in with this modern crowd in Fort Worth."

Kurina keeps her eyes closed and doesn't acknowledge his remark.

"And now Billy has got all riled up and turned against me. I wanted to make a go of it here. I wanted to have our own land and place to live—it seemed good. And y'all are close by. But it's not working out."

"Bobby, you're giving up too easy."

"We're leaving, Patsy, and soon. We're moving on to bigger things."

When he was near death, Bobby would write to me: "If only my mother had bought that five acres and a barn for me, I would have stayed in Texas."

**

"He…whose nature it is to tire of everything in turn…tired of common sense and civilization."
~ *F.L. Lucas*

Billy is alarmed when I tell him that Bobby and Kurina are moving to New Mexico.

All his anger is forgotten, and early the next evening we pile the children into the car and go straight to the barn—but not before Billy called Roland for advice. Roland was concerned that they were leaving their support system: family and church, so soon.

"Bobby, what do you think you're doing, man?" Billy demanded as soon as we pulled up to the barn.

"Moving to New Mexico, brother. The mountains and desert are calling me. Living here is not working out."

"What are you talking about? Of course it's working out. Things are great. You've practically got a career now and your own place to live."

"I'm soured on that so-called career."

"Don't be. That job in Garland was unfortunate but in the long run just a temporary setback. People forget."

"Well, I don't forget. And besides, I'm just not into it anymore. I'm ready to move on."

I am thinking to myself: With those itchy feet, no wonder Virginia is hesitant about buying this property for you. But joining the conservation, I say, "Bobby, at least don't be in such a hurry. Please stay here until this baby is born. Kurina is not doing well. You know that."

"Most days she's okay; and she wants to go as bad as I do."

I know this is probably true. I know she aches when other women and Bobby exchange glances, and I've seen it—it happens every time he leaves the house, even at the grocery store. Her presence with him is barely noticed, and when it is, it is with disbelief.

I look across the sitting area to where Kurina is listening to our conversation. I see the same tired excitement in her eyes that I saw yesterday. I think she would like for us to leave this alone. She joins in and confirms my suspicions.

"Patsy, I do want to go. We're going to drive to my mother's. The baby will be born in California. Like Bobby says, I'll be fine."

"It's such a long trip, Kurina, and you haven't seen a doctor here. You don't know—"

"Patsy, I don't go to doctors," she interrupts. "Bobby is my doctor."

All right, I am thinking, he's your doctor, but not such a caring one, it seems.

"She's right, Patsy," Bobby says. "Nothing will happen that I can't handle. I've made every kind of tricky delivery there is. Besides, Kurina is a fine, healthy woman. She was born to have babies."

Stupid statements like that are infuriating—and so easy for him to make. Oh you just know everything, don't you, Bobby, I think! Out loud I say, "Okay, you two agree, and it's your call. Kurina, I'll keep you in my prayers. Please write to me."

This is sounding too decided for Billy; he jumps up, walks over to the makeshift sink, walks around the sitting area, and comes back to sit at the table. Restless pacing like this is typical of Billy. I'm surprised that he sits back down. He probably does so because we have the only small fan in the barn directed at the table, and on this July night in Texas it is rather warm—as we sometimes say in understatement. His t-shirt is growing damp around the neck and underarms, not only with the heat but also with the physical effort he's putting into this argument.

I noticed, when we arrived, that Billy and Bobby were both wearing white t-shirts and blue jeans. I recall when they wore that James Dean outfit from the movie *Rebel Without a Cause* in high school. It drove us girls crazy. We would watch them walk down the hall and say, "James Dean, eat your heart out." We got very little done, academically, on those days. These guys haven't changed much.

"Bobby," Billy says, "I called Roland today. He's a smart man and I trust his judgments. He thinks you are too new and fragile a Christian to leave us and the church family. We all love and support you, and you need us right now."

"What does that mean, for crying out loud? I'm too new and fragile? And for his information, I really don't *need* anybody." Bobby seems outraged.

"He feels you may be led astray, Bobby, that's all. Like he says, you are practically a brand-new Christian."

I am thinking: led astray? I'm afraid it's already happened—and the one to lead Bobby astray is Bobby.

"Roland says Christianity needs to become a way of life for you—and maybe it hasn't yet."

"Yeah? Well, maybe it has." Bobby jumps up and starts pacing and gesturing. He says, pointing at himself and nodding his head, "I catch on pretty fast, Billy. I know the truth. Tell Roland no one can ever lead me astray. When I became a Christian, I became a Christian; that will never change. When people underestimate me, I wish you would take up for me instead of 'trusting their judgments.' You people think I need supervision."

It wouldn't be a bad idea, I thought; look at your life.

"Okay, okay," Billy says, "no offense. I believe you and trust you, but I still can't understand the *why* of your running off like this."

"I've got several reasons. Didn't Patsy tell you?"

"Yes, she told me—but I'm not riled up and I've not turned against you. Would I be begging you to stay if that were the case?"

And the pleading goes on, with Billy trying to persuade Bobby to change his mind—to no effect. The decision is final. They will be giving the donated items they can't use to Goodwill and taking the rest with them in the truck. They will be leaving Saturday morning— less than two days.

Billy's whole countenance sags with dejection. "Your decision is killing me. But I'll come over tomorrow and help you load up. Some of these pieces are heavy. Let's don't let Kurina lift at this point."

As we drive home, in an effort to lighten up, I recall a story that we haven't laughed about in a long time. "Billy, did you ever tell Bobby about your dad wanting to rescue him from Haight-Ashbury?"

"No! Can you believe it—I never did tell him. And Bobby would get a big kick out of it too."

"I think about that night every now and then and always have to laugh out loud."

"That was the craziest thing I ever heard of. I can't believe my dad came up with such a scheme. Come with me to the barn tomorrow and let's tell Bobby. At least we'll all have a good laugh."

"It will be their last night in Fort Worth. I'll definitely come with you. It makes me sad to see them leave. You'll be going early to help them load. Tell Kurina I'll make something to bring over for supper. We'll drive straight there as soon as school is out."

The truck is loaded, the few boxes packed, and we are finished with the two enchilada casseroles that I brought for dinner. The sun hasn't set and, for the time being, the children are playing outside.

"Patsy," Billy says, "while the kids are outside, go ahead and tell the story we were talking about last night? Bobby, you're going to get a kick out of this."

"Okay," I reply, "here goes."

I call this story "Let's Rescue Bobby," and it takes place in the fall of 1967. Billy is still in school at Texas A&M, and we are living in the house outside College Station. It is late in the evening, and I have long since cleaned up the kitchen from supper, slipped on my housecoat, and taken a seat at the kitchen table to read while Billy studies. We are deep into our books when we are startled by the blare of a l-o-n-g doorbell ring. We spin our heads, look puzzled into each other's eyes, and know that we are not expecting anyone. Who has come this late at night, and apparently with such urgency? We give the front door our immediate attention. Billy jumps up to answer the bell, which, in these few seconds, has just rung for the second time. I, in my housecoat, stay at the kitchen table.

"Dad!" I hear Billy say. "Is everything okay?"

This is the first time I.B. has been down here to visit us—and this late! My stomach tightens into a sudden knot; something horrible must have happened.

"I should have let you know I was coming down here. I officiated at the A&M game this evening and wanted to stop by."

I run in to hug I.B. and welcome him to our house. "We could have gone to the game if we had known you were there. How do you like our little house?"

"It's a great little place. I just didn't know you were out in the country."

"Yeah, we're on forty acres out here," Billy says.

"I.B., have you had anything to eat?" I ask, opening the refrigerator and handing him a ginger ale. I know that even if I.B. has eaten, he would like something else. While he and Billy talk, I quickly set out chips and start heating a can of Ro-Tel tomatoes and cheese for our favorite dip. I eavesdrop on them as best I can and hear I.B. talking about Bobby.

"I heard you talking about Bobby," I say, putting the hot dip on the table. "What's happened?"

"It seems," Billy says, "that Bobby has managed to overdose on drugs and get himself delivered, by ambulance, to an emergency room in Haight-Ashbury."

"Oh no! How is he?"

"They're keeping him in the hospital tonight," I.B. says. "His heart went into fibrillation. The emergency room doctor told me it was serious. I'll be calling them back in the morning. But even if he comes through this okay, what about the next time?"

"Dad, there won't be a next time—don't worry," Billy reassures him. "An overdose is so scary that people who survive rarely repeat the experience. Bobby won't do that again."

"Billy, of course he'll do it again. I don't think you two realize the seriousness of this; Bobby always does stuff again. The worse it is, the more I can count on a repeat."

Billy and I sit quietly, then Billy puts the words in my mouth, "I can think of a couple of times, Dad, when Bobby has 'learned his lesson.'"

"Well, I can't think of any—and besides, this is a matter of life and death."

"Dad, you're overreacting. It's not that bad."

"Believe me, Billy, it is that bad! I've heard of kids overdosing and dying—or worse, he could get brain dead."

"Well, what to do? Are you going out there?"

"I want to. I want to go to San Francisco, and I want you to come with me."

"Wow! I guess I could work that out. I'd love to see him."

"We aren't going for a visit, Billy; you're going to help me bring him back. He won't even know we're there till it's too late!"

This is getting very interesting, and I interrupt. "I.B., what are your plans? Are you going to kidnap Bobby?"

"Yep. That's exactly what I intend to do—kidnap him, with Billy's help. I want Bobby out of that place while he's still alive."

I turn to Billy, and the expression on his face is so comical I have to stifle my laughter. I am imagining the two of them struggling to hang on to a kicking and yelling Bobby. Billy is obviously thinking the same thing.

"Dad, how on earth do you plan to restrain him? Do you know what a fit he'll have? We'll never get him on the airplane, or even in a car. We'll be arrested."

199

And, I'm thinking, charged with kidnapping.

"I have a plan," I.B. says, "and he won't be struggling at all."

"Yeah?" Billy asks.

"I'm going to tranquilize him—shoot him with a tranquilizing gun."

We both gasp. I can't believe what I'm hearing.

He continues, "Don't act so surprised. Surely you both know all about how they shoot animals with tranquilizing guns—to capture and move them, or treat them or whatever? Well, it should work for Bobby too."

"Whoa, Dad; that can be dangerous! The injection has to be the right formula and right amount—and I've never heard of it being used on a human. And what if you missed?"

I.B. looks pained. "What if I missed!? Billy, have I ever missed a target in my life? If I have, it's been so long ago I can't remember. In fact, I would remember that, and I can't remember; so it hasn't happened."

"Dad, this whole idea scares me. Have you ever heard of it being used on humans?"

"Son, I was in the FBI for fifteen years; I'm not saying what I've heard of, but I've heard of a lot."

"Well, where would we get the human dose?" Billy asks. Then before I.B. could answer, he adds "I'm sorry Dad, but this is crazy. He's over twenty-one and it's against the law. And what would we do with him after we got him back? You gonna to keep him in a cage?"

"Yes. I think we'll have to. I thought we could chain him outside in your dog run," he says with a grin.

"Great idea, Dad. What'll we do when he starts barking—I mean yelling—for help?"

This whole picture triggers such a fit of laughing in all three of us that we almost can't stop. When we do, needless to say, I explain, the desperate rescue scheme was canned.

Bobby and Kurina are laughing hysterically—it's good to hear Kurina's laugh again.

Early next morning, before breakfast, our family once again arrives at the barn. Bobby told us last night that they were anxious to leave and would get breakfast on the road. Regardless, I brought them biscuits with Canadian bacon as well as deviled eggs and donated Billy's thermos full of creamy coffee. "This is good traveling food," I say to Kurina. "Especially for the children. You can eat these while you drive."

We stand forlornly in front of Bobby's barn and wave goodbye to him and his family and his truck.

It will be almost nine years and a lot of living before we see them again.

17. THE FAMILY ADVENTURE

"Experience: That most brutal of teachers."
~ C. S. Lewis

It is midnight in Fort Worth, and those of us traveling are bustling with excitement and a spirit of adventure. We load our suitcases, boxes of food, sleeping bags, hiking boots, and winter jackets into the cargo-carrier on top of our diesel Suburban, then all pile in for our sixteen-hour drive north to, and across, the Texas panhandle and into New Mexico. We are heading to the Sangre de Cristo Mountains to visit Bobby and Kurina and their children. The SUV, less than two weeks old, is Billy's purchase. Of course, it is the most comfortable and expensive model sold by Chevrolet.

Nestled in this big car, each with his or her favorite pillow, are nine of our family members. We are four generations ranging in age from our two-year-old granddaughter, Nichole, to my eighty-two-year-old mother. Allison and her husband, Ronnie, are along for the ride as well as Austin their four-year-old son. And because Will and Katie are away at school, there is room for Stevie, a friend of our son Ben; they are fourteen.

By starting our trip at midnight, Billy and I figure the children and my mother will soon tire and, with any luck, will sleep for most of the drive to Amarillo. Amarillo, far into the panhandle, is our halfway point and where we will have breakfast.

It has been a long time, almost nine years, since Bobby and his family left Fort Worth. A lot has happened in that time. Billy and I have sold our home in Fort Worth; bought a historic, three-story house from inside the city limits; relocated it to part of my dad's four-hundred-acre estate west of Fort Worth; renovated the house; and established ourselves on our new small Texas ranch.

Bobby and Kurina have been busy setting up their new home also. They have renovated and furnished a log cabin; established a herd of sheep; learned necessary farm skills; become proficient as artistic handicrafters; built self-sustaining solar energy lighting; and built water cooling and freezing devices. In addition to all these accomplishments, they have three more healthy children.

Over the past two years, Bobby has beguiled us with a multitude of letters and pictures urging us to come and visit them at their mountain ranch. He recently sent cassette tapes of himself playing the guitar and his young family singing to our family. How could we resist that? Charmed and flattered, even I am ready to forget that Bobby had once been a Morning Star, and forgive all the folly and hurt that name evokes. In nine years, with God's help, one can forgive a lot.

It is past midnight now but Billy, Allison, Ronnie, and I are wide awake and still making plans and discussing all we will see and do on this trip. We plan to cover the eight hundred miles to Ledoux and arrive there well before dark.

Ledoux, a tiny town in North Central New Mexico, is in the foothills of the Sangre de Cristo Mountains, about thirty miles southeast of Taos. According to Bobby, we will leave our car parked near the post office in Ledoux. He will pick us up there. We will finish the trip to Bobby's cabin in the same trusty old 1934 Army truck that brought the Morning Stars to Fort Worth. The truck can still negotiate the nearly impassible road to their mountaintop compound. In letters, Bobby has given us vivid descriptions of the rugged terrain where they live, so we are prepared for anything; even Mother brought her hiking boots. *Unfortunately, we will find that no amount of planning could have prepared us for this trip and Bobby's dark agenda.*

We speed along through the dim early morning, and one by one we grow quiet.

As my own thoughts turn to our prospective hosts, I notice an old familiar anxiety move into the pit of my stomach. It always happens. Why is it I feel foreboding when I am about to meet Bobby—or more precisely, when Billy is about to meet Bobby? Perhaps past experience is weighing me down. My thoughts are always toward the brothers being close, but that state of affairs, though easily accomplished, is never maintained. Since the sudden departure of Bobby's family, their truck loaded with food and clothes given them by our church and friends, I have been skeptical of Bobby's motives. Though he wouldn't say so, I could tell that it bothered Billy too that Bobby skipped out with lots of unfinished business, mainly regarding his wives and children. Billy and I rarely discuss how we feel about Bobby and his fickle past, but when we do, I ask for God's help and try to be sensitive.

A heaviness surrounds my thoughts as I remember the first letter I got from Kurina after their early-morning departure nearly nine years ago. It was a sketchy little letter, painfully printed, front and back, messy and childlike in its language, and it told a shocking tale:

Kurina was about five months into a troublesome pregnancy when the Moringstars left our family behind. The drive was long, and in that rough old truck the ride was not the smoothest. They were headed west, all the way to California. After a visit with her mom in Los Angeles and the birth of their baby in California, they would be backtracking to New Mexico. Setting up a homestead in the mountains, on a two-thousand-acre tract of land belonging to one of her mother and stepfather's friends, was their plan when they left Fort Worth.

This first letter from Kurina was much unlike her in that she complained bitterly about Bobby, something she had never done. She said that Bobby couldn't miss a pothole to save his life but had to hit every single one, on every unkept backwoods road. He was determined to go the roughest and longest and most backward way possible to get to their destination. I could feel the hurt in her tone as she complained that the drive was hard on her. Even so, she was unable to convince Bobby to stick to a logical route. She commented that Sheba, Bobby's beautiful mare riding in the back of the truck, was more restless and fitful than she had ever been.

Events took a horrifying turn when Kurina began to have labor pains, stronger and stronger. Bobby finally showed a little mercy and stopped the truck to give her some rest from the bouncing and pounding and to size up the surroundings—perhaps wondering what to do.

When he returned to the truck, the starter would not turn over. Kurina wrote that she had a scary feeling, like things were all wrong. She had hoped the baby would come in California at her mom's; but now they were broken down on some little side road and her labor was starting early.

Accepting that they were going nowhere, Bobby finally got some pillows and had her stretch out on the front seat. By this time, he was in a panic himself and could barely take care of the other two children. He slapped together some baloney and bread for them and turned his attention back to Kurina. Bobby was adamant that she not have the baby early, and went on and on about relaxing and telling her how to breathe; and it seemed to actually work, because the pains began to slow down and let up a little.

In only a short time, a man in a pickup truck saw them sitting there—which one really couldn't miss, this strangely renovated army truck contraption sitting on the side of the road. The man stopped, and it didn't take him long to size up the situation. Without hesitation he told them he would drive them to his house a short distance away, explaining that his wife was a nurse. He assured Kurina that whatever happened, her family could spend the night with them.

Bobby, almost babbling to this stranger, started telling him how he had delivered hundreds of babies, including the two that were with them now. He told the man that it was too early for this baby; if Kurina could rest for the night, the early contractions would stop. So with the understanding that the man would drive Bobby to a truck salvage yard in Albuquerque tomorrow, Bobby staked the two horses, gave them water and oats and left Sebastian, their wonderful dog, to guard their abandoned camp.

The family squeezed into the man's pickup and he drove them to his house for the night.

The man's wife also had compassion for Kurina and made the family comfortable in a guest room; Bobby telling her that he had everything under control and they would be leaving tomorrow.

"By the time tomorrow had come, our baby, Grace, had been born, but she didn't get to continue breathing the gift of life." Kurina said she didn't understand

the why of the situation happening like it did, but she tried to be accepting. It was Bobby who was crazy with grief. Bobby worried her because he was more disconnected and despairing than she had ever seen him. He convinced the man's wife to put the lifeless baby in her freezer.

With that plain-spoken statement, the letter ended. I guess Kurina wanted me to know what had happened with that pregnancy because I had been worried about her. What I also want to know, but have not yet been told, is what happened to the poor baby's body. In my nightmares I see the little thing wrapped tightly—in what? a blanket maybe?—wedged under the vegetables and meat in a stranger's freezer.

I doze off, and when I open my eyes the morning has dawned. Billy pulls over for gas and lets Ronnie drive. We're only an hour outside Amarillo, and we are all ready for coffee and breakfast. Ben and Stevie want to go faster. As the car speeds up, Mother wakes up and exclaims loudly, "Ronnie, what's the rush?" We are all awake now and laugh heartily, as that is Mother's standard question when she thinks the driver is going too fast.

The remainder of the trip goes pleasantly enough, and little Nichole and Austin have entertained themselves and been well behaved. After Amarillo, the terrain has become barren and desert-like, and the mountains soar increasingly skyward as we approach the former Unexpected Guests' home in the Sangre de Cristo Mountains.

At about four o'clock local time Billy, who is watching the map and occasional road signs, informs us with a delighted ring to his voice that we are almost to Ledoux. To put a damper on our wild whoops and cheers, he drawls, in a tour-guide cadence: "Please continue to be patient, folks. When we park this car in Ledoux, we will still have a two-hour ride, in the old Army truck, up the side of the mountain, before reaching our destination—the Hale family cabin.

While he is still talking, Billy motions for Ronnie to turn left onto a more or less unpaved road, and within a hundred yards we are pulling into the dusty little town.

Ronnie stops the car dead still—for we are spellbound.

Ledoux is as small as any west Texas town I have ever seen; actually, smaller. On the left side of the gravelly road is a little post office, no bigger than my living room. Built onto the back of the post office is a tiny sheriff's office—declared so by a puny, faded sign above the door, barely readable from here. On the right side, across from the post office, is a white house with a front porch and a couple of low-spreading trees in the yard. Next door to it, probably a hundred feet away, stands a one room "hole-in-the-wall" Mexican restaurant, a Corona sign nailed to the side and one wooden, straight chair out front.

Not one of us says a word.

"Welcome to Ledoux, folks," Bill finally manages, in a subdued mumble.

Ronnie inches the car forward, and by the time we reach the flagpole we spot the Army truck. It is parked behind the post office. When that truck had pulled away from the barn in Fort Worth, I thought I never wanted to see it again. That was then. Now, after driving sixteen hours and winding up in this Godforsaken town, the infamous truck looks like a welcome wagon from heaven.

Bobby must have heard our tires on the gravel, for as we pull into the empty area where the truck is parked—obviously what serves as the town's parking lot, he is running up behind us from somewhere, probably the restaurant.

Bill jumps out of the Suburban and yells, "We are here, man! We've come to the big city!"

After their long separation, the twins embrace and laugh and jump around with joy. If it wasn't for the sun shining, this scene would be for all the world like the long ago night of Christmas Eve, when the unexpected guests showed up in our backyard. I watch them for a moment, feeling happy that we are here, then hurriedly join the children who are piling out of the car.

Immediately we are surrounded by the expanding Bobby Hales—five children now. I calculate that Naomi is eleven and James nine-and-a-half. After about ten minutes of frolicking and craziness, Bobby hollers for the kids to come around and tells us, "We need to go up the mountain now before it gets dark." Then, behaving like a prince, he glides over to my mother and croons, "Mrs. Dorris, you have your own special chair in my humble vehicle. Let me show you to your seat." He takes Mother by the arm and ushers her up the same horse ramp that I remember, and seats her in a special rocking chair. It is padded with pillows: seat, back, and both arms. He has done a great job to cushion a lady in her 80s because it looks more like a nest than a chair. He has also secured it with ropes for the occasion. He says jokingly, "Now your ride up the mountain will be as smooth as a Cadillac." Then he hollered, "Load up!" The remaining sixteen of us scramble up the ramp and over the side into the bed and cab of the truck. Allison with little Nicole and Billy, and I with Austin climb into the cab. (Thankfully that horrible wad of hair and beads from nine years ago is gone from the mirror.) At last, all of us except Bobby are either seated or hanging onto pillars and posts and planks, and every one of us is raring to go... But in the next few seconds we learn that actually we are Bobby's captives. He is standing outside the truck between the cab and bed, so he commands both sections and, raring to go or not, crowded, uncomfortable, hungry, little ones whimpering, it makes no difference, we have to endure not just a welcome prayer of thanksgiving but an endless, tiresome tirade from Bobby, what he calls a prayer. But before it is over, I think is an insult, not only to us but to God himself. I'm sorry, but this is awful!

Bobby is finally revving up that ancient engine—oh what a welcome sound it is—and as we start to pull away, we hear someone loudly yelling, "Preacher Bob! Preacher Bob, wait a minute." Running across the road, a tall, slim Indian lad is waving and calling to us. "Preacher, don't forget to bring your visiting folks to Taos with you to the trade fair. You did hear that it is being held early this year?"

"We heard all about it, Miguel," Bobby answers. "We will bring my brother and his family," he says, looking at Billy, who is nodding his head. "We've got lots to sell, including a litter of nine healthy Pyrenees. If you spread the word, I won't mind."

"I will," he says, smiling and craning his neck to see those of us in the cab and those in the back of the truck. It is probably a rare occasion for him to see this much activity in Ledoux. We are still hanging on and still, same as thirty minutes ago, raring to get out of town, but we return his friendly grins and nods. The young man seems amply rewarded with our attention and, spinning around, he quickly covers the few steps to the only house in town.

I immediately have many questions to ask about the fair, but Bill interrupts and questions Bobby incredulously, "Did that young man call you Preacher Bob?"

"He sure did. That's what I'm known as in these parts."

"Can we go to the fair, Bobby?" asks Allison. "The children would love it."

"More than likely," says Bobby. "This year, for the first time, they've changed the fair's date. It's usually in October, not March. We've got lots of stuff to sell, but in the long run it depends on God's will and the weather. You know, the snow has just cleared enough for us to come down here and get you."

"It *is* cold." I look over my shoulder and see Ronnie and the boys struggling to keep their footing while rolling down the side tarps against the wind. "Will we encounter any ice?" I ask, imagining us sliding off the road with children in the open truck.

"A little ice is the least of our worries," Bobby says. Within the next minute the truck lurches and pitches violently as we take the first bend. Ahead of us is not a "rocky road," as described by Bobby, but a boulder-strewn ravine. "You'll see," he warns as he grows quiet and tightens his hands on the steering wheel into a vein-popping grasp.

Alarmed at this sight, I yell to the children in back, "Hang on!" as the first jolt nearly smashes my face against the window.

We said very little on that bone-rattling climb. Before a sentence could be finished, the words would be forced out of the chest in unintelligible bursts as the truck crashed over yet another bolder or rut.

First Night at the Homestead

At last the way grows smoother and Bobby announces with a "Whew!" of relief, "We're almost there." He relaxes his white-knuckled grip on the wheel and starts to sing his favorite song, "The Lighthouse," an old hymn I taught Bobby and Kurina when they were the Morning Stars in Fort Worth. Soon we are all singing joyously, "Jesus is the lighthouse, and saves us from our sins," as we marvel inwardly at the beauty of the landscape we are passing through. We are in awe at the awakening wildflowers and the tall trees with pinkish sunlight filtering through the branches—light from heaven surely.

"This is my home, Bill," Bobby says soberly as we pull into a clearing. Off to the right, standing in a small field of wildflowers, I spot three crosses—large, life-size crosses. I quietly punch Bill and nod my head toward the crosses. He spots them and stares at them for a minute but doesn't say a word. In fact, on the whole trip he never mentioned them at all—at least not to me.

The evening sun has beaten us here. It casts a crimson flush across the compound, giving the cabin and its outbuildings a fairy-tale glow. "The famous Sangre de Cristo sunsets," Bobby says, seeing our captivated faces, "The Blood of Christ."

Before the engine stops, Kurina runs out of the cabin and, like a good mother, is seeing to her children in the truck before turning to us. I hug her and say the standard womanly thing: "Kurina, I can't believe you've had three more children since we last saw you. You look great." *Actually she has had four more births, but I deliberately don't mention little Grace, who was born and died nine years ago on the road to California.*

Kurina laughs her loud happy laugh and returns the compliment. "You do too, Patsy. And you're a grandmother!"

"What about that Allison, making us grandparents at our tender age?"

We stand together, looking proudly at her children and my grandchildren running around like young puppies. This gathering feels like the family reunion I had hoped it would be.

Bobby is helping Mother out of her chair, and as they inch down the ramp she smiles at me. "The whole setting here is marvelous!" she declares in her good strong voice. We all agree, and she continues, "The sunset will be spectacular. Look how red everything already is." Bobby tells again how the crimson color inspired the Spanish explorers to give these mountains their name.

"Follow me a little way through those trees, and I will show you my favorite view," Kurina says. We eagerly follow her, and Mother, holding Bobby's arm, is striding straight and strong. When we get through the trees, the view is like a Remington painting.

"Tomorrow you need to come here again and watch the sunset," Kurina says. "It is always different. They say it changes as the sun moves. Bobby and I watched the sunset on this very spot the first night we got here. It was so beautiful I cried. I think Bobby did too."

"That's true," Bobby says. "They were tears of joy for I had never felt so right before. Do you know that feeling, Bill? Like everything is just as it should be?"

"Yes," Billy says. "I've had that feeling more than once, and it's awesome every time."

I can smell the scent of wood smoke rising from the valley and mingling with the fragrant sage growing prolifically all around us. I turn to Bill and, breathing deeply, say, "Wow, just smell this air."

His dry remark is, "You know I can barely smell anything, Patsy, good or bad." It is true; he can't smell very well, and now in particular it's a shame.

"I miss Will," Allison says. "Wouldn't he love this whole experience? At the sight of that *town* and the ride up this mountain, he would have had us all in stitches."

"Changing the subject, folks," Bobby says, "but if you don't get unloaded, it's going to be pitch dark." He turns toward the clearing and walks as briskly as Mother will permit him.

We fall in line and walk pretty fast. "I bet it gets really dark up here with no outside lights," Ronnie says.

"Unless it's a full moon, it sure does," Bobby agrees.

Back at the truck we look at the daunting pile of suitcases and boxes, and Bill says, "Can't we just get out what we need for the night?" I frankly don't feel like unloading all this now. All I need is my toothbrush."

I agree with him completely and so does Ronnie. Allison, on the other hand, would be unloading all night then go to a nearby supermarket—if such a thing existed—for more. I looked at her and said, "Allison, I'm taking my makeup bag and gown, that's all."

She looked at me like I was crazy. "Why do you need makeup here? I think your gown is plenty." She continued, "But I am taking the diaper bag, my suitcase, and the children's suitcases, all of our pillows, and my house shoes; also the grocery bag with the cereal and applesauce… And who knows, I just might need my sunglasses and hat."

"Miss Prissy—you little toot!" I slap her behind, and grabbing Mother's overnight bag, I climb out of the truck and head for the cabin.

On entering the dimly lit cabin, I immediately notice things familiar to me—several of Virginia's primitive antiques: the oversized hand-hammered copper pot hanging on the wall—Bobby had asked her for it before he left Fort Worth; her blue Persian rug, an interesting contrast to the rough-hewn boards of the cabin floor; a primitive hutch and round stool that she told me she had bought on one of her antiquing forays with friends around Austin; her brilliant green shawl draped over a small straight armchair; and her collection of primitive hand-carved wooden bowls, stacked on the rough-hewn dining table. Somewhere in my first impressions of this rustic cabin I registered how interesting it was that years ago, Virginia, owner of rooms-full of fine, inherited antiques, had become a collector of primitive crafts, and how well they fit in her son's mountain home.

The dining table takes up most of the back wall and has benches on each side. At one end of the table is a rocking chair, and beside it sits a small potbelly stove. I remember his obsession with our stove in Fort Worth and surmise that the rocker beside the stove is Bobby's seat. At the other end of the table is a straight, straw-bottomed chair—Kurina's? Probably. This room is also the kitchen. The sink and kitchen cabinets are against the left front wall, behind the door when the door is open. An impressive wood-burning cook stove, a gift from Virginia, stands against the left wall. I am intrigued by this "modern" stove and watch Kurina for a minute—her face florid from the heat, as she stacks her thick, homemade tortillas on the cooler side of the stove, for warming, and stirs a huge pot of deer meat stew on the other, hotter side. Over all the other aromas, I think I detect something baking. Kurina confirms that she is baking four loaves of sweet bread. "You'll like it, Patsy," she says. "It's like your pound cake."

"Oh, speaking of cake, Bobby wanted me to bring his mother's recipe for the family's Christmas fruitcake. Do you remember that cake, Kurina? We served it on your first Christmas Eve in Fort Worth. I brought the recipe, along with Virginia's kippling cookies recipe. Don't let me forget to give them to you when we unpack tomorrow."

Bill and Bobby come stomping through the door and close it against the cold. Bill's first comment is about the three kerosene lanterns that sit around the room for light—the same lanterns Roland had spotted in the truck years ago. "This place is great, brother. You've got all the conveniences, even our old hunting lanterns."

Bobby shows Bill and me our bed, which is separated from the common room only by a sheet hanging from the low ceiling. Mother's bed, just a comfortable cot, is separated from our bed also by a hanging sheet, not bad innovations considering how small the place is. The only other room is tiny, and it has bunk beds against two walls for their children and a bed in the corner for Bobby and Kurina. That is pretty much it for what we ironically come to call "the big cabin."

It's dark by now, but I step outside to check on the children's sleeping arrangements. A short distance from the big cabin is a little cabin, used primarily for storage and clothes. Kurina has cleared some space in this cabin for Ronnie and Allison and their two children. In here, too, is a little potbelly stove, and she already has a fire burning in it. My assessment is that they will be warm and pretty comfortable.

Between the two cabins Ben and Stevie have set up a tent brought from Fort Worth. This sleeping-outside adventure was highly anticipated by the boys before we left home, and they have brought their heaviest sleeping bags.

The trip from Fort Worth has been a long night and day for us, especially Mother and the children, and after the hearty but hectic dinner and kitchen cleanup, I am hoping we can all go right to bed. But that does not happen. Even as Allison and I wash the dishes, Bobby is drawling, "This evening I would like for my brother and his family to join with us in our family hour." Allison punches me hard with her elbow, and I shrug at her helplessly. "This time is sacred and traditional for us, and I hope we'll keep it up while y'all are here."

Billy strongly agrees that it will be our planned activity every evening.

Bobby takes his seat in the rocker and, to our surprise, explains how all of us will sit on the floor around his chair while he teaches. Then he will play the guitar, and we can join him in singing hymns. "Kurina," he says softly, "bring your chair into the circle for Mrs. Dorris."

"Yes, Master" is her soft-spoken reply. *This is the second time I have heard her call him Master.*

Hey! Didn't we agree on an hour, I want to say? It has been two hours now, and the young ones are asleep, in our arms and on the floor. Mother is dozing in her chair, and has been for a long time. Allison has pinched my arm black and blue. We have heard Bobby "teach" some strange stuff tonight—mainly his interpretation of the Scriptures. He is playing the guitar now and, thankfully, singing; we all join in and it wakes us up a little. At least he can't *interpret* the hymns, so far anyway, so we aren't subjected to his interpretive nonsense at the moment. But how long, I wonder, can this go on? How does his family put up with it? But Kurina sits mesmerized through the long, misguided homily and is now singing heartily. I guess you learn to put up with a lot if you're captive at the end of an unimproved road like we had just traversed a few hours ago. Allison abruptly gets up and gathers Nichole off the floor. "I've got to go to the bathroom and can't wait another minute," she quietly and firmly announces, and leaves the cabin—pronto.

Bobby, in his own "other world" barely notices as we all squirm. I thought it would never happen but finally, when Mother nearly falls out of her chair, Billy catches her and says, "We're losing my family,

Bobby. It's been a real long day."

Living in the Picturesque Past

I open my eyes and step around the hanging sheet. It appears that everyone is already up and out. Wandering over to the kitchen sink, about ten steps away from my bed, I splash my face with cold water, pull on yesterday's clothes, and find a partial pot of coffee on the stove. Five minutes after my feet hit the floor, I step outside with a blue-speckled porcelain cup of hot coffee.

Kurina, finished with milking her three cows, is struggling across the yard balancing a deep, eight-quart milk pail nearly filled with milk. Allison and the younger children are following her, when they spot me watching them. Instantly I am barraged with excited explanations of seeing the cows milked—each child trying to yell the loudest and each one adding his or her own descriptions. "It must have been wonderful!" I shout happily, scooping Nichole into my arms and smelling the flowers Allison has pinned in her silky white hair. "I think you kids are having fun. No?"

Again, more shrieking and laughing. "We saw baby lambs too!" Austin tells me.

"Mother, I thought you would never get up," Allison says. "This place is like one of those living museums. You won't believe what all Uncle Bobby and Kurina have devised up here. You said something about science projects? Wait till you see all these things!"

I look, bug-eyed, straight into Allison's face, shaking my head at her and laughing. "Ears, I haven't seen you this excited in I don't know when."

Kurina puts down her pail to open the cabin door and lets out with a loud laugh at us. "Look at where your boys are." She nods her head at the improvised hot tub. Ben and Stevie are sitting with all their clothes on quiet as mice, wanting to surprise us, in a round, galvanized tub with a fire burning underneath.

I read about the "hot tub" in a letter from Bobby, so I was not surprised. "Are we cooking them for supper?" I ask. They slap the water trying to splash me. I pretend to run away, then I remember my mother. "Where is Grandmother?" I call out to no one and to everyone.

Allison approaches me and says discreetly, "She's at the outhouse."

"Good, because I'm on my way there too." I notice as I leave the yard that the men are unloading the boxes of food we brought, taking them from the truck into the little cabin. I wave at them as I head down the hill to get Mother.

The outhouse sits a little downhill from the cabins in a shady spot with a panoramic view of the valley. Fragrant breezes are always blowing up from the valley floor; pretty chilly breezes too in the wintertime, I imagine. If you're not in a hurry, you can take up residence here for a while. That's where I found Mother. "Mother, you didn't even close the door," I tease her.

"If I close the door, I can't see the view," she replies, as unconcerned as a child.

Walking uphill, back to the clearing, Mother tells me she likes this place except for the "uphills." "It's like living in the past, like when I was a girl. They do all the things, and then some, that we used to do eighty years ago on the farm."

"Mother, can we make a small detour? And it's not uphill. I want to check out those three big crosses we passed by last evening."

"Well, I do too," she replies, "since I didn't even see any crosses."

"They're right over here." I turn her slightly to the left, toward the road. I am holding Mother's arm, and on the uneven ground we are watching our steps pretty closely, when we notice flowers at our feet. Stopping to look around, I exclaim, "Look, Mother, there they are." We spot, more or less, the top parts of three crosses. Within fifty feet we are there, standing in awe of the heavy, bigger-than-life-size wooden crosses.

"Look at this, Patsy." Mother rubs her hand over the wood, inspecting it closely as I steady her. "These are handmade—and they're huge. I bet they're eight feet tall. Do you know how much time it would take a man to hand-hew these? The cuts are so even, they remind me of fish scales."

"Well, Mother," I remind her, "Bobby fancies himself a Christian, above all other Christians, so I imagine these crosses were a labor of love. I think they must be a sort of shrine."

"I guess they are, Patsy. I just didn't know he was such a perfectionist at something like this—just like Billy."

"He hasn't always been. I guess the obsession has grabbed him now."

"Can you see those little crosses, Mother?" It looks like there are three more little stick crosses scattered around."

"Yes, I can." I hold her as she bends closer. "I think these must be little burial markers—kinda looks like it. But no writing that I can make out. What do you think?"

"Most likely they are…markers for their animals, probably." I wonder, but don't mention to Mother, if one of these marks the spot for little Grace. I hope so.

When we get to the cabin, Mother and I inspect the elaborate hot tub arrangement. A small fire is still burning beneath it to keep the water warm. We can see that Bobby built a wooden platform to support the weight of the tub with water and people inside. He cut a hole in the platform so the fire underneath couldn't burn the wood but is focused, by a metal cone contrivance, onto the tub's bottom. All of this is sitting unmovable and sturdy on several heavy legs to a height of at least thirty inches. It is very well built and quite nice, except I probably won't be using it. I can't abide the idea of everyone wearing all their clothes into the tub to bathe—and that is Bobby's rule: "We bathe fully dressed." As it turns out, the kids think it is great fun having their clothes-bubbles floating up around them.

In the clearing, on a tall pole, there hangs a bell. Its ring is loud and clear. At mealtime the rope is pulled two times to signal that food will be on the table shortly. These bells have long been used in remote places everywhere. Mother remembers this same bell in her family's yard eight decades ago. In an emergency, the rope is pulled many times, urgently calling for help from anyone within earshot.

At lunchtime I notice that Billy and Bobby are long in coming after I try my hand at pulling the rope. By the time they arrive, we are almost finished eating our lunch: sandwiches of homemade bread and cheese, leftover boiled eggs, and the fresh milk from yesterday that has cooled overnight in the spring. The men sit quietly at the table and don't really get into sharing our stories about the morning. When they finish eating, they abandon the compound, as far as we can tell, for they are nowhere to be seen or heard.

I notice that after lunch, Ronnie does not go out again with Bobby and Billy but stays behind with the women and children. After a few pensive minutes of watching us clean up, he says softly, "I think I'll take a nap. I got up real early this morning."

"I'm with you Ronnie," Mother says. She tries to push her hanging sheet aside but winds up pulling it down from the ceiling. That doesn't faze her in the least. She pulls the sheet off her head, piles it on the mattress and lies down, pulling it over her. Mother is pretty funny, and we have to smile at one another.

But I don't like the sound of Ronnie's voice, and I watch out the kitchen window as he and Allison and the two toddlers walk toward the little cabin. Before I can finish the dishes, Allison is walking back across the yard alone. She spots me in the window and gives me our "we need to talk" signal. She and I are the only ones in the house except for Mother, and Mother is breathing loudly—she doesn't snore, she says, she just breathes loud.

Allison is pretty wound up: "Mother, Daddy and Bobby are fighting! Ronnie says it's so bad he doesn't want to be around them. You know Ronnie doesn't know about their fighting, and he is worried. He said they nearly came to blows. He thinks that if he stayed with them, he'd have to break up a fight."

"Oh God, where are Ben and Stevie?" I ask, alarmed. I'm thinking that Billy may not have the same resolve that he had when Bobby was a Morning Star. If Ronnie is this concerned, it must be bad. "I know how violent and crazy Billy and Bobby can be. I don't want those boys to hear and see grown men act like that—especially Stevie. His parents would be horrified. We've got to find them now. Let's go!"

"Don't wake the kids!" Allison warns as I leave the cabin at a run. Allison doesn't follow, but as a result of her caution I don't start calling at the top of my voice—yet. I'm going to wait until I reach the corral.

But when I come tearing up to the corral, the boys are alone, talking their teenage banter and enjoying the horses. Ben notices that I am breathless and look half wild. "Mother, what's wrong!"

"Oh you guys scared me to death," I gasp. "I thought I had lost you."

Stevie looks at Ben and makes a goofy face as if to ask, 'Has your mother lost her mind?'

"Stop it Stevie," I tease him. "There are lots of ways you guys can get hurt up here."

Ben, screwing his face into an overblown question and lifting his shoulders in an exaggerated shrug, asks, "How?"

Before Ben's shoulders can fall into place, a powerful rifle shot explodes—at close range.

In half a minute, all hell breaks loose. Allison runs out of the big cabin slamming the door and yelling, "Mother!"

Ronnie flies out of the little cabin shouting, "Doc!" The toddlers start screaming bloody murder, and Kurina runs into the clearing from somewhere with her terrified children. They all see us and run toward the corral and the gunshot.

The two boys are actually funny. They have the most alarmed looks on their faces and are turning in every direction, flapping their arms, without the slightest idea of what the commotion is all about, scared because everybody else is scared.

The whole crew of terrified and crying family members reaches the corral just as another shot rings out. The gunshot sounds like it is very close by, and Ronnie, his face as white as chalk, shouts louder than before, "Doc!" and heads through the trees, straight toward the blast.

Allison, terrified for both Ronnie and her dad, starts screaming for them, and every one of us run toward the gun sounds. Kurina runs too, without even knowing why, but she is screaming for Bobby.

When we burst through the trees to the nearby meadow, Bill is holding the gun, and both men are just breaking into a run toward us screaming and yelling maniacs.

In an instant we all hush the racket and slow our pace to a stop—us looking at the men and them, with eyes like saucers, looking at us. "What in tarnation was all that about?" Bill directs the question at me.

"I don't even know," I pant, "but next time, tell us when you plan to target practice."

Ronnie glances at me a little sheepishly as we both spot the target the twins have set up, then says to Billy, "Doc, I bet these boys would like to target practice. That looks like a powerful gun."

"It's the rifle I use for killing wolves and bears," Bobby jokes with them. "I sure enough do; and deer too. This thing is awfully powerful, too much for you sissies. It might throw your shoulders out."

"Don't let them get hurt," I caution Billy.

"They couldn't shoot more than a couple of rounds with this," he says, showing me the rifle, "or they would be hurting. And Bobby wouldn't want them to use this anyway." He hands the gun to Ronnie and calls to Bobby, who is having the boys set up targets. "I'm going to get the twenty-gauge," he says and starts walking with me toward the clearing.

Kurina, who I think left in disgust, is way ahead of us, and we lag behind Allison and the children. "I'm going to ask you again," Billy says, "what was all that commotion about?"

"Billy, I'll try to explain the best I can: Ronnie told Allison that you and Bobby were fighting. The poor boy didn't know how you two go at it, and he was scared to death. He thought you were going to come to blows. Well, that scared me—not only for you, but I didn't want Ben and Stevie to see and hear such stuff. Then I ran calling for them. They saw me looking, I don't know, wild and frantic, and just then the gun goes off... You know the rest."

"Well," Billy explains, "when we went out after lunch, we decided to call a truce. We are okay for the time being. But let this be a lesson to you, Patsy...a lesson in mass hysteria and how easily it can take over."

That night we had the "family hour," but it was much more acceptable this time, shorter and less controversial. I thought Bobby was genuinely trying to get along with us.

Later in bed, I whisper to Billy, "The boys told me this day has been their best day ever. They loved everything about it: the hot tub and milking, the horseback riding; but the most fun, Ben said, was the target practice." Bill doesn't answer, so I continue, "It's been a great day for all of us—except for the 'mass hysteria' episode."

"Yeah, that was something," he whispers back. "And I might as well confess: I'm afraid it's not over. Bobby seemed okay tonight, but I know my brother. He believes a lot of wrong things, and he wants to convince me. He'll come at me again tomorrow. Truthfully, in my opinion, he's got his own religion. What's really bad is not that he's teaching it to his family, I can't help that, but he's trying to teach his heresy up and down this mountain. He claims to have a following. I pray to God he doesn't, but you know as well as I do how people follow Bobby. That's the way cults get started."

"It sure is," I agree glumly. "And think how horribly they usually end." We stare at the ceiling with our own thoughts. I remember how Roland warned me before we came up here: "He will be deep into his own fantasies by now. Bobby will never accept a concept not his own, and there's no telling how delusional he will be. Just pray and be cautious." I can't tell Billy about Roland's warning. Ironically my husband is so defensive of his brother and what other people say about him that he just might incline toward Bobby in a twisted effort to protect him from criticism. I've seen this strange behavior in Billy before and try to save him from that destructive urge by not repeating anything negative, especially what someone else might have said, about Bobby—even if Billy himself brings it up.

To lighten up a little, I whisper to Billy, "How do you like sleeping on my favorite feather mattress again? I don't know how it found its way up here."

"I didn't notice it, frankly. Who cares?"

"Oh I don't care; it's just interesting. Something else is interesting, and it was a huge relief to me: Mother didn't mention the quilts. Hopefully she no longer recognizes them because she is sleeping under one right now."

I turn over and settle into my pillow—but sleep doesn't come. "That's the way cults get started," Billy had said of Bobby's wrongheaded proselytizing.

Billy doesn't know this, but before Bobby's family left Fort Worth, I had overheard Bobby describing his future plans to Kurina: "When we get out there, when we set up our ranch, I'll have influence again. We'll have our own following." Those words have been chilling to me because he was already twisting the Scriptures into unrecognizable meanings known only to him; but I chose not to tell anyone. I figured his failure to win Billy over was the basis for his talk to Kurina anyway. Why admit my eavesdropping? Let them have their dreams.

Now, in light of the reality that people here are calling Bobby "Preacher" and with the possibility that, according to him, he does have his own "following," there are grim memories that keep me awake:

Billy graduated in the spring of 1969 and had secured a position in Ohio. We were leaving Texas at the end of August. A small group of us friends decided to say a long goodbye, spending the weekend in our favorite celebration town, Galveston. Our group includes our longtime school and college friends Jana and Wendell; blond-haired, blue-eyed Doug, who had lived and went to school with us in Fort Worth; and Carol, his wife from New Orleans. Doug met and married Carol after college when he moved to New Orleans. Also with us are Bobby and his girlfriend, Tammy, who met at a ski resort in Colorado where Bobby worked as a ski instructor.

We are entering Guido's Restaurant on Galveston beach when I notice that Bobby, a few steps behind us, stops cold in front of the newspaper stand outside the door. He is mesmerized, obviously, by the headlines. No one is watching him but me. I see Bobby purchase a paper. Gripping it to his chest, he steps in behind us and draws Billy aside. "I've got to make a call." He looks shaken and serious.

Billy pulls the newspaper down so he can see the front page. I look over his shoulder and see that the whole page is devoted to a story about some brutal murders that have just taken place in California. "What has this got to do with you?" Billy asks, studying Bobby's stunned face.

"Nothing," Bobby answers. He is staring at the page. "I'll join you later."

Billy intensifies his question. "Bobby, do you know these people?"

Bobby is walking away, "I don't know. I don't think so," he says over his shoulder.

As the hostess seats our party, Doug, who had noticed the whispering about the newspaper, catches up with us, carrying his own copy. He spreads it on the table and proceeds to read. The story describes five people, one of them the movie star Sharon Tate, Roman Polanski's pregnant wife, being cruelly murdered in a wooded neighborhood in the suburbs of Los Angeles. Pictures taken inside and outside the house look bloody and horrible, like a massacre. The house belongs to Terry Melcher, son of Doris Day. Tammy registers a surprised and painful frown as Doug reads Melcher's name. I think I am the only one who notices her, and neither of us says anything.

"Horrible!" Doug says, shaking his head. "But I'm wondering about Bobby. Aren't you?" he asks, looking at Billy.

"Well, yeah, but I think I understand what's going on."

"You do? Then tell us," Wendell says.

"Well, y'all know he spent some time out there and had friends. He most likely wants to talk to one of them to find out more about this killing."

I add, "He probably wants to find out if he knows any of the victims." We all look at Billy, who is staring into space, lost in thought.

"You're mighty pensive, Billy," Wendell observes.

"He could be remembering K.K," Billy says. We watch him—waiting to hear more. "She was pregnant with Bobby's baby when she died. Can you imagine the room after that gun blast? It must have looked like these pictures. And Bobby was right there, in the room. This death of a young pregnant woman—and these bloody pictures—just think about it. Don't you reckon it brings back awful memories? I think I can almost feel what he's feeling."

We ordered earlier, and our food arrives—but still no Bobby. Tammy goes to look for him and finds him still on the phone. He wants us to go ahead and eat; he doesn't care about food, she says.

I ask Tammy if she knows what is going on. She says she and Bobby knew a guy who knew Terry Melcher well. She thinks the man had some kind of business plan with Terry. She says Bobby met him—his name was Charlie—in San Francisco. She thinks Bobby has probably called Charlie.

(We had no idea who this Charlie was, and that he would be far too busy and distracted at this time to be talking by phone to a mere acquaintance like Bobby.)

When at last Bobby finds our table, he seems considerably settled down. He orders "something quick—fried shrimp and a Coors." Always enjoying the spotlight, he wants to pursue the murder topic. He doesn't have much to add but pretty much repeats what Tammy told us. (Bobby, being exceptionally good-looking and charming, met people easily and had been to parties with a lot of celebrities in Hollywood during his early days in California—when he was still "Mr. Neiman Marcus" and vaguely interested in acting.) He wanted to be sure these murders didn't involve anyone he knew or had met. And, no, Terry was not even at the house, and no he didn't get to talk to Charlie.

We were to have this day brought back into sharp focus when months later, at our new home in Ohio, we received a phone call from law enforcement. "What do you know about Charles Manson?" "Why did you call him?" "Do you know he's been arrested for the Tate/LaBianca murders?" Unknown to us, either Tammy or Bobby had placed a call to the Spann Ranch, Charles Manson's hangout, from our telephone in Texas. Once again, Bobby's deeds were following us.

We could easily vouch for Bobby's whereabouts at the time of the murders—he and his girlfriend were with us in Texas. We did find out though, that Bobby had known Manson from his time in Haight-Ashbury and that he and Tammy had attended an elegant candlelight dinner with Manson and his other friend from Texas, "Tex" Watson. They also had visited Manson and "the Family" at the Spann Ranch.

I lie awake now thinking about that time and what it must have been like—the acquaintance and interaction of those two men—both zealots in the making, each trying to win the other to his own way of thinking, no doubt. Thank goodness Bobby had the stubbornness not to be swept up in that Manson family mess.

But now Bobby has apparently made up his own strange doctrine that, by using Jesus' name, he can dignify by calling it Christianity—by saying that God has revealed *the truth* to him. How troubling that he is teaching this to his family and, apparently, getting converts outside.

I listen quietly to Billy and hear that he is still breathing the breath of the wakeful—soft with an occasional sigh. I know he is lost in his own dark thoughts, and I keep my silence.

Planning for the Fair

In the morning, same as yesterday, everyone is outside when I get up. It's not that I didn't wake up but, not caring for breakfast, I just didn't get up. It was nice knowing that Kurina and Allison would take care of everything, and for once in my adult life, I could lie in bed and listen to the morning stir.

Now, sipping my coffee at the door, I watch Mother walking up from the chicken yard with a basket of fresh eggs on her arm. She hands them off to me, and I set them by the sink before going out to join the group. Kurina and eleven-year-old Naomi want all of us to watch them get ready for the Old Taos Fair. The plan is for both families to attend tomorrow, with the possible exception of Ronnie, who grudgingly offers to stay here with Mother and the two younger children if necessary. Right now Mother says she wouldn't miss it for anything, though going involves another drama with the infamous rocky road.

I scan the compound but fail to see Billy and Bobby. "Where's your dad?" I ask Allison.

"They went toward the corral. I heard Bobby tell Dad there are a thousand more acres of this ranch he hasn't seen."

"Yikes! They're fixing to ride out then. I need to speak to your daddy." I hand her my cup and run toward the corral. "Kurina, wait a minute for me," I call. "I'll be right back."

"You're not going with the men?" I holler at Ronnie as I run past him.

"Not invited," he calls after me.

I throw my hands in the air as a shrug, and keep going. "Me either," I yell back.

I spot Billy and Bobby at the corral looking around inside the sturdy lean-to which is Bobby's equivalent of a tack room.

"Good morning, men-folks," I say sweetly as I approach. "Billy, I need my good morning kiss before you ride off." I put my arms around him.

"Gal, you sleep too late," Billy teases me and continues with what he is doing. Turns out he is inventorying and organizing the medicines and first-aid supplies that he brought to Bobby, not only for his animals but for his family too. I notice quite a bit of polycillin, a reliable antibiotic for people living so far from medical help. Scalpels and simple surgery and sewing tools are also included. I'm sure Bobby could use them with skill in an emergency. After all, he has delivered hundreds of babies; and in Fort Worth, after he transformed into the *Marlboro Man*, he watched Billy in surgery several times. "That's a lot of stuff," I comment.

"I've got a lot of kids and a lot of animals," Bobby answers. "Y'all haven't even seen my flock of sheep yet."

"No. I thought you'd have cows."

"Naturally I wanted cows. And started out with cows in spite of being warned against it. The fact is it's hard on cows up here, and real expensive to raise and feed them. I just went ahead and switched off to sheep."

"Where are they—these sheep?"

"They're foraging around—no telling where. You know we got two thousand acres. I got to get out and check on them."

"You say they can be anywhere; how do you find them? I mean on two thousand acres and it all rugged mountains?"

"We'll just ride out and I'll call them from time to time. My sheep know my voice and they will eventually hear me. And when they hear me, they will come to me." He says this while staring intently into my eyes. I figure he is trying to load biblical meaning into those words, but I'll not acknowledge the connection.

"And I guess you've learned approximately where they might be foraging—where the grass is greener so to speak, at certain times of the year, right? And that would make them easier to find?"

"That's part of being a good shepherd—knowing the habits and inclinations of your sheep; and they'll never be too far from water. So you're right; and I figure now they're on the outer edge of the property, down the mountain a way. Billy and I are going out to have a look."

"Okay, enjoy yourselves, but remember that Billy gets uncomfortable on horseback pretty quickly." I say this hoping he wouldn't stay out all day. They don't need enough time to start fighting.

I step over to Billy and give him a tight hug so I can whisper, "What do you think? Will your truce last?"

"Probably not. But I'll ride back in if I have to. And yes," he says in answer to my questioning frown, "I'll find my way back; I've never been lost before, and it won't happen now."

Please don't lose yourself—or your way this time, I think, recalling Roland's warnings. I look into his beautiful eyes. "I just hate to think of you out there being badgered by him for hours. Do be strong. I'll see you at lunch."

Walking back toward the cabin, I see all of the others, including the children, Allison, Mother, Ben, and Stevie following Kurina and Naomi to the workshop, which is situated downhill a bit, near the cow shed. I join them at the workshop, where, as planned, we are to watch Kurina and Naomi get ready for the fair. Kurina opens a large cabinet above the work shelf and removes two large stacks of woolen blankets. They are brightly colored and have Native American patterns. "We made these blankets," Naomi says proudly. "And guess what? I am the weaver of the family."

"Well, you're growing up to be a very smart girl," I say with admiration. "You wove all these beautiful horse blankets? And you're going to sell them in Taos?"

"Yes, Aunt Patsy, and the ladders too; we'll make lots of money!"

"Ladders too?" I ask with mock surprise. "And I see moccasins. There's so much here." I turn to her mother. "Kurina, I want my family to learn about all these things. Actually, I've been reading a little about the sheep, and I can tell about them—unless you want to."

"Go ahead," she says.

"Well, children," I say, addressing everyone from the young children to my mother, "these sheep are Churro sheep, and you kids played with the little lambs this morning. The Churro were the first domesticated sheep in America—that means sheep that were raised by people on ranches and farms. Spanish missionaries brought these big, tough guys all the way across the ocean from Spain. People, mainly Indians, have lived all around in these parts, growing these sheep and weaving their wool, since way back then. Kurina, tell us about the wool and weaving."

"We cut the wool off the sheep first. Then we get it ready for weaving. We just weave the wool like the Indians do. Like Naomi told you, she is our weaver. She is the one who will sell her blankets."

"Do each of you make different things to sell?"

"Yes. And Patsy, you saw the moccasins. Well, Bobby learned to tan. He works with leather for hours—suede too."

"He's like Billy then. Remember the suede jacket Billy made?"

"Yeah. And the moccasins are made by Bobby. He will sell those and the litter of nine puppies that were weaned last week."

I am getting really excited about the fair. "Kids," I say, "I can't wait till tomorrow. This fair is going to be fun."

"I want to buy one of those big Pyrenees puppies," Ronnie joked.

The boys start cheering, and Allison playfully wags her finger no.

"Here are the Kiva ladders that Naomi mentioned." Kurina points at an open doorway leading to another large closet. Most of the work on them I did, and John helped. There's a man who will buy all I can make."

Allison beats me to the next question. "This is great," she says. "Each of you makes something different, and you sell your own things. How many ladders do you have?"

"This time I have a hundred. I've been working on them all year."

"And what are they for?"

"They used to hang Kivas on the side of adobe houses. They could climb up on the flat roofs—guess they still do. Now people mostly like them for decoration."

"What else will you be selling?" I ask.

"Not much else. Most years I have a hundred pounds of cheese to sell, at least. But this year it's too early. The cheese has to get ripe, but it's not ripened yet."

Naomi says, "Sometimes we have wool to sell, but it's still cold and the sheep would get cold if Daddy sheared their wool off now."

"They usually have the fair in the fall," Kurina said, "but we've got a lot to sell anyway."

Hearing all these plans for the trade fair, the mystery of how Bobby's family survives on top of this mountain is clearer to me.

"Oh, I forgot to tell you," Kurina says. "Bobby hopes he will get two jobs building freezers for two families that, we heard, are moving onto the mountain. They are bound to be at the fair. They'll need to meet everybody and see what is available around here."

"Like the freezer he built and sent us a picture of? We haven't seen that freezer yet, and we would like to," I say, looking around to confirm with the others. "It's an interesting design, kids, and they can freeze food without having electricity."

There were questions all around, and Ronnie says flatly, "A freezer without electricity. How does that work?"

"Let me show you." Kurina walks to a grove of trees. Under the thick foliage sits the strange, freezer contraption. We look at the thing so ogled-eyed, you'd think it had just landed from another planet. And this is what we learned: They had built a large water trough and in autumn pumped water from the nearby brook to fill it. The water froze in winter, making a huge block of ice. They then covered the ice with a large box built of plywood—this is the freezer storage. Then they sealed the freezer all over with Styrofoam. On top of that, they poured loads of sawdust, which kept the food frozen and near freezing all spring and summer, until the next fall.

"Amazing what people can do when they put their minds to it," Ronnie says.

So it is, while Billy and Bobby are exploring the ranch and finding the sheep, the rest of us are having another wonderful day. It is beautiful and sunny, with a crisp touch of departing winter in the air. All of us are excited about the fair tomorrow and continue to make ready. Since there are no perishables this year, like cheese and bread, we are finished packing all the wares before lunchtime.

Thoughts of the tension between the twins surface to worry me as soon as we stop for lunch—though Bobby had seemed fine this morning. "I'm going to ring the bell for Billy and Bobby," I call to Kurina.

"You don't need to," she answers. "Bobby had me pack up the leftover cheese and eggs for them. He told me they would be gone from the house until supper."

Allison shifts her eyes from me to Ronnie and back to me. "I don't think your dad knew that," I whisper. We keep our thoughts to ourselves.

Kurina stacks our lunch items on a couple of Virginia's antique platters and hands them off from the stove to the table. Everything is homegrown and homemade and consists of fried egg sandwiches, cheese, pickles, butter, and milk.

I compliment Kurina on the hearty rustic food and continue, "This has been a great day, Kurina. We've all learned a lot."

"Well, the day's not over yet," she replies. "The babies need a nap, but Naomi can take you for a walk on my favorite trail." Naomi nods a hearty agreement. Kurina continues, "None of you have seen it yet, and today's a good hiking day."

Yes, I thought, Kurina is always too busy to take more than a few minutes' break. I know our hike will be a good opportunity to get this crowd out of her hair for an hour or so.

"A hike sounds great," I say enthusiastically, "and along a path— what fun! We'll be like Goldilocks. What do you think, kids? "And," I further propose to a chorus of approving cheers, "when we get back, you can get in the hot tub! Ronnie, let's start the fire before we leave."

There is something about a path. One steps onto a path and expectations quietly surface. Caution is suspended. Something unknown lies tantalizingly out of sight—not far; maybe around the next bend. To start down a path is a commitment—to whatever lies ahead. Which direction? Choose with care.

So, with some playacting on my part, it is with excitement and primal curiosity that we step onto the path. It has a mood all its own, and what I mysteriously whisper is, "We have entered the realm of the path." I feel we have taken our journey to the mountains to another level—pure nature, touched only by this small, secret trail.

The path is easy to walk, and I am glad Mother is with us. Even the fourteen-year-old boys are into the mood and feel of this place and time. The path has occasional grand views of the valley below and the mountains beyond. It curves through the scattered trees and wildflowers to skirt the icy, little snow-fed brook. This brook and the rain-catchment tank, located uphill from the cabin, are the family's sources of water. We follow Naomi's example and scoop into our palms the tingling cold ice-melt for delicious frigid sips.

On our way back to the cabin, we help each of the small children pick spring flowers for Kurina.

Throughout the mountains another remarkable evening is claiming our day. Rose-colored shadows are stretched across the clearing by the time Billy and Bobby ride in.

The boys and Naomi are still in the hot tub, and I can hear their happy young banter as they plan their adventures at the fair tomorrow. I'm on the front steps surrounded by the younger children, who with serious, quizzical faces, are helping me trim their flowers to fit a porcelain pitcher Kurina gave us as a vase. That's when I hear horses gallop to a stop at the corral. Shifting my gaze downhill, I watch Billy dismount in silence and, abruptly, hand his reins off to Bobby. There is no eye contact between them. Billy climbs toward the cabin, slow and deliberate, staring at me without smiling or speaking as he climbs. Ben and Stevie, seeing his demeanor, watch expectantly, and when he tosses his head and calls softly, "Get out of the tub," they climb out pronto, dripping and steaming; clothes stuck to their bodies. "Where's Ronnie?" he asks me.

Ronnie heard the men ride up, and he is just now walking out of the little cabin. I point in his direction and mutter to Billy, "There."

Bill picks up Ben's and Stevie's dry clothes and lifts his hand, tapping the air toward Ronnie in a "we're coming to you" signal. Wrapped in towels, the boys trot behind Billy downhill to the cabin. Giving me a backward glance, he lets the boys in and closes the door behind him.

The hushed drama I've just witnessed can only mean one thing: that peace in the twins' relationship was unreachable. I'm glad Allison is in the cabin with Ronnie and the boys and Billy. I can't join them—I still have all the little ones pressed around me, wrestling with this weighty task of trimming and arranging flowers—but Allison will let me know what goes on.

The evening air is getting chilly, and I usher the children inside where we join Mother at the table and continue our bouquet. "This is just like when I was a little girl," she says, "picking wildflowers in Texas."

About the time Mother sets the flowers in the middle of the table, Bobby comes in noisily and hails the children with, "I see some kids have been picking flowers in the woods today." After their happy exchanges, he turns to me and my mother. "How has your day been, Mrs. Dorris? Patsy? Have all of you had a good time?" And the chatting goes on, Bobby's mood directly opposite from Billy's. Why the big contrast, I wonder, as I play along and tell him of our lovely walk along the path.

"What about you and Billy? Did you have a good day? Did you find the sheep?"

Bobby pauses and seems to have a sudden change of mood: "Yes, I found the sheep." His voice is strangely loud. He is staring blankly into my eyes. Is this the way he mesmerizes his animals, I wonder?

He continues in the same weird voice. "I found the sheep. I am always finding sheep."

I am feeling so strange that I want somebody in this room to react—to confirm that this scene is not right—but Mother is involved with the children and she doesn't hear very well anyway unless the talk is directed at her. Kurina has not even glanced in our direction.

"Sheep will surprise me sometimes." Preacher Bob draws his head back and feigns shock. "They may not want to be found. They may not be where I expect—but they're out there." He moves in closer, peering right into my face, "Sometimes I find sheep; sometimes they find me."

I feel chills break out on my arms, and I start to shiver. Okay, I think, you are freaking me out and I am not going to continue this conversation.

"Mother," I say to get her attention, "watch Nichole and Austin." Running across the floor, I exclaim, "Kurina, I'm going to get my family for supper." I bolt out the door before another word can pass Bobby's lips.

A Sudden Change of Plans

I run to the little cabin and throw open the door so hard, everyone in the room turns and stares at me. I must look like I've seen a ghost. I am breathless and shaking from chills. (But seeing Ben and Stevie's faces, mouths agape in surprise, I have to smile inwardly. They must be thinking, "Not again.")

"Well," I gasp, "Bobby has just entered the Twilight Zone!"

"What did you say?" Billy grabs both my arms to stop the shaking. "What did he do?"

"It's not so much what he did, as what he said—or how he said it. He's talking and acting like a lunatic."

"Mother," Allison says, handing me the cup of hot tea she is drinking, "let's not do the mass hysteria thing again. Drink this and slow down." She places a warm blanket around my shoulders and pushes her chair closer for me to sit.

"Now," Billy said, "tell us what happened."

"All I did was ask him if he found the sheep. Remember from this morning, you and he were going to ride out and find his herd of sheep?"

"Yes."

"Well, that's all I said, 'Did you find the sheep?' And he goes into his full Preacher Bob mode. At least I guess that's what it was. He starts telling me about him finding sheep and sheep finding him— he's practically yelling all this, and staring weirdly at me. Is this the kind of stuff you've been putting up with, Billy? Because I can't put up with it. He's acting scary."

"I haven't heard what you're describing," Billy says. "But in his mind, there's no telling how it all ties in."

"He relates so strongly to Jesus," I point out, "he probably thinks his Churro sheep are the biblical equivalent of…"

"Oh I don't even want to hear it," Billy interrupts. "I will say his reasoning is way off."

"We both know that Bobby never seems to do anything in moderation," I say. "He is just compelled to be different and extreme. The way he's handling his faith is just another example of this inclination."

"And he wants me, and the rest of you, to believe like he tells us to. Bobby has convinced himself that he has special messages from God. Roland thinks Bobby has a messianic complex. I didn't like it when he said so, but now I think Roland is right."

We sit pondering what Billy has said and wait for him to continue. "I'm deeply concerned about my brother, but I've gone beyond thinking I can help him. I give up. And you won't have to put up with him much longer, Patsy, because I can't either. I told Bobby— and probably shouldn't have—that we're leaving tomorrow."

Supper is a tense, almost silent affair, with Allison and Mother doing most of the talking, and that centered on the children. Since my seemingly harmless question had set Bobby off so, I'm afraid to speak. An innocent word or slip of the tongue might stoke some smoldering ember in his brain and set off another barrage of nonsense. Kurina, too, is uncharacteristically quiet. I found out later that Bobby had already told her Billy had threatened to leave the next day.

After supper the "family devotional" was more awful than I expected—though Billy had warned Ben and Stevie earlier, when we were all in the little cabin together, to brace themselves for plenty of condemnation from Bobby. "I want you boys to understand," he said, "that Bobby has become very confused. I pray that in time he will think straight again, but for now let his words roll off you."

So we all sit in a circle on the floor around Bobby's rocking chair and endure his ruthless criticism of Billy. "Billy, you are leading your family astray," he says. "All you are about is money and prestige. All you do is of the devil. All the fine things you surround yourself with is vanity."

Surely in most families this kind of talk is way off-limits, but with the Hale twins, put-downs are typical—fuel for the inevitable fights that flare between them.

Fortunately, Mother seems oblivious to Bobby's insults. I think she knows his so-called teachings are erroneous and she has just politely tuned him out, probably from the first night.

Finally Billy interrupts, "Bobby your hour is almost finished and Grandmother is getting tired. You need to wind this up. I would like to request that we sing our old favorite, 'The Lighthouse.'"

Before dawn I wake to whispered, heated words between Bobby and Billy. They are seated at the table, less than three feet from my bed. I smell their masculine scent of confrontation and hear their every word.

Bobby is pleading, "Billy, listen to me... Didn't I listen to you? You've got to see how deceived you are. It's important for you to listen to me. It's not just you—you're leading your family astray. And your poor mother-in-law, what a shame. That sweet lady, after all these years of doing what she thought was right, will die and go to hell—because of you."

I hear Billy clear his throat and push his chair back. I am breathless, waiting for his next move. I listen, absorbing every sound in the room. But without saying a word, he walks over to the stove and scrapes around with the coffee pot. I try to guess what his tactic is—to let Bobby wear himself out? Unopposed? After a minute or two of silence, Billy asks, "Bobby, are you finished?"

"No, I'm not finished!"

"Then keep your voice down; everybody else is asleep."

Now that Billy is seated, I hear Bobby get out of his rocker and start to pace the floor.

"How can I be finished when you're still lost?" Bobby rails on—a little quieter maybe. "Why won't you believe that all the many things you have are just vanity? Why can't you see that all your niceties, the big house on the hill, they're all from the pit of hell? Billy, it's materialism, it's wrong!" Bobby is getting more worked up with every sentence. "You need to suffer—leave all this behind you. I'm trying to tell you, you and Patsy need to forsake everything. Leave that hospital. All those years getting your 'doctors' are in vain, and a model of a sick society. Remember you told me how proud Dad was when he first called you Dr. Hale? How sick! How prideful! You are just a pleaser of men. If this is your pursuit in life, you aren't even saved. I'm telling you the truth, you are following the wrong spirits."

Billy finally breaks in. "I'm sorry you feel that way, Bobby, but you're the one being deceived. God doesn't expect everybody on earth to live the same lifestyle. If that were true, we would still be picking berries. I'm not criticizing your life here; I think it's fine. But give me the same respect. I feel comfortable with my life. But since you insist on condemning me in front of my family, and continue trying to confuse them, we will be leaving here. Today."

"Well, good luck getting off this mountain," Bobby says, "because I'm not helping you. It would be a sin for me to help you. If you leave here, you'll do it on your own. And if you leave, there is no salvation for you. I've told you the truth. If you reject the truth that God has revealed to me, then you are lost, absolutely, and there is nothing I can do for you." Bobby storms to the door and gives it a slam on the way out.

I jump off the bed and, brushing the curtain aside, throw my arms around Billy. "I heard him say all those awful things to you, darling, and you didn't give an inch. I'm so proud of you."

I feel his body tense and realize that, for an impulsive instant, I have forgotten the "Twin Rule": When they are in conflict mode, I am to keep out of it. Billy twists away from me and stares out the window, following Bobby's progress toward the corral. "I don't care about your being proud of me," he states flat and cold. "I care about my brother."

I stand meekly beside Billy at the window. Sunrise is in progress, and in a flash the clearing is shot through with brilliant rays of light. We watch the corral until we see Bobby, with all the drama of a western movie, mount Sheba, turn his head to cast a malevolent glare at our window, and ride away.

Billy, his mood suddenly all business, turns to me and says, "Okay, time is of the essence. We've got to gather the family and make our plans now, while Bobby is away."

"You think he really is away, don't you?" I ask. "I mean he's not hiding in the woods watching us, is he?"

"We've got enough trouble without looking for it. Assume he's gone. But I can tell you—he won't be gone long. And when he comes back, he will cause trouble." As he goes out the door, Billy says, "Hurry up and meet me at Allison's."

I watch out the window as Billy, standing at the tent, is obviously telling the unhappy boys to get up. He waits until they are standing outside—poor kids looking half asleep—and I see by his motions that he is telling them to take the tent down and roll it up. He snaps his fingers—pronto!

I quietly throw on jeans and a heavy sweater, leave Mother breathing loud and Kurina and her children sleeping, or pretending to sleep, and rush down to join my family.

In the little cabin Billy is in restless turmoil. And I understand; getting out of here will be a huge undertaking. Billy is almost always restless anyway—forever moving, and rocking slightly—and since he stopped smoking, rarely without his cup of coffee. Allison is making coffee now, in an old percolator pot on the small potbelly stove, and Billy is impatiently waiting, not only for it to perk but for Ronnie and the boys to wake up and join us. Allison opens a box of granola bars and passes it around. Before the coffee has fully perked, Billy pours himself a cup.

Everyone is in place and waiting for Billy to speak. "I told you last night that we'd be leaving today." There are moans from Stevie and Ben that fall to silence with a withering look from Billy. "Ronnie and the boys and I are walking down to Ledoux for the car, and someway somehow drive it up here."

Ronnie slaps both hands over his mouth to stifle his own moan of agony.

"I know," Billy leans against the wall and shifts from one foot to the other. "Getting that Suburban up and then back down will be almost impossible, but we've got to do it. Getting off this mountain will be one of the hardest things we've ever done."

I thought of the large rocks and boulders—some of them lying loose but immovable, and some of them half buried in the "unimproved road." "Billy, Bobby's not trying to hold us captive, is he? Are you sure he won't take us out?"

"Patsy, he won't!" Billy snapped. "How can you even ask after what you heard this morning?" And I knew he would not ask Bobby again—for any kind of help.

Billy turned to the others. "We've got to move fast. Bobby rode off, but that's been at least half an hour. I want to leave here before he gets back."

"Agreed," Ronnie says, and he looks at Billy expectantly.

"I don't know if you noticed coming up here, but there were a lot of old tires propped beside the road and along the fences. I think we can push those tires close to the rocks—a tire in front of a rock and another tire behind the rock, then drive the car over the tire-padded rock. We can do this one rock at a time, being careful not to tear up the bottom. Do you get the picture, Ronnie?"

"There's a lot of that road, Doc, that the boys and I didn't see. It was cold and I let the tarps down. But whatever you say. The tires you're talking about might cushion…the way you describe…fill gaps too deep for the car. I think I get the picture."

"You'll see for yourself soon enough," Billy says. "Okay, we have our plan. Patsy, you and Allison have Grandmother and the babies ready to leave the minute we return. Pack everything and sit it all outside with the bedrolls and tent. Guys," he pauses a moment and breathes deeply, "let's go."

I follow them outside and walk a little ways with them. "This is going to be a lot of work," I remind them. "You will be walking how far? Eight miles at least. All that going back and forth and dragging those tires around; I hope you're up to it."

"Yeah, that's what I'm thinking about," Ronnie says. "Dragging those tires around. Doc, I hope your back's good."

"Oh, I thought I'd let you boys do that," Billy teases. "Seriously, whatever happens: blistered feet, strained backs, even busted-up car—everything will have to wait till we get off this mountain."

"Don't let the car turn over on the boys" was my parting plea as I turned back. My family accuses me of having a vivid imagination, and it's at work right now, picturing the huge Suburban tilting and lurching over those boulders.

Allison, expecting to stay several days, had unpacked nearly every item from her family's suitcases. While she tries to find all their things and repack, I take Nichole and Austin back to the main cabin to feed and dress them.

While I was away, Kurina and her children left the cabin and are still not back. Mother is up and tells me she has just finished the last drop of coffee. "There wasn't much. Maybe you can fix some fresh," she says, "while I go down the hill for a minute."

I put the coffee on and decide to go ahead with breakfast and not wait for Kurina. She will probably appreciate my help. Hoping I have the hang of this stove, I put in a couple of sticks of wood. Within twenty minutes I have a pan of biscuits made, eggs cracked in a big bowl for scrambling and a huge skillet of bacon frying. We had brought the bacon and flour from Fort Worth. While things are cooking, I run back and forth the few feet from the stove to my bed, packing my and Billy's things. Most of what we brought to wear is still in our small bags.

I sit Nichole and Austin at the table with Mother and serve their food. "Mother, you and the babies go ahead and eat. I'm running down to get Allison."

I'm trying to hurry, toting both bags down the front steps, when I see Kurina and all her children coming uphill, Kurina carrying the heavy milk pail, Naomi carrying the baby boy, and John carrying the basket of eggs. Ruth and James have other provisions, probably cheese and jelly. I stop and wait for them, unable to take my eyes off these beautiful, hardy children: Naomi and her little sister Ruth, just as rosy-cheeked and pretty as they can be, with all that blond hair. They are trudging uphill in their long, colorful skirts and little hooded jackets; both the girls and the boys are barefoot on this chilly morning. I think about how wonderful these couple of days have been and regret that our children will miss traveling to Taos with this mountain family.

When they get near, I ask—not really knowing what else to say— "Kurina, what time are you leaving for the fair?"

She answers in a voice that cracks with emotion, "Bobby said last night that Billy wants to go home. If you all leave, I doubt we're going to the fair."

"Kurina, don't say that. You've got to go! Look at all your hard work. What difference would our being here make?"

"Patsy, it's so important to Bobby that you stay. A lot of people know you're up here. They expect you to come with us. Why does Billy think he has to go home?"

Yes, and Bobby will have to make excuses for our sudden departure, I think; that could be embarrassing. But I say, "You've heard as well as I have the badgering Billy is having to put up with from Bobby. You must know, Kurina, there will be no peace between them until Bobby stops his preaching—and we both know he won't stop."

"But why don't you and Billy listen to Bobby?" she pleads. "He's only telling you the truth."

Do I see tears in her eyes? "Kurina, stop this! You are making me feel sorry for you. You are such a puppet in Bobby's hands. And he is using the excuse of our leaving for not taking you to the fair? After all the work you've done? You have a customer who wants to buy a hundred Kiva ladders. That's important. You'll lose your customer."

"Then stay with us, Aunt Patsy!" This is Naomi and James; they are in unison, and they have moved in very close to me.

"Children, excuse me, I'll be back in a minute." I maneuver through the group of five children with my bags, trying not to bump their little bodies. "Let me by, kids." What's going on, I wonder. These children haven't grouped around me this close since we picked flowers.

I hurry downhill to the little cabin, and Allison promptly lets me in. "Let's leave our suitcases in the cabin. I think the children are being put up to something. They might take something to force us to hang around."

"Mother, I heard all that and saw it too." Allison points toward the open window hung with thin curtains. "I don't want to go back up there. Are my babies okay? Can you bring them to me?"

"Yes, I'll bring them and bring you breakfast too. Something good—a bacon and egg biscuit. How's that for service?" I hurry out the door and run up to the cabin.

In the few minutes it takes me to walk to the big cabin, there is not a crumb of food left unclaimed. As I return to the little cabin, I announce, "Here are your babies, but the granola bar will have to do."

"Please, Mother, I'm not thinking about food," she whispers, focused attention in her eyes. We are on our guard as I, too, hear boot-steps crunching outside. The boots stop at the door. Even the babies are silent. There wasn't a soul or a sound in the clearing just a second ago when I was out there. How did someone appear from nowhere? It's got to be Bobby. I know Allison is thinking the same thing I am: "Please go away." The footfalls start again and continue climbing the hill. I peek through the curtain and see Bobby going into the cabin.

"Allison, can you believe how spooked we are?" I draw my breath, and so does she. "This is ridiculous. I'm going up there. I don't want to leave Mother alone with him. Allison, please be ready. I've got everything ready to go except Mother's things, and I haven't told her yet that we're leaving. She's going to hate hearing it."

When I get to the cabin, Bobby has already cornered Mother. "Mrs. Dorris, Patsy and Billy are not treating you and those kids right. You've all been having a good vacation up here with us, and now Billy wants to go back to Fort Worth—after just two days! Can't you talk them into staying?"

"Bobby, Mother doesn't even know that we're leaving." I pull a chair next to Mother and sit down.

"What is he talking about, Patsy? I thought we had a fair to go to. We can't leave."

"I'm sorry, Mother. None of us want to leave, but Billy feels we are being driven out." I look at Bobby. "As usual, these twins can't get along for any period of time, and in spite of our hopes and wishes, this trip is no different."

"Patsy," Bobby says, "I'm repentant that I didn't talk more to you about God's wonderful revelations to me."

"Oh, please, Bobby. I know what I believe, and you can keep your personal insights to yourself. Unfortunately you've driven Billy away."

"My 'insights,' as you're calling them, are from God. You ignore me to your own peril."

"Oh, good grief! I wish you'd stop!"

"I'm doing my duty, which is to tell you the right way. You and Billy are so in love with your big mansion on the hill—it is a rival for your love of God."

Bobby's accusations make me furious. "I need to get some things straight with you, Bobby," I say, far more boldly that I have ever been with him. "First, what do you know about our 'big mansion on the hill' that you keep talking about?"

"I've got the pictures Billy sent me. So prideful. So sinful."

"I guess he didn't tell you the whole story, Bobby, but I would like to: Billy and I spotted that old house in an area of Fort Worth that was scheduled for demolition. We researched the history of that house and discovered it was owned by a couple who promoted Western art and culture. It had been a famous landmark between two counties. Even with its important history, the house would soon, and without ceremony, wind up as a pile of rubble. As you ought to know, this is how cities lose their history. We wanted to save that house. And you, Bobby, of all people, should know that feeling, given your family's love of its own history. Remember—we celebrate it every Christmas Eve. It's almost like we bring your family members back to celebrate with us."

"Patsy, it's vanity! Can't you understand? Vanity! All that history and culture is just baggage! It keeps you from what really matters— your salvation."

"Excuse me for getting off the subject. Please let me finish about this so-called mansion. I do think you need a clearer picture: Billy found that the construction company would practically give that house away if someone would just move it off their property. We literally had the house taken apart, each brick numbered, and moved to my father's land. That's when the hard work began for Billy and me. It took three years and all our spare time to restore that house. We worked every bit as hard as, and probably harder than, you and Kurina worked setting up this ranch for your family. Every family needs a place to live, Bobby—and you know what? Billy and I feel good about saving that old home for our family to live in. If you feel that we committed a sin, then that's just too bad, because we feel we did good. I hope you won't badger us again about 'that big mansion on a hill,' because I'm sick and tired of it!"

My story doesn't even slow him down. He starts to plead again, "But your soul, Patsy? Your everlasting soul. What about that? What about your children and mother? You could influence Billy—you could all accept the truth and be saved." And he just goes on and on...

I have been putting Mother's things together and am ready to go. "I'm tired of this, and we're leaving. Mother, I've got your things."

"Okay, Patsy," she says, "I see what you're up against." On standing, Mother seems older and more bent than usual. She shakes her head and says sadly, "I don't even know why all this was brought up."

Our new, three-week old Suburban weathered its climb up the mountain poorly. It appeared to have been in the strangest possible accident. Its front and back bumpers were badly dented. Climbing over the rocks, it had swayed and tilted so far on its sides that the running boards hit the ground repeatedly. They were bent up at such sharp angles the car doors could not be opened. Billy and I stood on the running boards and carefully bounced, causing them to bend down enough to open the door and free the entrapped driver—Ronnie.

As soon as the men drive up, Bobby, probably surprised that they got that big car up here, levels a barrage of angry, threatening words at "Dr. Luke." Dr. Luke is his new name for Billy.

When at last Ronnie is freed, he and Billy practically hurl our stuff into the car. We will pack and arrange things later. Allison, the driver who weighs the least, will drive the car out. We secure Mother and the babies inside, and the rest of us will walk down. Bill and Ronnie walk ahead, on each side of the car, so they can clear the way and add tires to the rocks where necessary. The boys and I walk behind. Thus we begin our descent. We go fast at first, out of the clearing, for it is fairly even and unobstructed ground. We are determined not to be distracted, and we look neither left nor right.

A loud drama is being played out behind us—actually following us through the clearing. Bobby, unable to get Billy to even look at him, much less listen to his tirade, has sent Kurina and the children out to do his dirty work. They are all screaming at us to please listen to their daddy and be saved, begging us not to leave until we repent. Thanks to Bobby's unreasonable demands on his family, we have to run from them—literally escape. As we lunge onto the road, past the point of no return, the last thing I hear is the precious eleven-year-old Naomi: "God have mercy on you, Uncle Billy," she wails.

Three days ago we had a joyous arrival in Ledoux—a romping good time. The contrast between then and now gives me a feeling of unreality. I would have preferred to hug Kurina and tell her what a wonderful time we had, what a hard-working hostess she was, how much I loved and admired her. And it would have seemed so right to hug those precious children, kiss them good-bye, tell them to be careful and be good, promise an early return visit to their mountain home. But it was not to be—and probably can never be.

I always think about this trip with sadness and thoughts of how it should have been different. At those times there is an old Texas saying that I recall. It warns about dwelling on the past, wishing things had been different: "It's a waste of time, all that regret" the Texan says, "like chasing rabbits."

18. THE RETREAT

"Let not your heart be troubled.
If you believe in God, believe also in me."
~ John 14:1

Billy seems troubled. He has become increasingly moody and hard to get along with lately. His fiftieth birthday is only a few weeks away, and I would like to throw a party for him, maybe cheer him up. But he considers that date a sobering milestone, and he will not hear of it. His father died suddenly at the early age of fifty-four; and though that was some twenty years ago, the memory and shock of I.B.'s unexpected death still eats at Billy. With the concern that a fate similar to his dad's might await him, Billy is not interested in a celebration. I think he feels, more than most of us, that the calendar is not his friend.

I've been told that some men in their thirties and forties are haunted by the specter of their own deaths. I believe this was the case with Billy. He often reminded me, through the years, that when he turned fifty he wanted to get an arterial angiogram to be sure there was no "blockage" anywhere that might take him out like it did his dad. The truth is we are not sure what killed I.B. In spite of his sudden death at a young age, with no history of health issues, no autopsy was performed. For that reason, the theory of the fatal blockage is only Billy's guess. At the time, we did not question or think twice about the fact that there was no autopsy; now we wonder why.

I think it is worth noting here that when I.B. died we did not know how to get in touch with Bobby. It turned out he was in Spain working for the Maharishi. Somehow he showed up briefly, just for the funeral. He told us that J. Edgar Hoover had found him and flown him over. It seems that Virginia, though she did not feel free to attend the service herself, had called Mr. Hoover and told him that Bobby should be at his dad's funeral.

The security force that I.B. had trained at General Dynamics guarded his body and coffin day and night for two days until the ceremonial funeral and burial were held.

When I bring the subject of his "fiftieth" up to Billy a couple of weeks early, I learn that though he wants no birthday party, what he does want is to go away on retreat. "I've been thinking about it, Patsy, and for my birthday I would like for you to drive me to Mineral Wells. I want to spend a few days alone in the park—to read and pray and set some goals for the coming years."

Mineral Wells State Park is only about thirty miles from Fort Worth, and Billy has camped there before. Because the park is on the western side of the low Texas hills, the lay of the land is beautiful there, with large rock formations everywhere and sparse trees.

The truth is I welcome Billy's occasional retreats. He always gets a great boost from being alone to reflect and sort things out. Once he returned from a retreat and wrote this note in my Bible:

My Dear Patsy,

You taught me how to sing, love, work and play. You must understand I don't know why I do those things sometimes that I don't want to do and don't do the things I should. It's as if a darkness overcomes me. Thank you for trying so hard, and for supporting me in more ways than one.

Love, Billy

"I'll be happy to take you, Billy. I'd like to see the park again myself."

I tell him how I love the rugged aspect of the park, with the rock formations and the Brazos River running through the campground.

"That's Proctor Creek that runs through," Billy corrects me. "It's a tributary of the Brazos, though, so you're close."

"You're going to pitch the tent there—right?" I'm thinking of Billy's very pricey North Face tent and how comfortable I can make it for him.

But he answers, "I've been thinking about the tent, but being April, it's liable to rain or even flood the campground. My best choice is to stay off the ground and camp in one of the open-air cabins."

I remember those cabins, and they are nice. "I think you're right, Billy. The views from the cabins are peaceful, and there'll be no weather problems to interrupt you."

Billy says he would like me to drive him out a day or two early and then, on his birthday, come back and bring two steaks to his cabin and cook my famous campfire baked beans, spend some time with him, and depart. When the time comes, I am glad to do as he instructed, and we enjoy our time together immensely.

Bill remains three more days—fasting and reflecting and enjoying the serenity of his environment. Renewed and deeply affected by his retreat, he returns with new optimism and affection. On the night of his birthday, he had written me a sweet, insightful letter:

4-7-91   9:00 pm

Tasty

I look around @ all thing in my little cabin – its put together by you, bought, organized & packed. 3 cans of deodorant, 2 box powders, more food + provision than I would ever need + all you could say do you need a ice cooler or steak or this or that. Three fourths of this stuff is your effort, your initiation + represents your love. I'v got your antique lamp, your antique quilts, your feather pillows + half of the stables from your kitchen. You'v always been this way – caring and helpful – Trying your best to do whatever it takes to make me successful + happy.

But look what I give you in return – I don't yell to loud, I manage to give you whatever I have left over after buying everyone else gifts to make me look good. When you care about the Ride I allow you too – as long as you don't get carried away – after all it might look as though you were supporting me. In fact I have thought of you so much as try to show you how to be perfect by making you all over again in Bill's image; so you could really enjoy life like I have in the past

Well with all that aside I have let you express yourself through the finances($). I have let you all by yourself struggle, toil, manipulate, sceme + never give up trying with more fortitude than five husbands could ever muster together – the $ situation in our home – and show you the confidence I had in you, I let you do is

All by yourself — without any support from me. Of course most of the family by this time realizes all my so called "spiritual" support in all your effort — But I got one problem — I've never convinced myself.

Here I sit on my Fifty I^st and In all honesty all I have to show for it is a nothing if I don't some how make up to you the specialness you have shown me me these last 28 years. I have misused you and mistreated you and exploited you and may God forgive me. If God gives me 4 more years, may they be committed to you — The word talks of Two union in life — The first is with a wife — for this reason will a man cleave from his mother & father and become united to his wife and the two will become one flesh

The second is w with the death & ressurection of Jesus the only Son of God — which of course is pictured in the first union as a man & wife. Please forgive me — it may be?? - possibly?? understandable if you were lost, a wh, whore, druggy, mean & etc - even then I would be without excuse - but you — the only things you lack are those that I block you from — don't stand the gap - consent too becau in your failure perhaps it builds me up — With True Repentance of Acknowledging the Truth — with EYE, that only God Can Give — I REALLY LOVE you
BMI

This letter gives me new hope. It appears that his mood is lifting.

Eight months later, after a separation of more than six years, Bobby begins to write to Billy—seemingly chummy, harmless letters—after all, they are brothers, and Bobby misses his twin. That's what I try to believe. But a couple of months after the letters start, the benefits of Billy's birthday retreat are lost forever. All those goals for the coming years are cast aside. Bobby has other plans for him.

19. KATIE'S DREAM

"…being warned in a dream, a vision in the night."
~ Bible

My family and I were quickly soaring through the water in a taxi-boat that my Uncle Bobby had arranged for. Our destination was a lighthouse shining in the distance. Our family loved lighthouses, so we were happy and excited. With my first glimpse of the land and seascape around the lighthouse, it reminded me of that old prison Alcatraz, in San Francisco.

As we approached the lighthouse, I looked back across the water and realized it was a long, treacherous way back to land; and instead of the brilliant display of lights we had seen when we set out in the boat, the building was actually without any semblance of light and very dismal.

Upon arrival, we were told to get off the water taxi. We had to walk up a flimsy, rotten-looking plank to an old eroded building. We looked at each other with shock and bewilderment. Bobby smiled and looked at us in a peculiar way. In a very strong voice he relayed the message that we are not all here by coincidence, but for the sole purpose of surrendering to a higher authority. We somehow realized that the higher authority was Uncle Bobby himself. We knew he wanted our submission, even to the point of calling him Master.

My father's presence began to weaken in my mind at this time. My other siblings surrounded me, but they had no remembrance of his journey with us.

We walked into the dark so-called lighthouse. Inside the second room I noticed a trapdoor, and we were told that this would be our dwelling place. Uncle Bobby shoved us, one by one, down the trapdoor for his safekeeping. It was so dark that we could not see each other or even our hands in front of our eyes.

I was striving to communicate with my brothers and sister, and with our mother, but I was not succeeding. Our mother had been put in a special cage in another room. We could hear the cage squeaking loudly as it was raised and lowered from floor to floor at different times of the day and night. We would call and cry out to her, but it was to no avail. She was actually farther from us than we thought.

In the dungeon at twilight a small sliver of light would shine through an opening in the wall. That opening appeared to lead to the spot where, in the past, the lighthouse beam had been sent out to the sea for direction. Most of the time we found ourselves in total darkness.

All at once I could see the shape of a hand reaching down through the trap door. The hand would grab one of us children by the hair of the head and pull that child up to him—him being Uncle Bobby. The rest of us siblings would just cringe and wonder when our turn would come; and when our brother or sister would be dropped back down. This was a ritual that happened every day. When each of us, in turn, was in Uncle Bobby's presence, he would look closely into our eyes, then grab us and push our nose and mouth into a giant slice of a huge molded cheese. He would demand our grateful thanks for this bountiful provision. If we didn't adhere to his demand, we would have do without. It was wretched. My uncle would scream at me and say, "Eat it. Your Master has spoken."

I was quite young, only about twelve or thirteen at this time, and was tormented with a strong sense of fear about what our outcome would be. I somehow realized, however, that I would never submit.

As Uncle Bobby would ramble and rave, to whichever one of us was his victim at the time, he would shout, "Just repent, you are of the world!"

When we would drop back into the dungeon, Will, Ben, Ears, and

I would talk about our feelings and tortured experiences. Ben started to stutter like he had done when he was a young child.

My biggest fear was for Will, my older brother. His anger was growing, and rightly so; but I knew he would be severely punished if he expressed any of those feelings.

Allison, still not eating the cheese, was growing weaker with each passing day.

I somehow knew that Uncle Bobby was planning to start bringing us up by age and I knew that, since Ben and I were the closest in age, we would be brought up together. I began to whisper to Ben about a plan to distract Uncle Bobby. In my mind I knew that I was going to have to break free for all of us, and felt the evil and danger of my action.

Somehow the plan involved taking away Uncle Bobby's ability to walk. I told Ben that he had to move quick and hurt Uncle Bobby's legs. Then I could get to the window and climb out to the thin railing.

The time came, and it all happened so fast that I scarcely recognized the railing as I climbed onto it. Now I was out here all alone in this physical world. In my mind, it was communicated to jump and swim across this never-ending body of water to get help. It was as if I was being pulled or maybe even pushed. I knew I was leaving Will, Ben, Allison, and my mother all alone. It was devastating. Darkness and shadows were all around me. I seemed to be melting, just melting away.

My eyes sprang open wide. I jumped as though I had stuck my finger into a wall socket. Screaming for my mom, I discovered I was wringing wet—like I had just crawled out of an ocean. My tears were unstoppable as I explained to my mother that my Uncle Bobby had been so cruel to each of us. It all seemed so realistic. I immediately wanted to look for my other siblings, but then remembered that Allison was not living with us at this time, only Ben and Will. Mom looked very sad as she said, "Katie, darling, this was just a dream."

Katie Hale
15 years old

My darling Katie, it is inconceivable to me that at only fifteen years old, you had a dream that so closely foreshadowed major events that manifested in my life and in Kurina's. "You will call me Master," Bobby will demand."

The dream appears to be strong insight of devastation to come.

20. THE TRANSFORMATION

"A wildness, a strangeness,
can erupt and carry us into realms of unreason…"
~ *Tess Gallagher*

Pleasant memories and a troubling announcement

Our household was devastated when my tough little mother, at age eighty-nine, was felled by a stroke. She has been left physically impaired and requiring a wheelchair, but her memory is untouched and her voice is still strong. Today is her first foray into the yard since her return home. It's early spring, her favorite season, and I knew she would enjoy this warm afternoon. The oak leaves are turning their deepest green now, and wildflowers are popping up everywhere. Mother especially loves the bluebonnets, and we have fields of bluebonnets here on the ranch. We still call it that, "the ranch," mainly because it makes Mother happy. Also to honor my dad—who, before he died, had nearly four hundred acres here, and it was indeed a small working ranch with horses and cattle.

Mother and I are sitting near the swimming pool which is shaded by our tallest and oldest oak trees. "This is so beautiful, Patsy," she says. "I never tire of being here. This is just about where the old barn stood; do you remember?"

"I remember well, Mother." Dad had died of a heart attack right outside that barn. I would never forget it.

But the time came when we had to tear it down. Billy wanted to situate our house—a historic home we were saving from demolition—much too near to where the barn stood. That particular spot was the highest and hardest ground and, indeed, the perfect location for the house.

"And what about the time when you had to burn the barn down, Patsy? Do you remember that?"

"I sure do, Mother." She likes to remind me of that conflagration, as she calls it, so I let her go on.

"Can you remember how many rattlesnakes were in that barn, Patsy? I never saw so many rattlesnakes in all my life."

"Yes, Mother, there was a big den of them. Billy couldn't get any help tearing the barn down because of all those snakes."

"So he had to burn it down. And you called the fire department to come out and stand by."

"Then what, Mother? Do you remember?"

"I sure do. Billy poured gas in a circle around the barn and started the biggest blaze you ever saw. I can see it now."

"He sure did, and I can still see it too. You and me and the kids ran way back, past where the drive is now, and watched all that fire and smoke. And, Mother, do you remember Billy walking between us and the fire, with his six-shooter drawn, peering at the ground? He was ready to shoot any escaping rattlesnakes headed our way—our hero!" Mother chuckles at that picture. I'm glad she's enjoying herself. It's good for her to talk and remember.

"Don't you love to hear the windmill, Mother? It still screeches like it did when I was a little girl."

"A lot longer than when you were a little girl. That windmill has been singing its screechy little song for a hundred years."

"Well, not everybody appreciates its little hundred-year-old voice, Mother. Did I tell you about the midnight call we had from our neighbor down the valley? She said she couldn't sleep because our windmill was making her dogs howl. Poor Bill had to climb the rickety ladder, all the way to the top, and push the wooden handle down to stop the windmill. And that was in the middle of the night."

"Patsy! It's a wonder he didn't get killed—you know that ladder is probably a hundred years old too."

"I know it, Mother. I was afraid that one of those old rungs would break, and it scared me to death. It was cold that night, but I came out here and huddled in my blanket, holding my breath with his every step, as he climbed higher and higher. Fortunately we had a full moon that night, so at least he could see. I'm sure it was the moon, not the windmill, that made her dogs howl, because he started the windmill next day, and we haven't heard from that woman since."

We sit for a while without talking—each of us enjoying our own memories. I can see, in my mind's eye, myself as a little girl, probably no more than seven or eight years old, sitting with my dad almost on this same spot, under these same trees. Every Saturday, Daddy and I would drive out here to the ranch from Fort Worth. On the way, we would stop at the Old Corral drive-in restaurant, where we would pull in and order our po-boy sandwiches from the carhop. This was our ritual, and he would always get us the same thing, a po-boy sandwich and a drink—me a Yoo-hoo chocolate and himself a coke—which we would enjoy right there in the car. But I'm not sure he got to enjoy his sandwich or his coke very much. I would be so impatient to get to the ranch, I would nag, "Daddy, Daddy, hurry up, hurry up." When we got to the ranch, I would climb on my little mare, Cricket, and challenge Daddy to race me and Cricket to the water tank.

Dad was riding Gary Cooper, a Tennessee walking horse chosen by the famous Western actor as his namesake. This horse was a beautiful deep-chestnut-colored stallion with four white stockings and a white blazed face. Daddy came by that famous horse because he could not keep his stride—he broke "the running walk" that the breed is famous for. I had gone with Daddy when he decided to buy a stallion, and when we saw Gary we didn't care whether he could perform his gaits perfectly or not; we both loved him. Gary Cooper was a truly fine horse and it amazes me, now, how I almost always won that race. Just imagine—almost every time, Cricket was faster! I was so happy and secure as a child. I would not change my parents or my childhood with anyone.

There was another man in my life, my older brother Ken. When I was riding Cricket, I thought I was Dale Evans, but Ken was the real cowboy. All my friends and I had such respect and adoration for Ken—which he richly deserved. He was, and is, a wonderful older brother—protective and loving, almost like another father. Perhaps the men in my life, and their caring, respectful ways, were what made me feel secure with all men. I grew up believing they were all like Daddy and Ken, and I trusted that that masculine quality would always be present and flourish in my marriage to Billy.

The cool shadows are lengthening across the yard. "Mother, we ought to go in; it's getting toward evening. Billy will be here soon, and I need to start supper." I do my best to make our meals healthy, but sometimes they are haphazard affairs; the quantity varies almost every night, depending on which of the children are here and whether Billy springs someone on me at the last minute.

As I roll Mother through the front door, I notice Billy on his blue bicycle, approaching down our long, winding drive. About three years ago he started riding his bicycle to the hospital—for exercise. That's a thirty-two-mile round trip every day except weekends, and in any weather except ice! My husband has a hard time doing anything in moderation.

From Mother's room I hear the door open at the portico, on the far side of the house, then close with a slam. With an "I'm home" call and lots of noise, in comes Billy. To my dismay, he has failed, again, to take his bike shoes off, and I hear them clicking across the hardwood floors—floors that he had, with painstaking care, refinished himself. His clicking and clacking seems quicker and more noisy and determined than usual. I run to meet him in the front foyer, and he is obviously excited. I get a quick peck of a kiss as he lays out his upcoming plans.

"I'm going to visit Bobby," he announces. "I'm taking some young people with me."

This news tightens my throat, and I freeze to the spot. He is animated and rattles on about his plans. "I'm taking some young people with me," he repeats.

Speechless, I watch him take off his shoes.

It has been years now since our family's disastrous "adventure" to the Sangre de Cristo Mountains, where we were subjected to Bobby's relentless tirades. He told us in no uncertain terms that vanity ruled our lives; that we were all proud, vain, and going to hell—treatment we had not bargained for. Bobby had become obsessed with his own new version of how to attain salvation: "The truth as revealed to me by God," he said. Bobby especially hounded Billy, warning him that he was leading his whole family, even my mother, astray. When Billy couldn't take the harassment anymore, and decided we had to leave, after only two days, Bobby turned the embarrassing job of our conversion over to his family. I sometimes wonder, when recalling that episode in our life—Kurina and the children crying and pleading with us to stay and be saved—if his giving the responsibility to his wife and children allowed him to blame them for his failure. At any rate, Bobby's glaring stare and his family's wailing forced our humiliating escape down the mountain—practically destroying our new car in the getaway.

On that long stretch of road back to Fort Worth, Billy had been in a black mood. What few words he said had a cutting edge. And no wonder—with what we had just been through. At the time I figured he was questioning, as I was: What kind of theater have we been involved in? Why did Bobby invite us all the way to New Mexico, encourage us to bring the family, promise excitement and adventure, only to start a big fight with him on the very first day? After our return home, we discussed Bobby's motive. "I think he wanted us out there so he could convert us," Billy said. "That seemed to be the only thing he was interested in. He wanted to add us to his new following." Shortly thereafter, Billy began to receive letters from Bobby. These letters were addressed to "Dr. Luke's Deception." I read a couple of them, and they were just ranting crazy. Billy stopped reading the letters after a while. He was as determined as I was to either ignore or reject everything Bobby said—or so I thought.

Billy is staring at me. "Have you heard anything I said?" he asks.

"You're going to Bobby's. But why? Have you forgotten that last miserable trip? You know you two will fight bitterly, just like before."

"I don't think so. He's had a long time to think things over, and I believe he's changed."

"Why would you think that? What's your basis?"

"His letters."

"I thought you had stopped reading those."

"I did, but recently he started writing again—and not to 'Dr. Luke's Deception.' You have noticed his letters addressed to Dr. Hale? He's settled down now."

The disappointment and fear is rendering me speechless. I stare at him and can't bring myself to say a word.

"And I want to see him! That's all there is to it. This will be a good trip.

I do know there has been a flurry of communication between the twins lately, but it is like that sometimes—a lot of communication and then nothing for years.

But, in all truth, I was not unsuspecting s. Something feels insincere about the change to "Dr. Hale," a title Bobby hates. He has said more than once, "I could have got a doctor's degree too, but I didn't want it." Too bad I had pushed away that disquieting alert. Now the uneasy feeling sits in my throat—he wants something from Billy.

"Who are you taking?" I ask. "Some youth, you said?"

"Yes, I want to take our girls; both Katie and Allison."

There has been some tension in his and Katie's relationship in the past few months, so I'm glad to hear her name. Katie, our third child, now twenty-two, is a natural beauty and looks a lot like her dad. She is strong and has a lot of endurance. Katie has a big heart and wants to be everything to everybody, which sometimes gets her in trouble. Even so, she says what she thinks and doesn't put up with much.

But Allison? What is Ronnie going to think about being left alone with Austin and Nichole? I will ask him to stay here at the ranch. I can help him with the children while this select few travel. "Anybody else?" I ask.

"Yes, there are three young men from my Bible study class: Gerald, Tim, and Joe. I want them to go with me.

I know these names. Tim, polite and serious by nature. He has been a close friend of Katie's through school. He loves "Doc" and is loyal to our family. Tim is strong and rugged-looking with sandy hair.

Joe is a very good-looking young man with black hair and a broad, beautiful smile. He has a big red pickup truck that will be handy on a trip like this.

Gerald is tall and thin, and is a rather quiet young man. His dad is a professor at Weatherford College.

"I'd like Christie to go too," Billy says. "She's been attending Bible studies with Katie. Both of our girls enjoy having her around."

I know Christie well. She is a happy girl and Katie's good friend. She is taller than average, graceful and thin, with black eyes and black hair. Christie is competitive, and loves horses and the outdoors. She would like this trip, and our girls would enjoy having her go with them.

That's five young people ages nineteen to twenty-four, not counting our little blond Allison, who is twenty-six and mother of our two grandchildren. In all, seven of them will be going. "You will have your hands full," I say. For various reasons, our two sons were not included.

We walk into the kitchen, and Billy sits at the counter, looking hopefully at me. "Patsy, there's lots of preparation to be done. We need to take food and warm clothes."

"How much food?" I ask.

"I want to fill the pickup full—with stuff they can't get out there. You know as well as me. And pillows and blankets. April will still be cold in those mountains."

"Who's going to get all that stuff together?" I ask—knowing good and well he expects me to do it all.

"I'm hoping you will help me," he says.

"When are you leaving?" I ask glumly.

For the group going to New Mexico, departure time has rolled around, as time and occasion always do, and it is Friday, almost midnight. I'm exhausted from the hectic week of everything involved in getting the group ready for this trip; a trip I seriously didn't want them to take.

With a big smile plastered on my face, but with a heavy heart, I find myself waving goodbye to Mother's blue Oldsmobile, carrying Billy, Christie, and my two girls, and to the overcrowded, red pickup, carrying the three young men and every staple the truck bed will hold. I stand on the front porch and watch the taillights weave and bob down the long drive and disappear.

Flipping off the outside lights, I relax into the cool blanket of darkness; sit on the cool tile of the porch steps; listen to the silence. The rhythmic turn of the windmill is the only sound I hear…not even the call of a night bird or buzz of an insect. On this clear night, the sky is glorious. Out here on the ranch, away from the city lights, the stars are so bright and close I can almost touch them, almost pick the stars from the sky with my fingers. But even the majesty of the heavens can't ease my anxious thoughts.

As Billy's wife, I have never concerned myself with his absences for hunting trips, retreats, or campouts, even when I wasn't included, which more often than not I was included. I know Billy is a capable, creative man, and I'm not concerned about the usual types of occurrences like a flat tire, or being stranded, or even safety. My concern tonight is for what might emerge from Billy's own twin that could be frightening for the whole party, and above all for Billy. I wonder if he thinks the group he's taking with him will protect him from Bobby…cause Bobby to somehow moderate his behavior.

And what of this group: six unknowing young travelers who are driving through the night? Will they find fun and adventure, like they expect, or browbeating sermonizing by Bobby? I fear this party will endure the same hell Bobby put our family through on our first "adventure" to his mountains.

My thoughts keep returning to Roland and his warning to me years ago, when Bobby was still a Morning Star and even then arguing philosophy of another sort with Billy. *"If Bill ever starts listening to Bobby,"* Roland had warned, *"starts being influenced by him, it will be too late."* Regardless of what Billy says about Bobby's changes, I don't believe it. Bobby hasn't changed. Bobby is relentless. And for some reason, either because of sincere misguided convictions or out of mischief, he will not leave Billy alone. The reasonable tone of his letters, I think, is a ploy to reassure Billy, and this trip is a trick to entrap him. God, please let me be wrong.

Katie's Account

Mother, we had been driving all night and day, but we were getting close. You had told me what Ledoux looked like, and I recognized it. With only three buildings, it wasn't hard to identify. We had all switched around, and I was in the truck now. We were in such high spirits. I stood outside on the running board as we crept into town and yelled my first-hand report, "Look, I see the post office of Ledoux. And there's Uncle Bobby on Sheba." He was waiting for us like he knew exactly when we would arrive.

Daddy introduced Tim and Joe and Gerald to Uncle Bobby, and we girls gave him big hugs. He was sweet and real glad to see us. We parked the Oldsmobile behind that tiny little post office, and after Bobby said a big long prayer, everybody piled into the pickup truck with Gerald and me on top of the food.

Mother, you said the road to their cabin was rough; well, it was worse than rough, even in the pickup, and even though Uncle Bobby said it had been improved some over the years. Joe stood on the running board and Bobby warned, "Boy, you could smash all your teeth out on that truck roof. Be sure you don't break your jaw! There's some big ruts ahead."

Gerald and me, in the bed of the truck, could barely keep from bouncing out. Uncle Bobby was riding Sheba and kept circling around to see if we were okay. He might have been more concerned, though, about losing some of that food than losing us. Anyway, we started winding around and around, following Sheba's lead.

In about an hour or so, Daddy called our attention to the cabin, way up ahead, and to Kurina. She was sitting on a log and bending over an outside fire. I couldn't tell what she was doing at that distance, but Allison said, "She's making homemade tortillas." Allison didn't seem very excited, but to the rest of us hungry folks it sounded wonderful.

The cousins were so happy to see us—they are just stair-steps you know, and we had to hug and kiss every one of them, from one year old to teenagers. Some of them just clung to us. The girls, even the littlest ones, were wearing long, ground-dragging skirts, and all of them bright-colored; you know, Mother, how they dress, they just all looked so—fitting. Kurina stopped cooking and hugged each one of us with a warm, motherly hug, her face red from the fire and her clothes smelling of smoke. I loved it. It felt good being with her in that old-timey setting. Daddy and Uncle Bobby and the boys went one way, but we girls stayed with Kurina. We watched her finish cooking the tortillas and stack them in an oblong, wooden bread bowl. She carried that big bowl full of thick tortillas into the cabin, and we followed right behind. I could not resist the smell and asked if I could just break one in half for a taste. That tortilla was heaven! It tasted something like fresh corn smoked on the grill, and I could have gone through the whole stack. Kurina offered one to Allison and Christie, but since Allison wouldn't take it, neither would Christie. I realized right then that Allison was going to be a problem. You know how she won't eat anything new without picking through every bite.

Kurina took us to see our loft bedroom. She said, "Sometimes there will be animals bumping in the stalls under your loft. If you hear them, don't get scared—it will probably be one of the goats wandering around in the night. The dogs will take care of anything prowling around that would hurt you— like a wolf!" She still has her happy, loud laugh, and we all got to laughing with her.

I remember you telling us, Mother, that Uncle Bobby had rigged up some kind of solar lights. Well, those solar lights were over the beds in the loft. Kurina told us they collected the sunlight during the day and glowed for a while at night—long enough for us to get ready for bed at least, and they did. They worked pretty good.

The first thing I noticed in the main room of the cabin was a chair sitting all by itself in the middle of the floor. It was parked on one end of Nana's blue Persian rug. I remembered you telling us how Uncle Bobby made everybody sit around him while he preached and sang. Oh no, I thought, that big solitary chair is Uncle Bobby's pulpit.

I probably saw it first because I was looking for it.

I wanted to show the dreaded chair to Allison, but I noticed her staring at the cook-stove. She had noticed that the stove had two purposes: one purpose was for cooking and the other was as a clothes dryer. There were some thick, woolen socks hanging over the stove to dry, as well as some big pots of food cooking. When Allison turned around, I saw that her face was gray—I guessed with nausea. I figured the socks being that close to the food, even though the food was covered and boiling, was too much for her finicky stomach. "I'm going to get something to eat out of the truck right now!" she whispered to me.

Allison took the three quick steps to the kitchen door, swung it open, and with a little squeak of surprise, stopped dead in her tracks. That sudden stop was so unexpected, I almost pushed her down the steps…and then I saw: down the hill, at the truck, our huge pile of provisions had all the strapping removed, and those kids were having a field day. No wonder none of them had followed us into the cabin, or followed the men for that matter—they had spied that truckload of food and goodies.

You know, Mother, that Daddy and Allison had loaded up at Sam's with staples like flour and sugar and paper stuff. They also got coolers of bacon and meat. But what the kids saw was, boy oh boy, brownie mixes, cake mixes, boxes of cookies, bags of candy, marshmallows, every kind of cereal, and, most important to Allison, her boxes of granola breakfast bars.

"Tell me it isn't so!" she moaned when she finally found her boxes. They had all been opened and, to her horror, most of the bars had been dumped out of the boxes. Some were a little crushed, but none were eaten. Though each bar was in its own wrapper, that was not good enough for Allison—she wouldn't touch them. We were surprised that, even unsupervised, the children had eaten almost nothing. I think they just wanted to take an inventory for later. Allison salvaged the few bars that were still stuck in the three boxes and carried them, right then, to the loft.

When Kurina got supper ready, we couldn't find Daddy or Uncle Bobby or the boys anywhere. She had to ring the bell in the front yard to call them. The little kids and I were starving; but no one was allowed to have even one bite until Uncle Bobby got there and said his blessing. Right then was when I began to understand how *iron-fisted* he was with his family. I felt he was very inconsiderate. And, Mother, when he finally got there, what a terrible imposition that prayer of his was. We had to sit, wasting away, while he repeated almost word for word what he had already said when we first got in the truck in Ledoux. I forgot to tell you about that prayer in Ledoux; it took at least half an hour.

When we finally got to eat, which was a good hour after we first sat down, Kurina had salsa and cheese and deer meat to go with her homemade tortillas. The boys and Dad and I thought it was delicious, but I noticed Allison kinda pushing her food around on her plate. I know she was wishing that one of the dogs was in the house so she could drop her serving of deer meat on the floor. She ate maybe half a tortilla and a little salsa, and that was only because we had brought it from home—Joe T. Garcia's salsa in a jar. Christie is thin, and almost as picky as Allison, so her meal was just about as skimpy.

After supper, even though it was dark, we girls were ready to clean ourselves up after such a long drive. Mother, I'm sure you remember the big hot tub under the kitchen window? It looked so inviting, and we were told it had fresh water in it. Then we learned the water was not heated yet, so we could not bathe till later—about an hour, maybe more, Kurina told us.

Uncle Bobby, hearing that we wanted a bath, gave us a lesson in bath-taking at his house: "Keep all your clothes on except your shoes," he said. "Remember that modesty is a much sought-after virtue. You shouldn't look at each other's naked bodies—you know it's sinful."

I spoke up. "Uncle Bobby, it's only us girls. It shouldn't be a problem."

"You all need to be steadfast in avoiding vanity and the ways of the world," he said. "By the way, Christie, could we visit for a minute?"

Allison and I couldn't help overhearing Uncle Bobby talking to Christie. He proceeded to tell her that she had a very "worldly look."

"Those earrings and makeup are uncalled for," he said. "And your clothes are too provocative."

When he said that, it made me furious... Blue jeans and a big thick sweater? That's what Allison and I had on too. You can't even dress "provocatively" up there or you'd freeze to death. Anyway, he just wouldn't leave her alone. I wanted to go out and take up for her—and Mother, you know I would have, in a minute, except that I have not been getting along too well with Dad. So I chickened out and kept my mouth shut. When Christie came back inside, she looked very upset. Allison and I didn't have a chance to even speak to her because Daddy and Uncle Bobby summoned all of us to what we girls called "the throne room."

Sitting at Uncle Bobby's feet and looking up into his face was real hard for me. But you know, Mother, while I was sitting there, I realized that this was what Daddy, in his secret heart, had always wanted us to do—sit at his feet.

It took a while, but I finally got into the whole scene: Uncle Bobby, looking like he was wearing a wild-man costume, with hair and beard flying, was flailing hard at his guitar; Naomi, in long sleeves and long skirt, was singing loud and clear—her head thrown back so far she was looking at the ceiling; she also sawed at the fiddle, sounding kinda good. One of the boys had a good voice and played a Dobro. It was pretty good stuff. All the rest of the children sang as loud as they could, and Kurina drummed the big bass fiddle keeping time. Dad kept telling us girls to sing louder, but we couldn't sing louder. I'm not even familiar with some of those songs. One of them was called "Don't You Want to Be a Shepherd?"

After sitting on Nana's rug for over an hour listening to Uncle Bobby, all of us visitors, except Daddy, were ready to collapse. Uncle Bobby's topic of the night seemed to be vanity. I'm not even sure he knows what the word means. But he kept on about it till I thought I would scream. You know, Mother, he does not permit a single mirror in that cabin? To look at yourself in a mirror is vanity! To look at your naked body is unspeakable vanity. And to let somebody else "gaze on your nakedness" will send you straight to hell! I have never heard the word "naked" used so many times in my life. And sitting there with the guys—it was embarrassing!

We need to get out of this room, I thought, and I'm not attending this mess again. I've got to get in that big tub, and not just to take a bath; I need to wash away all those vulgar words. "The water is the cleanest it will be," I whispered to Christie, "and we are first." Sooo… we squirmed and changed positions every few minutes, each time inching closer to the door. Finally we got to the door, stood up real quick, and scooted right out. There was a camping lantern sitting in the yard, so we were able to find our way.

There we were, in the middle of the night, in all our clothes, sitting outside in a tub of hot water. It was pretty funny, and Allison and I were feeling pretty good about our successful escape. Christie, though, was still mad. She said, "I'm twenty-two years old, and your crazy uncle is treating me like a baby! I think he's a dirty old man, and I want to leave this place!" But I laughed when she said, "Or maybe I do look trashy! Do I look trashy?"

Allison and I didn't blame Christie for what she said about Uncle Bobby. We felt he had insulted her. But the water was very warm and relaxing, and she began to calm down. We all laughed at the whole episode. Believe it or not, we really enjoyed bathing in our clothes.

All too soon we had to get out of the tub and make way for the boys and Dad. Daddy said, "I hope you girls got good and clean because these baths won't be frequent."

We tried to blot ourselves and our clothes dry with the big beach towels you made us bring from home—thank goodness for them. Even with those big towels, we still had wet clothes to contend with. All the hiding around we had to do, and trying to change into something dry without being seen, even by each other, was a huge, stupid production. But we were finally in bed, and bed never felt so good.

Mother, I don't know how this happened, but next morning I was alone, and I ran upon Uncle Bobby training his young colt. He was in a clearing beside the corral. I think he is kind of famous for controlling and training his horses with his eyes because I've heard the family talk about it. I stayed in the shadows and watched him in secret. He was standing in the bright sun, still and quiet, his eyes shining with sunlight. Right in front of him stood the colt; and Uncle Bobby was staring, with those shining eyes, right into its eyes. All at once the colt lay down and rolled on its back, and rolled all the way over, and stood up. That seemed so strange to me. I wanted to find Daddy and tell him about it and see what he thought. Then Uncle Bobby noticed my presence, and his strong stare met my eyes, and for some reason I blushed. To account for myself, I said, "Uncle Bobby, is it time for our hike?"

"I think you girls can handle that by yourselves," he said. Just turn at the big tree stump past the outhouse, and you'll find the trail. And by the way, you girls are not ever to use perfumed soap in my tub again. Not only is it ridiculous, it's also vain."

"I'll tell them, Uncle Bobby," I said. "We meant no harm." He halfway smiled at me.

I turned around to go back and find the girls. But I was preoccupied with the strange stuff that had just happened. To tell the truth, Mother, I don't even know if it was strange, but it made me feel strange. In fact, not many hours after we arrived, I had already started to feel uneasy about being up here in this place. After first loving Uncle Bobby's pioneer ranch, it seemed creepy to me now.

I wandered around a little but couldn't find anybody. It seems that everyone had got up at different times this morning and just wandered off on their own. Then I heard Allison call, "Oh there you are, Katie. Are you ready for our hike?"

"Where is everybody?"

"No one's going with us except Christie," she said. "Daddy wants to show the boys some things Bobby has built, mainly the freezer. Kurina says for us to follow the path by the creek till we come to 'the beautiful view.' I know which view she means because we went there last time. You will love it."

We had not been walking any time—had not even reached "the beautiful view"—before Allison wanted to go back. She said, "My sweater's not enough, I'm cold." I let her know that I was aggravated because I was enjoying the walk, but she convinced me. "Kurina is going to make cheese and butter this afternoon. I want to watch her. Don't you?"

Dressed in extra pullovers, we joined Kurina in the shed. The little children were all over the place, and it was fun to watch her and Naomi make cheese. It was goat cheese, though, and we didn't like the smell. Kurina told us she stores the cheese in the root cellar for a few months to ripen and then sells lots of it in the fall, at the Taos fair. Then she took the butter that had formed in her churn and put it in half-pound wooden molds. I couldn't wait to enjoy that delicious butter, spread thick, on her homemade bread—or even leftover tortillas.

After a while, we eased away from the shed, and I lured the girls out to the path again. "I want to pick sage and wildflowers and surprise Kurina," I said. She had little bunches of flowers and herbs all over the house, so we knew she liked them.

We were hoping to run into the boys on our walk, but unfortunately it was Daddy and Uncle Bobby we saw first. They were in a heated conversation, each of them taking his Bible out of its leather holster on his belt. And each of them pointing and showing the other something in the Bible. "Oh brother!" Allison said, "I hope this doesn't end in a fight. Let's just scoot by before they see us."

When we brought Kurina the little bouquets we had picked, she said, "We are having cheese and the fresh butter with wild turkey tonight." That sounded okay to me, but I've been worried about Allison—she hardly eats anything. Somehow I know she will eat tonight, though; she just has to.

We went back outside, and Daddy saw us and came over. He looked like he had something important to say. "How was the hike, girls?" But before we could answer a single word, he began to lecture us. "I want you to eat more food tonight. You don't feel like coming to Bobby's teaching because you're not eating anything. You girls need to be following these insights Bobby has. The guys all seem of one accord, except Tim."

You know, Mother, Uncle Bobby's teachings aren't worth two cents to me, and I was glad to hear that Tim wasn't falling for them either. You know Tim's history. He's had such a hard life and has overcome so much. It hurt me that Dad was wanting any of us, Tim especially, to follow Uncle Bobby.

I wanted to change the subject and talk to Dad about something else. I wanted to remind him of our horseback rides tomorrow. "I want to talk to you, Daddy," I said. But he wasn't listening. "Do you have just a minute, Daddy, for us to talk?" I repeated. His mind was a thousand miles away. He didn't even reply.

Allison and Christie had stood by and watched and listened to me and Dad. "Did you hear what he said?" Allison whispered. "Uncle Bobby must have won that argument we saw earlier in the woods. Mother would be sad to hear Dad say we should follow Bobby."

Allison did, at least, eat the butter and bread at supper. Uncle Bobby walked over to her and said, "Allison, aren't you going to eat the cheese?" For some reason, even though I wanted her to eat, I was hoping she wouldn't eat the cheese. I whispered in her ear, "It's putrid!" I was so fearful of her eating the cheese that I made a quick decision to run to the loft. Allison and Christie were inches behind me. We kicked off our shoes and dove into bed. I whispered to them to be very quiet and maybe no one would find us. Christie started giggling at that, and so did I. We all knew there was no way we could hide in such a small house. Sure enough, here comes Dad.

"Why are you girls running and hiding?" he asked.

"Because Allison isn't feeling well," I answered. "Neither is Christie. They both feel sick."

"I told you that you need to listen to your Uncle Bobby. I want you to come to the teaching!" He sounded pretty mad.

"We just can't," Allison groaned.

"Anyway, Daddy," I said, "we can hear him perfectly well from this loft."

He stormed off to join everyone else sitting on the floor around Uncle Bobby. I think he and Daddy made real sure that we heard them *perfectly well*. What a racket! Since we couldn't talk over all the commotion, we tried to fall asleep. But sleep was impossible. It was a little like being tortured.

After all that carrying on last night, the morning seemed normal—quiet and slow. From the loft we could hear that everybody was at the breakfast table, talking or mumbling. Breakfast sounds different there. We could hear Uncle Bobby's rocking chair, and Kurina opening and closing the stove, and spoons scraping wooden bowls and plates.

We climbed down from the loft, one by one, to the floor. Oh, I meant to tell you, after that first night, we slept in our clothes, even socks, so we didn't have to "hide our nakedness." It was just a lot easier.

We girls grabbed some bread and butter and boiled eggs. This was the third day, and it was the first meal Allison had eaten… that is if you call a hard-boiled egg a meal. We excused ourselves from the table with the angry eyes of Dad and Uncle Bobby following us.

"We're going to the corral to see the horses, Daddy," I said. "Remember, we're going horseback riding today." The guys confirmed that they were going with us and would meet us at the corral when they finished breakfast.

Uncle Bobby stared at us, real cold like, and listened to us make our plans. Then, before we could leave the room, he thumped his empty cup down and backed out of his earlier promise: "There's only one horse will be available," he said. "The other two horses are going on a long trail ride— carrying your Daddy and me."

Allison and I were shocked. We knew that our Daddy didn't even like horses. Remember how he liked to quote that writer, I don't who he was: "A horse is dangerous at both ends and uncomfortable in the middle." And he was going on a "long trail ride" with Uncle Bobby? I looked at Daddy like, "Is he kidding?" But Dad didn't look like he wanted to explain.

When they finished breakfast, Dad and Uncle Bobby left on that "long trail ride," not even taking us into account. They saddled up, real quiet, not talking to each other, and never looked back.

Allison and I were still puzzled and angry. I think all six of us felt pretty let down. The only thing Dad had wanted us girls to do since we got here was to sit at Uncle Bobby's feet. And now he had abandoned us, and the guys too. We all felt pretty resentful, but

Christie definitely was more miserable than any of us. "I'm sick of this place," she said. "Maybe we should call your mother to come after us!" This was not like Christie, and I had never seen her this close to tears.

Allison and I reasoned with her, "You're talking about a long drive, and Mother's got our grandmother to look after." And we can't call anyway. They don't have a phone. She got hold of herself, but I felt sorry for her and regretted that Allison and I had talked her into coming on this trip. She had ever experienced anything like what Uncle Bobby and daddy were putting us through. She thought things weren't going right and was concerned that something bad might happen. Remember, Mom, we had all heard about that first trip, when you all tore up the car leaving early.

We were in the yard, and considering the nature of our conversation, we were sitting close together for privacy. Gerald and Joe didn't seem to like us talking about how unhappy we were. And they didn't like us complaining about the way Daddy and Uncle Bobby were treating us. They let us talk but didn't join in.

Mother, you know how serious Tim is; he was getting worried about Daddy. Tim whispered, "What's going on with Doc?"

"What do you mean exactly?" I asked.

"Katie, your dad is very disturbed," Tim said. "I just want to know what you and Allison think. He's not acting like himself."

I told them that actually, the few times in my life when I've seen Daddy and Uncle Bobby together, they've always acted crazy to me.

Allison and I told them that you, Mother, and Nana have said that Uncle Bobby and Dad could never be together without fighting, even as little boys. But the family, I think, just figured it was because they were twins. So, I told Tim, I guess this time *is* different. If they were following their usual behavior, Dad would be arguing and fighting with Uncle Bobby.

"They have been arguing," Tim said, "but in the end, seems like to me, Doc gives in to his brother. And Doc is trying to convert all of us? Frankly, I'm pretty disgusted." We were all staring at him saying this stuff. "I'm sorry, but that's the way I feel," he said.

During this whole conversation, Joe and Gerald hadn't said a thing and looked real sour. Then, all of a sudden, Gerald snapped out, "Just drop it!"

Our moods were terrible, Mother. You know that Christie is almost always easy going, but she stood up and said, "Let's get out of here! If we can't ride, can't we at least walk?"

"Let's walk down to Ledoux," Allison said. We all thought that was a good idea, so we took off.

It is a long walk, and when we got there we were real hungry, even Allison. Looking at the one tiny place in town serving food, she said, "Does Mexican food sound good?"

"I don't think we have a choice," I said. The señora brought the greasy enchiladas and salsa to the table, and we all dug in, even Allison and Christie. Mexican is what we were used to, and it was good. We ate like pigs and sat there drinking cokes and talking for a while.

Mother, you told us about a young Indian who lived in Ledoux. He is probably about our age now. There wasn't anything to do in *town*, and it was too far to walk to Taos, so we were looking for him. But he was not in Ledoux that day.

We got a little way up the mountain on our return when, all of a sudden, Gerald broke away from us and ran into the woods. We put two and two together and figured Gerald was not feeling well— probably from all that greasy food he had gorged on. Joe and Tim said they would go on back with Gerald.

We girls were fine with the guys leaving. We were in no hurry to get back to Uncle Bobby's *enclave*, as Tim had started calling it. Christie said that place gave her the creeps, and I agreed. We just took our time and enjoyed being away from there.

In a little while, we came across an interesting little trail, clean and "well trod," as I've heard you say, and decided to check it out. The little path was so pretty. We were examining every little plant, when we ended up in a beautiful, flowery clearing. The ground was covered with pinkish-white flowers. You've seen them before, Mother, because Allison told us, "They are the first blooms of spring, and Mother and grandmother loved them when they were here."

We were just awestruck at how pretty they were and wanted

Kurina to have some. We were looking around trying to find the most perfect blooms without stepping on them when, to our amazement, facing us, and riding out from under a tree on horseback, was our Daddy. Uncle Bobby had said they were going on a "long trail ride." We knew this wasn't that far from the cabin, and Daddy was by himself, and looked lost. I wondered if he was lost. I think we were speechless because none of us three said anything. I thought, is he just wandering around? His countenance seemed totally different, Mother. His eyes were vacant. He looked like he couldn't focus on us. I got goosebumps. When he spoke, he sounded mumbling and, you know, almost like a robot, and didn't make sense. He motioned us to come close to his side, by the horse. He dismounted and tried to look us in the face. His words were without expression, as if he was reading something. He looked at me and said, "This is a time for all to choose what is right—and that's what I have done. Bobby has made things clear to me. Now I understand. When you get back to the cabin, get it all together. We are leaving in the morning. Do not worry about coming to the teaching time after dinner."

I thought to myself, it's nice to have your permission, Daddy, but I wasn't going to that mess anyway.

We brought so much with us but had so little to take back— "getting it all together," as Dad had told us to do, was a snap.

The drive home was wretched. We had to endure Daddy's deadly silence. He didn't say six or seven words the whole trip. And he didn't take the wheel a single time. I drove most of the way, and he sat in the front. He rocked in his seat endlessly, just rocked and rocked and rocked the whole way. And he grimaced, popping his jaws over and over. I don't know what was going on with him, but it made us miserable.

When we finally drove up to the house and I saw you, Momma, standing at the door, I was so relieved—you just can't imagine how good it was to see you. When you asked me, "Katie, did you enjoy yourself?" I almost cried.

The Transformation

"A very troubling story, Katie," I say. "When your dad first mentioned his plans for the trip, I felt it wouldn't go well."

"I knew you were worried about it, Mother, but now that I've told you my account, I'm so sorry to say this, but you're probably going to be seeing less of me."

"Katie, darling, why are you saying that?"

"From the first morning after we got to Bobby's, I started to feel uncomfortable. I tried to enjoy all of it—Kurina and the kids, the mountains—but by the time we left that place, I felt a cloud over us. What happened up there with Dad is not good. You said he and Uncle Bobby have always fought something awful. Well, now I think the fighting's over. Mother, I think Uncle Bobby has won."

"If that were true, Katie, it would be terrible—surely not."

"I'm sorry, Mother, but I do think Dad was deceived by Uncle Bobby. He wanted Dad to be his little puppet, and now I think he will be. I'm afraid Daddy will want us to sit at his feet like Uncle Bobby's family does. I won't do it, so I need to stay away. And, Mother, did I tell you that Kurina calls Uncle Bobby *Master*? I hope that doesn't lie in store for you."

"Katie! Why are you being so dramatic, baby? You know I would never do that—either sit at Billy's feet or call him Master; nor would he expect such a thing. It sounds like you think your Dad is transformed into another Bobby."

"That's about right, Mother. That's what it seems like to me. To Allison too. You noticed how quick she left after saying hello to you and getting her children. She doesn't want to be here around Dad."

"I don't understand this behavior you're describing, Katie, but it won't last long; it can't last. I just need to talk to him."

"Well, Mother, I'm not sure he will talk to you in any meaningful way. Where do you think he is now? He hasn't even come to the house."

Our conversation is interrupted when we see Christie and Tim, looking at us through the window and waving. "It looks like Christie and Tim are leaving," I say. "Let's tell them goodbye."

We hurry out to the porch. "I can put dinner on the table in no time," I tell them. "Why don't you two stay and eat?"

"I called Mother and told her I was hungry for her cooking," Christie said. "She's fixing dinner for me and Tim. He's taking me home."

"Tim," Katie says, "can you drop me off at Melvina's? She asked me to stay with her any time, and now's the time; I'm taking her up on it."

"Katie, you're leaving just like that?" I say. "Shouldn't you say goodbye to your Dad? Where is he anyway?"

"That's a good question, Mother. Where is Daddy? Out somewhere praying and singing with Gerald and Joe?"

"That's exactly what they're doing," Tim says. "Something happened to Doc on this trip, Mrs. Hale. His brother got him way confused and off track. The way he's talking now, I'm sorry to say this, but I don't think he should be teaching our Bible study."

"I've heard Bobby's claims, Tim. He says he's had special revelations from God. But all of us know better, and so does Bill."

"I don't think Doc does know better," Tim says. "I think Doc's bought all that garbage, Mrs. Hale. I'm telling you, he's talking just like his brother."

It sickens me to hear Tim say these things. "Katie has told me of Billy's changes, Tim, and now you're confirming them. I can't tell you how worried I am about my husband."

"And," Katie says, "I'm worried about you, Mother. I'm going to call you soon. But I've got to go." She turns to follow Tim and Christie to where Tim's car is parked in the yard. "Dad's not around, and I'm not going to interrupt him. Why should I? He won't care anyway."

I sense the sad truth of Katie's statement and watch the three of them drive away. When they turn onto the lane, I can barely see through the back window, and I catch a last, faraway glimpse of my daughter before losing sight, and then sound, of the car.

I can't go looking for Billy. I just can't do it. It would mean getting caught up in all the heresy he has brought back from Bobby's. Out of my reverie, a Bible verse comes to me: *We war not against flesh and blood but against the principalities of darkness.*

I wander room to room through the house before seeking solace in my favorite space, the kitchen.

The kitchen window is almost floor to ceiling and overlooks the deck, then out to the swimming pool, the grove of oak trees, and the field of bluebonnets. Everything is beautiful. It is my land and my history. Regrettably, I had made the mistake of my life when, in a moment of feminine weakness, I let Billy persuade me to add, to my deed and trust, the name William K. Hale—the man whose own father had warned me was not a very good manager.

For a moment I can see my dad—out among the bluebonnets, riding Gary Cooper. Daddy was hesitant for a long time; he really didn't want me to marry Billy. In the end, after a long talk with Billy, Daddy was convinced, and he gave us his blessing.

What does the future hold for us, for Billy and me? The room seems dark and closes in. The floor has turned to glass. The slightest move will make me fall. I feel that things are coming undone.

I step out on the deck. It is early evening, a good time to reflect. Katie surprised me today. She was so plain-spoken—analytical even. That was a young woman talking, not my carefree little girl. She has seen some troubling things on this trip, and she is worried about her dad. Tim, as well as Katie, said Billy is changing. I think it's true for I have observed some troubling signs over the past year or two myself. For instance:

Something very disturbing to me was that Bill decided one day that the Italian tile in our large, third-floor spa looked pink. Nothing would do him but to tear out that beautiful, expensive tile and replace it with even more expensive, stark-white tile with dark green geometric edging. My protests and reasoning meant nothing to him. What a costly decision that turned out to be: tens of thousands of dollars. But at the time, it seemed I had no choice. I had signed my trust to him. With a lot of misgiving, I resigned myself to the loss.

Another incident was in March, only a few weeks before this trip. We had a barbecue for our Sunday school classes. This big cookout at the ranch, and greased pig chase, was every bit Billy's idea. And it could have been a great party. But on the day of the cookout, he decided he had to read his Bible and study—all day. He wouldn't even come outside. He just glared at me when I tried to reason with him and snapped. "Can't you see I'm reading my Bible!"

We had more than a hundred people in attendance, and he left me to do all the work and supervise the whole incredible operation. I was miserable! And not only miserable but terribly embarrassed that my husband was acting so strange. That night I paced the floor in anger and frustration. To add further injury, he acted surprised that I was upset! And I didn't know what to make of the hard look on his face when he said to me, in a hushed tone, "You didn't need me anyway—look at all the help you had."

I am filled with dread. Billy returned from New Mexico over three hours ago, and he still hasn't come to greet me.

Since there's no one around for the dinner I've cooked, I make busy work to distract myself. Organizing the dishes is as good a distraction as any.

I am reaching up to a high shelf when I sense a presence in the room. Glancing down, over my shoulder, I glimpse the surprising image of a mountain man. He is standing in the archway between the kitchen and butler's pantry. He is wearing a beard, heavy jacket, and a wide-brimmed hat.

I am confused. "Bobby?" I ask. "Where is Billy?"

I climb down the kitchen ladder, and those sea-green eyes meet mine. "Oh—Billy, it's you."

21. DUELING IDENTITIES

"God whispers to us in our pleasures, but he shouts to us in our pain."
~ *C. S. Lewis*

While on his retreat in Mineral Wells, Billy wrote lovingly to me. The handwriting is not very good, not the writing of a bright, accomplished man; but Billy had terrible penmanship and could not spell. Well, actually, he *could* spell—every medical word and term in the books—but other than medical, his spelling was abysmal. And Billy was also dyslectic.

This was a big difference between him and Bobby. Bobby was not dyslectic, had beautiful handwriting, and was a good speller. This may have accounted for Bill's having to struggle academically, while school came easy to Bobby. Despite that, Billy was the one who, through much effort and determination, achieved an advanced education—making extraordinarily good grades. He accomplished his education during the years Bobby was far from the scene.

Bobby attended ten colleges but accomplished little academically. He never received a degree, though he fell only about a single semester short. I felt he was jealous of Billy in this regard. He would say with a sneer that he, unlike Billy, didn't have to, and didn't want to, conform to people's expectations. My feeling is that he was either too rebellious to be motivated, or possibly he was afraid of failure. It was, no doubt, much easier for him to claim disinterest than to try, and then possibly fail to match, or best, his brother.

One day, Virginia revealed an interesting fact. She said that when the twins were infants, she and I.B. held and cuddled Billy much more than they did Bobby. The reason Billy got so much extra attention was because he cried more and was not content.

On their second Christmas, Virginia bought little rocking chairs for the toddlers. They loved those chairs so much that she used them as pacifiers; the little twins would rock and rock and rock. I.B. was so impressed with the rocking chairs that he bought two rocking horses and rigged them to the floor in their station wagon. There being no seat belts or toddler car seats in the 1940s, the boys got to rock both in the house and in the car.

The majority of the time, the twins got along well and were constantly together. Early on they developed their own language, which was in no way like English; not even a word of it could be understood by Virginia or I.B. She said it became a cause of much concern to them. It went on for so long, they wondered if the twins would ever talk normally.

As they grew up, even though they scuffled and fought a lot, they were dependent on each other. And though they were identical in looks, until Bobby's nose was broken more than once in fistfights, their character and inward feelings and responses were very different—so different that it seemed to me, that Billy had inward feelings of turmoil in relating to his twin. Some of Billy's actions and words were strong indicators to me, off and on throughout our marriage, that he wanted to be released and set free from Bobby. I believe this secret—maybe even subconscious—wish caused him guilt in some ways. For instance, I think he overcompensated when it came to defending Bobby. He wanted, despite the evidence of Bobby's behavior, to believe that his brother was good and basically harmless. He wanted me and others to believe the same.

But Bobby was not harmless. He was a bully, and a bare-knuckle fist-fighter. I've seen him at times have almost superhuman strength and energy, and he was admired greatly for this power by both males and females. He would go to extremes to get what he wanted, and he usually wanted what someone else had. Bobby was a womanizer in general, but a girl was much more interesting to him if she was dating another boy.

Another personality trait of Bobby's: He always had to be first in any endeavor, and if he couldn't come out winning—like the time he lost a fight to a football player who was much bigger that him—he would withdraw or escape, just disappear for a while. Bobby enjoyed withholding information—sometimes teasing, sometimes just to be mean. At other times he would tell outrageous lies, seeming to test his skill at deception—and that skill was considerable. Sometimes he would eventually admit that the story wasn't true. But what he called true wasn't always truth, only truth as he saw it. High school friends would gather around and listen to Bobby, and for good or ill, he took on a certain position of influence. He could rouse wild enthusiasm in his peers, and when he pledged Sigma Nu in college, he was a favored pledge. In the rope pull, for one thing, he could excite the other pledges to do almost impossible feats.

Bobby had no problem stealing; he would just take what he wanted. If he was caught, he would explain the theft away—he was so sorry, he hadn't been paying attention to what he was doing, and this was just a mistake. He always had a story, and the victim, the few times Bobby was caught, was apologetic to him.

In spite of—or maybe because of—these traits, some desirable, some undesirable, Bobby was a leader and had total confidence in himself. He had a lot of charm and charisma and could talk his way out of any situation: He once rented a car in New York City without a driver's license. And he traveled by airplane to Hawaii with no identification. That is just two incidents. Bobby was highly intelligent, and although he fell a few hours short of his college degree, he had a good vocabulary; and if he wanted to present himself to impress others, he could do so to perfection. He was adventurous, good-looking, and had great sex appeal.

But he could also be cold and selfish and opportunistic. With only a few exceptions, loyalty was not in Bobby's character—unless he would profit from the acquaintance. Bobby abandoned his children and their mothers with impunity, leading me to believe he had little compassion or empathy, even for his own flesh and blood.

Billy, on the other hand, was compassionate and had empathy. He loved his friends and was loyal to them—that is, until he fell under Bobby's influence. Billy was equally handsome and physically about equal with Bobby, but he was not a fighter; nor was he eager to take anything that belonged to others. He saw no victory in those hurtful behaviors. But Billy was insecure despite all his accomplishments. Although he was intelligent and creative and worked hard at earning his education and building our home, he was never satisfied that what he did was good enough. Being a perfectionist, he also wanted what he considered to be the perfect family. That fantasy is a recipe for disappointment and hurt. Billy was easily hurt, and he suffered from what he perceived as rejection. When he was misunderstood or his feelings were wounded, he would worry and brood and hold it all in. But Billy was well liked, and I know that most of the rejection he felt was his own imagination.

I think that having a brother like Bobby who, underneath his healthy external appearance, had a complicated, tricky mental system, caused Billy to often misunderstand people. Also, Bobby's total confidence might have been a factor in Billy's insecurity, for when they were young he felt Bobby had a stronger presence than he did, and Bobby became dominant. But in situations where Billy felt completely accepted, he let his guard down and became the star attraction of any gathering. He excelled when attention was focused on him or he was the center of importance, as in teaching a group. He was a wonderful teacher as well as a funny and entertaining storyteller. One of his good friends said, "You won't be around Billy long before the laughing starts." But, though it sounds contradictory, in spite of his outgoing personality, he was an introvert and struggled with low self-esteem. If he wasn't participating in a central, leading way, he would withdraw from a group. Sometimes this came across to others as Billy thinking too highly of himself, but what he was feeling was that he was in the way or detracting from the occasion.

Bobby was the opposite: assertive and an extrovert. Billy was not quiet able to compete with Bobby and all his flashy behavior when they were young teens, and this must have made Billy feel inadequate. Bobby usually laid the groundwork for any activity they were involved in, and he always drove the car. Though Billy might have been as physically strong as Bobby, he was not as aggressive and angry and he was unwilling to fight, whereas Bobby looked for fights. However, Billy would fight Bobby, until one day Bobby got the best of him. Their fist-fighting each other ended then—Billy saying, "Bobby's the fighter; I'm the lover."

So it was that Billy went through his teen years in Bobby's shadow and always wrestling with Bobby's reputation. The parents of Billy's peers judged him by what they heard of Bobby, and he was accused of much he had no part in, by association—Billy being the other twin. He was injured once when he was knocked off a barstool and rendered unconscious by a young man who mistook him for Bobby.

There were quite a few traits that Billy and Bobby did have in common; most noticeably, their looks and voices where almost exactly alike. They were both exceptionally skilled with their hands and excelled in everything from surgery and carving art, to building and renovating.

Billy and Bobby were both extraordinary animal trainers. Billy enjoyed training all of his dogs, but he had one special dog, an Australian shepherd, that learned forty-one commands. I overheard him trying to explain his talent to a friend. "Animals just watch me and want to communicate. They really want to cooperate with me." Of course, Bobby's communion with animals was no different.

Both the twins were subject to melancholy at certain times of the year, the spring in particular. Around early April, the time of their birthday, they were heavy in their moods. I don't know why it was that way for Billy, but for Bobby that was the time of year that Kathleen, his first wife, was shot and killed. It could be his dark April mood had something to do with her death.

Not only were Billy's mood swings yearly but they also went in five-year cycles. Something dramatic would change in the fifth year—like, "We won't celebrate Christmas this year." He would be consumed with a thing, but then he would decide right the opposite. We would have something planned when, out of the blue, he would change his mind. Billy was plagued by a destructive element or spirit in his life that repeatedly pulled him down, like he wrote in my Bible, "Patsy, I don't know why I do the things sometimes that I don't want to do, and don't do the things I should."

The fact that Bobby was dominant, and Billy had spent his youth taking up for Bobby and making excuses, even to himself, for Bobby's behavior, made it hard for Billy to resist Bobby when he came back into his life with such force and determination.

I almost forgot another interesting thing that is different about the twins: Billy had little sense of smell. I've heard the lack of smell curbs a person's enjoyment of food—I don't think it bothered Billy in the least.

22. THE LAST PARTY

"Like an ant on a twig, both ends of which are burning, I go to and fro, not knowing what to do, and in great despair."
~ James Whitaker

"Patsy, it's a shame you can't go with Dr. Hale to visit his brother. He says those high mountains in New Mexico are beautiful."

That statement, spoken in innocence by Leigh, the receptionist at the clinic, draws the breath from my lungs and starts my heart racing. To save face, this is going to take all the willpower I can muster.

"Yes, they are spectacular, Leigh," I answer, rather louder than necessary; she's sitting across the table from me and a couple of seats down. "I have been there, and they do keep calling you back—the mountains, I mean."

I turn to Bill, sitting beside me at the long dinner table, and look calmly into his eyes. I can read his face, and he is struggling too. Surely he knew someone would give him away? And the mountains calling him back? I know better than that. Bobby, of course, is calling him back. Bobby cannot leave us alone.

Leaning forward, I address Leigh again, and those around her whose attention I have. "I would like nothing better than to go, but I can't leave my Mother. She had a stroke, you know, and is confined to a wheelchair. A trip for me is out of the question."

The extravagant meal is served, and delicious food, which I should enjoy, is tasteless. Being with all these people seems surreal. I can only think of my situation—and Billy's.

So Bill has planned to slip away and leave for Bobby's without telling me? One of the employees has inadvertently given him away: "It's a shame you can't go with Dr. Hale to visit his brother in New Mexico." I handled that shocking announcement with the grace and diplomacy of a wife who, in the years since the Unexpected Guests, has grown used to surprises, countered with pretense and covering for her husband.

Billy and I continue on, for all anyone can tell, carefree and enjoying Dr. Ellenberger's birthday party. The whole group, within earshot at our table, wants to know about Dr. Hale's legendary brother in New Mexico.

"I hear he and his wife are eking out a living with their own hands," says Clay, one of the young techs.

"They do," Billy speaks up, "and better than eke; it's a pretty abundant life. And a great way of life." He is on the defense. "They raise their own chickens, milk cows, horses, and have a herd of sheep. They raise their own food, and Bobby's wife makes homemade bread and cheeses. They preserve food too—drying, canning, and even freezing. So in the food department, they are better off than most of us."

"Dr. Hale, do they—"

"Wait, that's not all," he goes on, raising his hand against questions. "They don't have electricity on top of that mountain, but they do have running water, solar power, and an outdoor refrigerator that keeps food and meat frozen and cold the year around. Clay, you would be impressed with that contraption—everybody is—and he builds these outdoor refrigerators for other ranchers. They live like people lived a hundred years ago—self-sufficient. Bobby hunts and dresses their game. There's a feeling of freedom and accomplishment that's hard to express when you, with only your good mind and two hands, are the one responsible for your and your family's livelihood—and you succeed."

Why do I feel that Billy's long, glowing spiel is for my benefit?

"Patsy, what do you think about all that?" This is from Dr.

Ellenberger, who, in making the rounds of his guests, is standing right behind us. "I'm just wondering about the personality and characteristics of such a man."

I know George Ellenberger has met Bobby at least once; I just don't know if it was when Bobby was a Morning Star or the Marlboro Man. Apparently he wants me, not Bill, to confirm, or perhaps refute, some of his impressions from that meeting.

"You're asking me, George, so I must tell you, one man can't accomplish all that by himself. Living the simple life is not simple. Kurina, Bobby's wife, is a big factor in the success of this pioneer lifestyle. She works hard morning till night; plus she has a baby every eighteen months or so.

"But you asked me about the personality and characteristics of Bobby. He is one of the most talented men I have ever known. Like his brother sitting here, he can do anything he wants to do. He has delved into many things and, I think, accomplished what he wanted to." The five or six employees around me are still listening, so I go on: "He has done everything from flying single-engine airplanes to midwifery to managing a large family on his own self-sustaining ranch. He is an animal trainer, a rugged individualist, and a former vagabond."

"I must include his one or two shortcomings," I continue, "the most obvious being his need to influence people. Sometimes I wonder, when he meets a person, if he thinks with the first handshake, 'How can I change you?' So if you ever meet him, don't think you will escape hearing his opinions—or his preaching about his opinions." Sorry Bill, I think to myself, but I had to say that. People need to be warned.

"And he plays the guitar!" Billy adds, strumming the air and acting silly, apparently unaffected by my last comment—or trying to cover it. We all laugh at his antics.

"Patsy, I appreciate the way you handled that news," Billy says as we get into our car after the party. "I know it was a shock. You were cool."

"Oh, it was nothing," I say sarcastically, "thanks for the

compliment. You handled it pretty well yourself. Now, please tell me what all that was about."

"I'm going to see Bobby. That's it. That's what it's about."

"You've made arrangements with the hospital for time off—for a trip to New Mexico, which is bound to take at least a week, and you haven't told me a word. How come? Why would you leave me out of your plans? Didn't you think I would miss you? That I would probably notice you weren't coming home?"

"I knew you would disapprove of this trip, and I didn't need to hear it."

"You're exactly right; I do disapprove. And I'm hurt. I'm hurt, disappointed, disapproving, and a lot more. I'm scared. You were just out there with Allison and Katie, and you came back in a terrible state. After that, I am sincerely and honestly afraid for you. Your time with Bobby is doing you harm; I can feel it. I think you feel it too."

He stares straight ahead as I drive and says nothing.

"You were at Bobby's three months ago. Since then we were making some progress, I thought, toward being of one accord about his heretical thinking."

"I thought so too, Patsy. I don't really want to go. I want to break away." He bends forward, rocking back and forth—as is typical of Billy in distress.

I remember Virginia telling me about when the twins, at twenty-four months old, got their first tiny rocking chairs—right after the scarlet fever. "Those rocking chairs were their pacifiers," she said. "They would rock for hours."

"You need to pray for me, Patsy. Something irresistible is drawing me. It won't let go." He sits up and asks, "What if he is right? What if Bobby is right? What then?"

"He is *not* right! Billy, if you have any reasoning left, you know he is just spouting religious legalistic nonsense! God doesn't give Bobby Hale tedious, universal secrets. He is manipulating you. Can't you see it? You're allowing him to manipulate you with doubt and fear."

He is rocking again. My heart goes out to him. "Why did you make this decision, darling?" I ask. "You know what a pull he has on you. Why would you tempt fate?"

"It's too late to ask those questions, Patsy. I'm leaving tonight. In fact, go to the exit for Love Field. My rental car is there."

"You've arranged all that?" I ask with tears in my voice. I can't speak above a whisper.

He doesn't answer. He is not rocking now, and again, stares straight ahead. His arms are tightly folded. He has shut me out.

"I'm surprised that you even went to George's party," I say, recovering my composure. You could have left for New Mexico in the afternoon. Why keep Bobby waiting?"

"That's what I wanted to do, but it didn't work out. My absence would have disappointed George, and then you were involved...logistically problematic, to say the least. And Bobby is not waiting."

I pull off at Lemon Avenue. "What now?"

"Go toward Love Field and follow the rental signs. It's at Hertz."

"They are closed, you know." I am still hopeful.

He doesn't dignify that with an answer.

I see "Car Rentals" in the distance. "How were you so secretive about this, Bill? I paid the phone bill just this week, and I didn't see any collect calls. I know Bobby must be tickled to have you pull this off without my knowing. And when were you going to call me? I would have been worried sick about you."

"Obviously I would have called you—after I got on the road. And stop being so hard on Bobby. I told you, he doesn't know I'm coming."

I pull to the fence, outside the company parking lot; we are looking at each other through the semi-darkness. "Then why? Why would you go again so soon? I figured he must be badgering you already."

"Well, he's not. I told you I'm being drawn. I don't know how else to explain it. I don't know what's going to happen, if anything. Just know that something is calling me. I want to break away, but something overpowering compels me to act...to go. And *you're* scared? So am I. Pray for me."

I can't speak to him. If I speak, the tears will fall. I watch him get out of the car, turn toward the back, and close the door. He quickly removes a duffle bag and some things he has stashed in my trunk, and walks toward the rows of rental cars without looking back.

That's good, Billy; I would like to hide my tears. Don't look back; if you do, I can't stand it.

I sit transfixed and watch him. He walks through some opening that I try to see but can't. Then I can see him in the distance look down and scan the numbered spaces, find the car he has reserved, and throw his belongings in the back seat. He gets in and starts the engine. He must know I'm still parked here—he must, because he flashes the car lights...but only once. Maybe he is just testing them, not indicating anything to me at all; not even that he sees me.

Hope drains away as I watch his headlights weave through the parking lot, enter the access road, and melt into the flow of midnight traffic—that bright, endless stream, moving west, that has nothing to do with me.

I recall I.B.'s counsel to me before I became engaged to Billy. Apparently he had mulled over our situation and felt he should warn me.

"Billy is immature, Patsy," he said, "and he is a terrible manager. Shouldn't you think this over?"

I can still hear my youthful argument: "I'm a pretty good manager, Mr. Hale. I think together we can manage fine."

I could see no wrong in Billy; I was consumed by him. I can't live without your son, Mr. Hale, is what I was thinking.

"Is your father going to be able to handle this?"

"Dad was worried, but he and Billy talked. Billy won him over because Dad is feeling fine now."

I.B. shook his head and said with the same big grin that Billy has, "Okay, Patsy, you seem as determined as he does. I hope you kids have the very best that life has to offer."

We subsequently had the biggest, most beautiful wedding ever held at my parents' church up to that time.

Perhaps I should have taken I.B.'s words to heart. Billy was indeed—and more often than not, still is—immature. And he has always been a bad manager. Unfortunately, as it turned out, there was little I could do about his management skills.

But Billy, I was safe with you then. And you made me laugh. And we had more fun than any couple I knew.

23. THE TIE THAT BINDS

*'The acid test of our faith in the promises of God is never found in the easy,
comfortable way of life, but in the great emergencies.'*
~ Ethel Bell

"Hello, Patsy, this is Roland. How are you?"

"I'm miserable, Roland. How did you know to call me?"

"From the news I got from Brother Miles. He told me Bill has gone back out to see Bobby."

"Oh? It's true of course, he has gone back, but I'm surprised Billy told him. He didn't tell me. But I guess you know that."

"He didn't tell Brother Miles either. When Bill returned from his last trip out there, Brother Miles advised him to stay away from Bobby. It's not likely he would mention another trip to him."

"Then how did he know?"

"He had stopped by the clinic hoping to see Bill. In the office they know he is Bill's pastor, and they alerted Dr. Ellenberger. He asked if Brother Miles would speak with him in his office."

"Really? What did he say? What did he tell Brother Miles?"

"Number one, that Bill is in New Mexico. Number two, Dr. Ellenberger told Brother Miles that he was concerned about Bill. He said Bill has become withdrawn, that he doesn't enjoy seeing and interacting with people like he used to."

"What he says is true, Roland. Billy has always been friendly to

293

almost everybody. You know how outgoing he is. Now I see our circle of friends grow smaller and smaller. Friends we've known for years, even went to school with, he's indifferent to most of them now. What am I saying? He's indifferent to all of them!"

"I can believe it, Patsy. He never calls me either."

"In truth, Roland, he keeps his own counsel. I miss our friends. I need them. To say the least, I'm unhappy about his changes.

"Dr. Ellenberger told Brother Miles that Bill has grown so remote, he only wants to do surgery. How do you account for all this, Patsy—these changes?"

"Because of Bobby. It's got everything to do with Bobby. He is ruining our lives. I hope Bobby doesn't cause Billy to ruin his career."

"The way I see it, he's been working on that for years—ruining your lives. And ruining Bill's career, for that matter. He had to get settled in New Mexico, but with that accomplished, he got right back to it. I'm sorry that he has. There is another purpose for my call, Patsy. I told Trish that Bill had left again and I was going to call you. She wants to stay at the ranch with you this coming week. Call her if you will, and you two set something up."

When we hang up, I almost laugh with relief. With our children moved out and at school, Billy has left me stranded with my bedridden mother. Without waiting a minute, I dial Trish.

"Trish, it will be wonderful having you at the ranch. Please bring Roland. You don't know how welcome you two will be. I can't tell you how grateful I am."

"I think you are pretty much stranded, Patsy, and I just couldn't leave you like that. Roland will have to come to town for office hours, but we can stay with you till Thursday or Friday. And you know, for us city dwellers, the ranch will be like a little vacation."

"You're right, Trish. We will have a good time—in spite of everything. Come on out tomorrow any time you see fit; obviously I'm not going anywhere."

I want to celebrate my dear friends' arrival at the ranch by serving a favorite Texas supper. We will eat on the deck and will have grilled steaks, baked potatoes, and marinated grilled vegetables. Later in the evening, while we watch a movie, or just sit on the deck and talk, I will serve vanilla ice cream with my strawberry-blueberry-raspberry sauce. In some places this sauce is called fruits of the forest, or something similar, but I call it TexasGrits. I feel infinitely better—which is still not great in light of my husband's behavior—knowing I will have Trish and Roland's company for the next few days; their compassionate company, I might add, because I will have two thoughtful people to help me through this difficult week.

The weather has turned dry, and the breeze, in crossing this hill, carries away what few mosquitoes and small insects there may be buzzing around. This evening will be perfect for dining outside. I must admit, it feels good to be preparing something special. Not since the big Sunday school barbecue that Billy planned, then refused to participate in, have we had company over. I lay bright place mats on the round table and get out my most festive, hand-painted and fired dinnerware from Pueblo Mexico. The start of my friends' self-proclaimed vacation will be a special event.

Roland and Trish arrive in the late afternoon, and I welcome them with tall, frosty glasses of my special peach tea. I usher them into the sitting room where Mother, already bathed and fed and in her wheelchair, is waiting to greet them. "Trisha," Mother says, "you've cut your hair! I love it."

Indeed Trish has a new geometric cut that brings her shining black hair swinging beneath her chin. She is a small woman with big brown eyes and a flashing bright smile. She adores Roland and laughs at his jokes as much as or more than anyone.

An hour later, Mother is worn out. Trish and Roland love my mother, and she has put a lot of energy into entertaining them, mainly with tales of the ranch when Dad was alive. I prop her up in her bed and turn the TV to a game show—she still loves to solve those problems. "Mother is comfortable, Trish; let's go out and start the coals. We can talk out there."

Roland is in an analytical mood when he joins us, and he recalls a conversation he and I had some time back. "Do you remember telling me that you felt one reason you are able to resist Bobby and his fallacies is because of your parents? That, since childhood, they have made sure you were well founded in their faith and their church?"

"Yes. I have my parents' upbringing to ground me. I won't be swayed by Bobby."

"But, Bill, you say, did not have this foundation?"

"No, he didn't. But he did eventually start to question. I guess it's normal for people to say, 'What's the meaning of all this?'"

"Sure, it's normal. And when he needed some answers, you took him to your church, which is ordinarily what happens."

"Right."

"He believed and was comfortable there until Bobby came along and precipitated a whole landslide of confusion for Bill.

"Yes. Billy loved Birchman Church, until Bobby decided he knew more than anyone there, including Brother Miles."

"This trip will be a struggle for him, you know. There is a tie that binds identical twins that we are only beginning to understand. They are basically the same person."

"But, Roland, even being genetically the same, they have always been so different. They looked alike, but they were not the same person at all. In fact, I would say that they were, and maybe still are, the opposite of each other. Do you think that's possible? Good twin, bad twin?"

"Maybe that's close to the truth. Mirror images? Maybe. But Patsy, I believe Bill, the man we both know, desires to be the man God wants him to be. But Bill finds himself overcome by the strong ties with his twin. On the other hand, I'm not convinced about Bobby. He is a complicated man, full of contradictions. Think of his past life. In one area, money—you said he loved all the finer things that money could bring."

"Yes he did, but he accused us of being vain! It was a while back, but he had to have fine clothes, fine cars, fine restaurants. And I told you he went through his uncle's inheritance like water."

"Yes, and, as you say, 'a while back' his tastes became so lavish that when the money ran out, he began to steal from others, even you, to satisfy his appetites?"

"Yes, he did."

"Then he decided—tell me if I'm wrong; I'm trying to get this sorted out for my own understanding—even before his conversion, that 'materialism' is wrong, immoral even. And to put it his way, things aren't important. Possessions don't matter. Property gets in your way."

"Yes, I've heard him say all those things."

Roland continues, "He doesn't want to own riches now, he wants to own people—and their minds. Bobby likes to be different, and he craves importance. He is again stealing to support his new appetite; he is stealing from the Bible by falsifying its meaning and claiming that he is the man with the answers. This is to confuse and draw people to him, especially Bill. In spite of his claim of conversion, I'm seeing with my own eyes, metaphorically speaking, evil triumph in his life."

I sit quietly and think about what Roland has said. I think of Bobby's life: the cruel fights in school, Kathleen killed and her family crushed with grief, money and goods stolen, wives and children abandoned. And I'm tempted to add: Roland, evil has been there a long time—we are seeing it triumph again in his life.

But Roland continues, "Bill has been acting out a lot of self-destructive behavior in the past year; or I would say even the past two years. He is going through a transformation. There is no doubt about it, and it could go either way. I am praying that he will not follow Bobby."

"He did tell me, Roland: 'I don't know what, if anything, will happen out there.' Like you say, I think he has a real battle raging within himself. From what he said, he doesn't have any definite plans to follow Bobby. And here's something else he said: 'I don't want to go. I want to break away; but something is drawing me.' He repeated that twice."

"That's hopeful, Patsy. We don't know how this will turn out, but remember he did return with renewed strength after your first family visit. Let's pray that he returns, this time strengthened and invigorated. "

I think we are ready to change the subject because Trish says, "We have a full moon tonight. Can we turn off the lights, Patsy, and enjoy these glorious heavens? It's not a sight that can be seen in the city."

"We certainly can. I do it often. The switch is inside. I will check on Mother while I'm in there."

I look in on Mother, whose room, once an office, is right beside the kitchen. She is still alert and watching her program. She looks at me and gives her head a little shake, meaning she is fine and doesn't need anything.

When I return, Roland and Trish are together on the double glider. "The moon is so bright, it dims the stars," Roland observes. "We've talked tonight about good and evil, but I've heard said that the full moon is associated with an increase in both good and bad events."

"How so?"

"A couple of my physician friends have confirmed that during the full moon, there is more activity in the hospital emergency rooms, for instance. More health traumas, more accidents, and more births."

"That's interesting. I remember that two of our babies were born during the full moon."

"See there?"

"I don't remember about the other two. The moon might have been full for all I know." I think about our four children and how fond they are of Trish and Roland. For the past couple of years, they have sought and trusted Roland's guidance much more than their dad's.

We talk on into the night, and finally, after years, I tell Roland and Trish about Bobby rummaging through my closet and about his eventual cleansing us of toys and television. "You had wanted him out of our house, Roland, which we wouldn't do. After refusing your advice, I was so embarrassed I couldn't bring myself to tell you."

"That was just a start," Roland says. "There is something going on here. I think he will do it again."

"I do, too, Roland. I felt it then, and I still feel it—that he will exact more from me than toys and a television set. When he was in my closet, he saw all the jewelry my dad had made for me over the years, and called it vanity. I could hear him slide my clothes hangers around, and he called my clothes vanity. He told Kurina that he held me responsible for Billy's materialism. 'What is she doing to my poor brother? She is the one responsible for his materialism' is the way he put it. I know, Roland, he wants to liberate me from my belongings."

"He is not like us," Roland says. "He has a sense of entitlement that is alien to most people. Who would prowl through another person's—even their own wife's—closet? Much less a sister-in-law."

"Billy never did, unless I specifically asked him to hand me a jacket or something. Other than that, I doubt he ever opened my closet door."

"Very few people would. It bothers me that Bill, while I'm sure he didn't think it was okay, was still unwilling to approach his brother about it. I guess you were afraid to confront either of them? Afraid of their ganging up on you, so to speak?"

"Right. And, despite my caution, that's exactly what they did do."

"That moon has moved across the sky quite a ways, Patsy," Trish says, yawning. "We're about ready to turn in. Let's just pray tonight that Bill's visit will have the good effect that Roland mentioned. Maybe Bill will throw off the hold Bobby has on him and return here the same man we used to know and love."

"Oh, Trish that's what I'm longing for. There has to be more in store for him than this downward spiral. Even Dr. Fields said so after Billy survived that awful boat accident."

"Yes," Roland says, "God gave Bill another chance." He made a long pause. "That's all I can say about that now. The rest is up to him."

24. I THOUGHT I HEARD MY BROTHER CALL MY NAME

"Be not deceived; God is not mocked."
~ Galatians 6:7

Ronnie called to let me know Bill had just telephoned him. "Doc is back in town, Patsy. I'm going to pick him up at the car rental then take him to the clinic for his bicycle."

Now Billy has finally made his way home from Bobby's. From the minute he pedals up to the house, I can tell he is restless and ready to talk. I am not ready. I dread hearing what he has to say. This trip has been just one too many trips to Bobby's lair. "Lair" is how I've come to think of it: a place that's risky for the unsuspecting. How has Bobby influenced Billy this time I wonder? I watch him take off his bike shoes. Again he has worn them, clacking and scraping, all the way through the house. I hand him a cool, wet cloth to bathe his face, and he finally looks into my eyes. "What's with this worried look?"

"I'm no longer worried, Billy. You are home safe. I guess it takes time for the worry to wear off." I give him the best smile my lips will permit. The truth is, how could I not be worried? Bobby's influence on Billy has proved harmful over and over. I doubt this trip will be any different. Even his close friend and partner, Dr. Ellenberger, had told Brother Miles, "Bobby is not good for Bill." So, though I dread hearing about it, I am being swept along. Bobby's clout has obviously consumed Billy, and I have no choice but to ride this out.

I pour us some iced tea, and we perch around the kitchen island. "Well, tell me all about it," I say. "Was Bobby surprised? What did you all do this time?"

Billy is antsy and within two sentences he jumps up and starts pacing—not looking at me very much, just pacing and talking. "Bobby didn't know I was coming. I didn't have anything planned, you know, like a big surprise or anything. I didn't know what would happen or if I would even be welcome. I was compelled against my will to go. That's the truth, and I told you that. I drove all night and most of the next day."

"I do hope you pulled off the road for a nap at least?"

"No. I was tired but wide awake, until I got to Ledoux. When I got to Ledoux I still had that mountain climb. Then I was tempted to sleep. But I didn't give in. Hiking up the road, I almost fell asleep on my feet. Then I came to a bend; it was where the property line fence comes out and meets the road and runs along beside it. Right there, hanging over the fence, I saw robes. They were white. I counted nine. I had no idea what the robes were for, but when I saw them, a chill went through me." Billy, still standing, leans over the kitchen island and looks into my eyes. "And I thought I heard my brother call my name. I was shocked to hear that, and I wanted to get away from that spot. I hurried on. Then I heard our secret whistle. We have used that whistle to call each other since we were little kids. I thought I was imagining things. Under the circumstances, you know, the drive, not sleeping, not eating, it wouldn't be the strangest thing in the world to hallucinate."

Wow, this is quite an admission. Billy acknowledges the possibility of wrongful thinking under extreme circumstances! Roland had warned me several times that sleep deprivation and fatigue, and constant badgering by Bobby, could lead Billy to flawed thinking, even brainwashing, but I had never heard Billy admit to such a thing.

"But I wasn't imagining. I answered the whistle, and when I got to the end of the road, Bobby was standing there. He said he had been waiting for me.

"'How did you know I was coming?' I asked him.

"'God heard my prayer,' he said. 'I knew you would come. You are here to be baptized. There are eight other followers here. You saw their robes hanging on the fence? The ninth one is yours.'

"'Baptized again? Why?' I asked him.

"'We will have a lesson on that very subject tonight. Then tomorrow I will baptize the nine of you,' he said, 'and it will be done God's way.'

"Patsy, that night I understood his teaching perfectly and powerfully. Before it was over, I had been awake almost three days, but what he said rang clear and true."

Roland's warning! The thought sits heavy in my mind.

"Before dawn, we walked to the bend in the road and put on our robes. In that cold little creek that runs down the mountain from behind the cabin, as the sun broke over us, Bobby baptized us—as is pleasing to God."

These words are chilling to me. It is obvious that Billy has attached a lot of significance to every word and gesture regarding Bobby. I nearly despair at the notion of trying to convince him otherwise.

"Patsy, you too, and the children, and your Mother, must be baptized again. Excuse me… I don't even mean 'again'; not again, because you weren't ever baptized. Not really. The sooner we can arrange it, the better." He says this with the urgent look of someone who is already making a plan.

"Billy, what are you saying? And why would you say such a thing?"

"Why? Because it's true! You're not listening to me!" All of a sudden, he is loud and excited. "You are not baptized! I'm telling you. And you are not living right. I'm not either! Brother Miles has deceived us. He needs to be exposed. He needs to be thrown out of that church. The man is a viper!"

Billy's words unnerve me to the point of panic. I stare into his eyes—they are anxious and empty, not familiar anymore. I don't know what to say to my husband. Bill has come back from Bobby's more misled than I expected. All of our hopeful prayers did not counter the strong tie between these twins. "There is a strong tie that binds twins that we don't yet understand," Roland had said. I wonder if it was inevitable, or at least predictable, that Billy's will would be weakened by that *irresistible pull*. He had told me, "Patsy, I am drawn irresistibly to go to Bobby—though I don't want to go. Please pray for me."

Not knowing how to answer Billy's awful charges toward Brother Miles or his demand that we all subject ourselves to Bobby's baptizing, I decide to stall. "Darling, we have a lot of things to talk about. I know you are tired and hungry. Why don't I fix your favorite meal, and then we can discuss everything while we have dinner? And it's so beautiful outside—you might enjoy a swim while I cook."

Half expecting him to turn angry and tell me how worldly I am, I'm relieved when he says, "Sounds good. Didn't I see some tea in the fridge?" I hand him another glass of peach tea and watch him wander haltingly toward the pool—a stranger with a strange step, who may not belong here anymore, who has been influenced from far afield, and who has brought back grim warnings and accusations that are not helpful. "You're not living right!" "You're not baptized!" And worse of all, "Brother Miles is a viper."

As I prepare Billy's dinner—pork chops on the kitchen grill, baked beans, grilled corn on the cob, and lemon icebox pie—I think about the things he said and ponder how to handle this situation. I cannot let his terrible statements stand without challenge. But challenging Bill is *not* something I do well. No doubt he will try to back up everything he says with Scripture. And probably most of his backups will be some remote verse from the Old Testament that Bobby has singled out to twist the meaning of. This is not going to be pleasant. I wish I had the children here… No, actually, I don't wish they were here. It would be painful for them to hear their dad talking like this—not that his evolving personality is anything new to them. The children have been witness to his changes and his unreasonable expectations, and to his distancing himself from our friends, and even from them. Yes, unfortunately, before long they will hear all his new demands. With Billy wanting us to be baptized again, and start "living right," he will—unless I can change his mind—be confronting them soon enough.

I don't know how this evening will play out, so I give Mother her dinner first. In case things turn unpleasant, I want Mother to be comfortable and in her room—let's hope distracted with her TV programs.

Not long after this, Bill—with the cruelty and selfishness of a fanatic—takes my mother's television from her room, carries it outside the house, and destroys it by stoning.

I gaze out the kitchen window and across the yard at Billy relaxing by the pool and think: Why interrupt a good thing? He seems to be almost tranquil now, so let's eat out there; it's our favorite spot for a meal anyway. Perhaps in that peaceful setting, our discussion will be more calm.

Everything is ready. The mouth-watering aroma of Texas barbecue follows me out the door. I load up a big serving tray, and in two quick trips to the kitchen, I have set up one of Billy's favorite meals in his favorite spot.

Since pork chops are Billy's favorite cut of meat, I have presented them to my family numerous times, and numerous ways, and they've always been a hit. "After fixing these pork chops for the thousandth time," I say, teasingly to Billy as I pour his tea, "I wonder if Julia Childs has any more talent than I do." He is interested in the food, but he doesn't give me so much as a smile, and his eyes are still strange and anxious. "Billy, this is your favorite meal, and I fixed a lemon icebox pie for your dessert." Even that fishing around for a compliment garners no response from him. I doubt he even heard me.

In spite of our idyllic setting, the air is tense with Billy's preoccupied mind. He eats his meal without so much as looking up and I wonder what is he thinking, planning, scheming? His behavior, distant and unreachable, fills me with dread. Soon he will once again assail me with Bobby's unreasonable demands and wrong beliefs. Watching him eat, I try to calm myself by thinking: Patsy, you've already heard the worst of it; he can't come up with anything more outrageous than what he's already said. *In a few minutes I will learn that I have not yet been hit by his 'ton of bricks.'*

Dessert is always mandatory for Billy. He has managed to be distracted and quiet through the meal, but as soon as he finishes the lemon pie he starts acting out of character. He is confrontational and is trying to bully me, not just convince me, of his newfound theology—if you can call it that. Charming manipulation is typically the way he finally wins me over, but now his approach is one of vengeance, of settling scores. It is as if a desperation to teach Bobby's belief has taken over. The main target of his anger at "having been led astray" is our beloved pastor, Brother Miles, who is a godly man and is well schooled in the Bible. Billy says that Bobby had, once again, reminded him of how badly we had been duped by our pastor, who was, after all, just a man—a man who doesn't know the truth and doesn't want to learn.

I counter him with his own prior belief and knowledge, and the fact that he once vehemently rejected Bobby's heresy. But reminding him of that only makes him angrier. "I was deceived!" He has both hands and his eight fingers pointing at his chest and is all but yelling at me. "We were all deceived! Can't you understand?"

No, Billy, I think, I don't understand; but I do understand this: My battle is not just with you but with other influences that have taken hold in your mind. "Darling," I try to reason with him, "how can you believe someone who has followed a Maharishi for years? And then he was led astray by gypsy philosophy? And what of the occult practices he told us of—witch-doctor stories with trees bending and sending messages, and all sorts of other strange phenomena? He would have had you believe all of that too. What if you had fallen for that?"

My efforts are useless. I am getting nowhere with him. He is bound up in Bobby's world and cannot, or will not, break loose. Bobby has always been the dominant twin; now it looks like Billy has, at last, truly become his pawn.

Abruptly Billy stops pacing, spins around to glare at me, and blurts out, "I will never go back to that church! And that's not all— we've got to sell this house and get out! I want to sell it now! Within twenty-four hours! You can give it away if you want to!"

My knees weaken. I can't see so well. Thin gray twists of something float before me, and between us. Things are terribly wrong. I'm bewildered by what I hear. He has already separated himself from our friends; now he'll never go back to the church? And his career and our security? What about that? Did he say something about the house? Did Billy just say we've got to sell the house? This house is almost paid for. Even with all of Bill's expensive updates and renovations, we've almost paid it off. We saved this house from demolition. It was a joint effort for us and the children. We all love our home. The house means the land too—Daddy's land, rich in memories for me and my brother. The land I've loved all my life.

If I didn't already fully comprehend my situation, I do now—my family, my world as I know it, is falling apart.

I watch him: angry, pacing, threatening, saying irrational things.

"Please stop, Billy!"

But he only grows louder. I listen in disbelief as a chasm drops open between us.

25. A LITTLE WHILE TO REMINISCE

"For everything there is a season."
~ *The Bible*

I realize now that from the time Billy entered the house yesterday, he was already consumed by Bobby's beliefs and plans. Knowing Billy, once he decides on an action—and it seems he has decided—things move fast. To avoid being swept along by arbitrary events, I have no choice but to steel myself and keep up. Last night, even though my heart was breaking, I was composed enough to realize that one of us has to remain rational. Since he has lost that ability, I figure that job will fall to me.

This morning, watching Billy sleep, heavy and loud, I imagine his exhaustion must be like a warrior after a battle. I think of the battle he fought with me last night: his urgency to move from our home, change our religion, and change our lives. That battle he partially won, I reflect as I walk softly to my dressing room, for I have been in battle myself, and have decided to yield to him—on one front, at least—the house. Part of my being rational is realizing that I cannot keep this big place without Billy's help. The other battle, he has lost—the duel between himself and his twin. A duel of identities that has lasted their whole lives, and has ended with Billy's surrender.

I prepare myself for the day ahead, wishing the weather would cooperate with me, turn sour and match my gloomy mood. Maybe I can dress the part. Pulling on my least favorite black sweater and black pants, I look in the mirror—not nearly bleak enough. Oh well, I've always looked good in black.

As I start to leave the room, I notice the telephone sitting inches from Billy's head. For one brief instant I want to pick up that phone and say loudly and vengefully, "Hello, Milton! Billy wants to sell the house... Yeah, in twenty-four hours. Think you can move it for us? No? Well, then find somebody and give it away. Yes, Billy says he doesn't care. He says I can give it away."

But I would never do that, especially now. I don't want to wake him. I don't want to hear him. I don't want to hear him rehash last night, or talk about Bobby, or about moving to New Mexico, or anything else. I leave the room, easing the door shut behind me. I need this morning to myself.

Downstairs I take my coffee and kitchen phone onto the deck. It's cool and fresh out here, and so lovely. My plan is to call Milton Harvey, a realtor and our good friend since high school. (He was even better friends with Bobby.) It's going to break my heart, but it is time to make this call—before I lose my resolve. I start to dial, hesitate, check my watch—it's so early. Milton won't be in his office for another hour or two.

Moving across the deck, I sink into a lounge chair and try to relax. There may not be many mornings like this left to me. Casting my gaze slowly around the yard and down to the valley below, I spot several deer, our wild and welcome residents, grazing where Dad's cattle used to graze. Continuing my visual sweep of the landscape hungrily, like for the last time seeing and remembering, my eyes come to rest on the pool in its beautiful setting among the oaks. When we moved the house, we built the pool before we started with any renovations. With the hard work we anticipated and the hot summer ahead, Billy and I knew that having a pool to cool off and play in would make our work much lighter, and our children much happier. And it did make them happy. I can almost see them dive and splash, and hear their laughter.

Feeling a timelessness around me, I continue my survey of the grounds. My gaze falls on our impressive dog run—Bill designed it and hired some of the youth from our church to build it. That was our first summer here. Billy paid them twice the minimum wage, and they worked on it all summer, putting in sleeping stalls, antique tubs for bathing and dipping, and a self-flushing cleaning system. There are actually seven runs, and the entire project is surrounded by the most expensive double-duty fencing money can buy. Like everything Billy sets his hands to, it was truly the Taj Mahal of dog runs, and became a sightseeing attraction for dog trainers and breeders. It sits empty now.

The dog run is so much like Bill—such a good example of his extreme perfectionism. But it is not the only Taj Mahal he built; he also built the Taj Mahal of duck blinds on Lake Proctor in Comanche County. That was years ago. His friends teased him about building such a fine duck blind, and they named it the Taj Mahal. But Bill had the last laugh. When a sudden violent storm came through, it wrecked and blew away all the blinds on one end of the lake. But when the storm was over, the Taj Mahal stood alone—almost untouched.

Mother and Bill are still asleep, but not for long, I'm afraid. Maybe Milton is available now. I will have him list the house with three-and-a-half acres of land. I want to keep the rest of the land; since Bill didn't even mention the land last night, I don't think it will occur to him. I dial Milton's number and get an immediate "Harvey's Real Estate."

"Milton, I'm so glad you're in."

"Patsy! We haven't talked in a while. How are you guys?"

"Not great, Milton, but we can talk about that later. Right now...the purpose of this call..." My throat tightens. My ears are hurting. I can't say the words—I didn't know it would be this hard. I take a deep breath.

"Yes, Patsy?" Milton quizzes. "Are you okay?"

"Billy wants to sell the house," I manage to say in a rush, my voice cracking.

"I'm sorry, Patsy. It sounds like this is not what you want."

"It's okay, Milton. I'll be all right. Anyway, he wants to sell it fast—within twenty-four hours, though I know that's impossible."

"Yeah, I would say so. I can try for thirty days. That, too, is unrealistic. But I can try."

"My point is, Milton, I want you to list it to sell fast. Bill even said, 'Give it away if you want to.'"

"Sounds like he is in a choice mood. I would like to talk to him, but he has dropped me like a hot potato."

"I know, Milton, he's dropped all of his friends. But I will work with you. I'm just saying, list it to sell ASAP."

"I'll do my best, Patsy. I'll be out later to take pictures."

"Milton, I hear Billy in the kitchen. I'm out of time."

26. THE JUDGEMENT TABLE

"Judge not that you be not judged. For with what judgment you judge, you shall be judged: and with what measure you mete, it shall be measured to you again."
~ Matthew 7:1/2

He hounds me now, day and night. Unless he's at work, doing mostly surgeries, Bill is harassing me. He follows me around the house so closely I barely have privacy in the bathroom, and he subjects me to his preaching late into the night.

It is in Bill's makeup to start a project and see it through to the bitter end. Now his project is converting me to Bobby's doctrine. He is obsessed with this mission, assigned to him by Bobby, I'm sure, and talks of nothing else. When he is here, I am a prisoner.

Word rapidly gets around of my predicament, from the clinic to Brother Miles to my friends at church.

Brother Miles—what a blessing he's been to us over the years—comes to visit. He would like to talk with Bill—try to reason with him. But his attempt to restore some sanity to Billy's thinking fails. Finally, he says, "Bill, you are scaring Patsy with the way you're talking."

Bill was ready to end this visit, and spat his angry reply as he showed Brother Miles the door: "If finally hearing the truth is scaring her, so be it!"

A couple of weeks ago I would have thought it impossible, but things are looking… I don't want to say so hopeless… I'll just say things look so unpromising that I am actually eager to sell the house.

I know how to get a house ready to sell; I've sold two of our houses in the past, and at the moment, I'm in the right frame of mind. I will prune the hedges, plant flowers, and hang baskets of shade-loving flowers and pots of ferns on the front porch. Inside I will polish all the hardwood flooring; touch up with a little paint here and there—it doesn't need much; organize and restock the freezer; clean, organize, and restock the pantry. Then I'll have Milton hold an open house. I want those potential buyers to feel they can't live without this house. The work will keep me busy. Work is my old friend when I want to focus my attention and lessen my discontent. I will start on my inside projects immediately and call my friend and his landscaping crew to help me next week. Also I can count on Allison and Ronnie to help me.

Allison and Ronnie were devastated, as were our other children, when I told them that their dad wanted to sell the house. I know all the children will grieve the loss of our home for a long time, but they are strong and realistic and have their own lives. They also understand that things have deteriorated out of control with their father. "I've already called Milton and put the house on the market," I told the children. "What I want to do now is prepare it to sell. If your dad turns around, changes his mind…it will be wonderful. But I can't wait for that unlikely event."

The short story is that in two weeks' time I, along with my wonderful friend and his Davis Lawn Service, as well as Allison and Ronnie, have accomplished everything on my to-do list. The spring cleaning—that's what Allison and I have been calling it—is finished, and I let Milton know that he can arrange an open house—the sooner the better. "The house and grounds are beautiful, Milton. I will bake fresh bread for the cozy aroma of home, and this place will be irresistible."

During all this "spring cleaning" Bill's lecturing never stops. In the evenings, until late at night, I stay busy polishing silver, folding clothes—anything I can lay my hands on while Billy follows me around, reading and interpreting the Bible. I know he is trying to wear me out and wear me down; Bobby has taught him well. But the sleep deprivation goes both ways, and finally, after hours of this, Bill falls asleep, exhausted, sometimes on a chair or the sofa. The next day, since he does most surgeries in the mornings, he gets up and leaves the house very early.

From my dining room window, I can see across the porch and front yard, through the scattered oaks, the length of the curving drive, almost to the lane that goes down to the access road. It is Monday afternoon and Billy is due to ride up anytime. Not that I look forward to his arrival and his haranguing, but I glance casually out the window on my way to the kitchen. I do see Bill's arrival—not on the blue bicycle, but in a familiar-looking red pickup truck. Yes, I believe this is the same pickup—Joe's pickup that he drove to New Mexico in with Tim and Gerald and a truck bed full of provisions. That was just a few months ago, on the boys' first trip to Bobby's with Billy and the girls. The truck is arriving, spilling over with people. I'm used to crowds, but at the same instant I think "no problem," I spot Bobby!

If my reaction isn't panic, it is close. I run through the kitchen and into my mother's room—I guess because it's the farthest room from the front of the house. I am as shocked as she is to find myself, my face drained of blood and my heart racing, in the room with my helpless mother. Poor thing. She is staring at me, her mouth agape.

"What's wrong?" she asks.

I laugh and hug her. "Nothing, Mother. I didn't mean to interrupt your program." I have done all in my power to insulate Mother from the turmoil around here; now, in my fear, I almost gave it away. She doesn't know our house is for sale… I don't know how I'm going to handle that. Something will come to me later.

I grab the telephone handset from the kitchen and run back to the front window. I need to call somebody. Someone needs to know what is going on here! I can't think straight, but I do remember a number—my old friend, Susanne. Her fiancé, Wayne, lives on the next hill to the east of my property. He and Susanne know a lot about our deteriorating circumstances—they are some of our friends who have been rejected by Billy and know that he is now a disciple of Bobby's. "Susanne," I get right to the point, "the last person on the face of this earth that I want at my home has just arrived."

"Bobby!" she guesses.

(She has had a low opinion of Bobby for many years, even though after his conversion, she still styled his hair and helped Kurina with what little Kurina permitted. She, like the rest of us, thought at the time that Bobby had changed. Her disappointment with Bobby had come many years ago when Susanne and her twin sister Zoë had lived in the same apartment house as Billy and Bobby. At that time she was establishing herself as a young hairstylist. She and Zoë invited Billy and Bobby to dinner one evening, and Bobby found the jar containing Susanne's tip money. Like a common thief to a stranger, he helped himself to her tips. That was pretty typical of his stealing; as though his victims wouldn't notice.)

"Yes, Susanne, and I'm watching him, right now, drag himself out of a pickup truck... I don't have time to talk. Just be aware that he is here, and if you want to stop by and see Mother, or check that I haven't been kidnapped—and I'm not joking—then please do. You know what I'm putting up with from Billy; now it will be doubled."

"I'll come see your mother when I get a break from the shop. And we will talk every day," she says.

At this front window, where I can look out without being seen, I watch the truck unload its cargo of unexpected, and highly unwelcome, guests. At least they must think they're going to be guests—Bobby has brought Naomi, his oldest daughter, and Leah, his youngest. These three are certainly a long way from home. Did they come all the way here in Joe's truck? Apparently they did, which tells me that at least Joe, maybe Tim and Gerald, too, have been with Bobby in New Mexico.

I will forever hold Bill responsible, and I think God will hold him responsible, for taking these trusting young men into Bobby's trap in the first place; right into his compound where he could infiltrate their minds and confuse their thinking. I thought Tim was finished with Bobby, but apparently not. As it turns out, it took years for those three to gradually, one by one, shake their puzzlement and clear their minds enough to function maturely.

Another thing that bothers me about seeing Bobby and Naomi here is that I know Kurina is well into another pregnancy. When I got her recent letter, she had the feeling, according to past experience, that she would have an early delivery. She needs both of them with her.

Billy lifts his bicycle out of the truck and rolls it toward the house. The entire truckload of passengers falls into lockstep behind him.

I sit inside the foyer on the bench across from the door and wait. When Bill opens the door, Bobby and his daughters push into the room. I cannot bring myself to stand. I cannot bring myself to accept a hug from Bobby. And I just can't be civil to him. I look past him, trying to see the young men on the porch. "Tim," I call, "you guys come on in." I don't know what Bill expected of me but I head straight to the kitchen while saying, "I'll get everybody some iced tea."

"Make mine coffee," Bobby orders.

"I'll make some," I call over my shoulder.

Bill comes into the kitchen by himself. "You're being very cold to Bobby. I want you to stop it. I want him respected in this house."

In answer, I grind the coffee as high as it will go. "I've got to make his coffee," I shout over the grinder. Then I turn to him. "I don't like him being here, Billy, I'm sorry. He's got a wife at home who is almost ready to deliver yet another baby for him. Where is his respect for her? You and he have just been together. He needs to be at home!"

I don't know what's come over me—I have never, in our marriage, talked to Bill like this. Before he can get over his shock, I apologize. "I'm sorry, Billy. I didn't mean to say those things to you. But I got a letter from Kurina just the other day and I'm worried about her. She thinks she might deliver early. And not only is Bobby here, but Naomi, too. She needs to be with her mother."

"Patsy, you worry too much, and you talk too much. Bobby knows what he's doing. A woman couldn't be in better hands than my brother's."

Even if those hands are eight hundred miles away? I want to ask. But I don't say a word. I've said too much already.

I put ice in glasses and ask him, "Billy, can you take this tray of glasses? I'll bring the tea." We set these on the dining room table, and I immediately leave the room, calling, "I'll bring your coffee."

I bring a jar of salsa, a bag of chips, and Bobby's coffee with whipping cream. I have the cream because Billy had started drinking coffee that way, too.

I watch this group from my chair across the room. I have the uneasy feeling that I know what is going on here. You're in Texas, Bobby, because Bill, failing to weaken me, has called in reinforcements. I know what your plans are, Bobby. I know because I got a letter from your wife:

Patsy, you will be so welcome in our home. We have prepared a place for you here... You know I am six months...

Those words of welcome from Kurina—so innocent—sent chills through me. She is expecting them to bring me back. But no, Bobby, I will not be going to the place you and your family have prepared for me. Though their intentions are naïve, yours are not. Yes, Bobby, though you can't tell from the pleasant look I have frozen on my face, I know you are here to strengthen Billy and kidnap me!

I need to say something; Bill will think I'm too unwelcoming. I ask the question that has been bothering me. "When you came out, did some of you have to ride in the pickup bed—on the highway?"

A moment's silence. The boys won't say anything that might indict Bobby. Then he spoke up. "Yeah, we took turns. We made it mighty comfortable back there, too."

And mighty dangerous, I thought, but I didn't comment further.

I go in and out of the room three or four times: refills, check my mother, anything to avoid sitting at that table with Bobby. As I stay busy, I do pay attention to the three—as Bill referred to them one time—*disciples*. The boys' attitude toward me has changed. Only Tim will return my smile—and only a quick, weak grin at that. They know

316

what is going on. They have overheard, and perhaps were part of, the plans that were made before they left New Mexico. Their countenances are altered from the carefree young men who left this house, with Bill and the girls to visit Bobby, only a few months ago. They have a hard, uneasy look on their faces and they watch, expectantly, Bobby's every move.

Naomi also seems remote. I feel very much an outsider—I would say I feel like a target. Bobby tries to engage me in some kind of friendly conversation, but I ask only about the children and Kurina. He leaves me alone as long as I am bringing out the food—now it's tuna sandwiches. I make tuna sandwiches just like Miss Ivory, the twins' grandmother's maid. They were a favorite treat of Billy's and Bobby's, and before today, have always brought back good memories.

Finally, everyone has had his fill and the group grows quiet. Bobby and Billy jump up simultaneously to revive the action. Both of them say, "We've got work to do. Let's go."

"We need to set up things outside," Bobby says loudly to Bill as the group files out the front door. I feign total disinterest and start to clear the table.

Within an hour I clean up the kitchen, feed and take care of Mother, and am thinking of the people who arrived this evening at my house. I watch them from the dining room window. I guess this will be my lookout since I have a clear view of what's going on in the drive. From here it looks like, in the driveway, at the point where the turnaround meets the drive again, they have set up...a table? A table with a big chair. And they are positioned so that no one can come near our house. On the table are two lanterns and they burn brightly in the early dusk. I see Bill and Tim set up Bill's North Face tent under the oaks right in the middle of our turnaround, squarely aligned with my front door. Who is going to sleep in the tent? Glancing again at the table and its lantern display, I realize that my car is blocked in place. Such a threatening thing for them to do! I am cornered. I call Susanne again and tell her of the continuing saga and that they have blocked my car. I also call my cousin Buck to let him know of my dilemma. I just feel it's necessary to let people on the outside know what's going on. I call Milton, too. "Milton, don't bring anybody to see this house after all. I don't think a potential buyer would be impressed with what's going on here."

The days go by slowly. The camping site, and the Judgment Table they set up has effectively barred entry to and exit from the property. These unwelcome guests have pulled out one of my beautiful antique tables, a small Queen Anne dining table that is over a hundred years old, and set it across the driveway. Lanterns are on the table, and on the ground beside the table, and they burn day and night. *These must be the same lanterns that Roland admired in the old Army truck so many years ago.*

When Bobby is not sitting in the chair at the table, one of the four young people is: Tim, Joe, Gerald, or Naomi. To visit the house—or leave it, for that matter—one must approach the person sitting there and be approved for entry or exit—thus the designation of it as the Judgment Table. It is a humiliating experience to be judged acceptable by this group, and after a couple of my friends from church came to check on me, nobody else came—other than Big Mike, Mother's beloved home healthcare nurse.

The first time the poor man drove up to the Judgment barricade and saw this ridiculous outpost, Big Mike sensed trouble. When Bobby judged him worthy to enter the house, Big Mike told me all about his encounter. He was incredulous. After seeing the campground in our front drive—kerosene lanterns burning and smoking in midday, and having to contend with Bobby, sitting at the Judgment Table, scowling at him—he didn't know what to think. I had failed deliberately to tell him of our predicament. Big Mike would not have needed to know, or be troubled about our problems if Bobby and his crowd had not showed up. With concern written all over his face, he asks me, "Patsy, what is happening here? Are you okay?"

It isn't long before Gerald's father, the college professor, gets word of what's going on and calls the house. "Mrs. Hale, I want my boy released at once, from your home and from your husband." I take the message to his son and to Bill, and the next day Gerald is gone.

At the end of another week, a new letter arrives from Kurina, this time at the clinic. Leigh, the friend from church with the beautiful voice and receptionist at the clinic, phones me. "Patsy, I think you need to know this. I'm going to read the front of an envelope that just came in the mail. It's addressed: *To my Master, Pilgrim Bobby, c/o His Brother, Pilgrim Bill.* It's addressed to the clinic and is from Maiden Kurina. And Patsy, Bobby is not only having his mail sent here, but he's been hanging around the clinic for the last few days."

I had noticed Bobby leaving in the red pickup during part of the day. "I knew he was bound to get bored just sitting around this yard, but I wasn't sure where he went during the day," I say. "I'm sorry to learn he's hanging out there. I know he must be disruptive. I guess George is thrilled?"

"Oh, yes, we all are. Seriously, Patsy, he has the run of the place when Doc is here. And you know how Bobby looks and acts. Yes, he is very disruptive."

"I'm sure Billy knows that he is, but I can't even talk to him about his brother, much less change things. Don't get me wrong, Leigh—I know this can't go on. I understand the strain he's putting on the practice by allowing Bobby to run wild."

"My words exactly, Patsy. He is running wild. The reason I'm even mentioning it to you is I'm worried about Doc; and I'm worried about you. What is going to happen? What is Bobby doing out here, anyway?"

I'm not going to divulge everything I know to Leigh. Some of this insanity I need to keep to myself. "He shouldn't be here, Leigh," I answer. "Kurina is expecting another baby soon and he's even brought his oldest daughter, who might have been some comfort and help to her mother, out here with him. He will have to leave soon. Surely."

"Well, I know you feel like I do—it can't be too soon. By the way, Patsy, as I see it, that poor woman Kurina is more slave than wife. How does he keep her living the way she lives...and calling him 'my

Master' and herself 'Maiden'? Is she being abused?"

"I think she is. I think she is being abused, threatened, brainwashed, intimidated—you name it. But I don't know if she understands that she is. He took her away, or she ran away, when she was so young, fifteen or sixteen years old, that she has had very few life experiences outside of her life with Bobby. Her own parents were divorced...therefore living separately. I don't think she knows how a husband is supposed to treat his wife. Anyway, Leigh, I'm sure you need to go and I do, too. Thank you for reading that envelope to me. It tells me a lot."

"Just one more thing, Patsy. I wonder if Kurina has permission to call Doc 'Pilgrim Bill'?"

"I seriously doubt that she has," I say. "I don't know where that came from."

"From her loony husband. Don't you think so?"

"It must have. Now you've got me wondering, Leigh, if Bobby will show it to Bill."

"That's a great idea. It says 'in care of.' I'll just give it to Doc first."

"No, Leigh, please don't. Don't give him anymore crazy ideas. Bobby has already given him enough. I've got to run. Let's pray that Bobby will leave town soon." Before it's too late, I think as I hang up the phone. George Ellenberger is a friend, but he is also all business. I don't care how valuable Billy is as a surgeon—this cannot keep up. And does Kurina have permission to call Bill "Pilgrim"? Of course she does. I don't doubt it one bit. If Bobby is "Pilgrim," then Bill is "Pilgrim," too.

A couple of days after their arrival, Billy appeals to me to come out and join the group in song. "You love to sing, Patsy, and we need your voice in our little choir. Bobby will have a devotion and we'll have a great evening."

I summon all the strength within me, and with a firm voice I tell him, "Billy, I will not listen to anything Bobby has to say. He is not of my faith and I will not participate. I don't agree with anything he stands for or is trying to do, and I don't condone him being in my home."

Bill is visibly shaken by my words, and very angry. Naturally, he would be angry; I had never voiced so strong an opposing opinion. I could have been frightened, and probably should have been, taking this determined stance, but somehow I knew a peace, and fear did not have its way with me.

Bill went back outside, alone—to face Bobby, I guess, with his failure, or more likely, my obstinacy. Late that same night, when I am asleep, Bill comes to my bed and startles me awake, yelling, "You need to come outside and worship with us!" He is fuming mad, but I stand my ground.

"There is no way I will go out there. It's unreasonable for you to expect me to. And why is he keeping you up all night? Don't you have surgeries in the morning?"

"You don't know what I've got to do in the morning, Patsy."

"Well, I know what Bobby has got to do—nothing. Absolutely nothing but sleep all day while you try to work." I want to say, "Or hang around the clinic, making a nuisance of himself,' but I've said enough.

After that night, I throw bedclothes on the floor of Mother's room and sleep there.

Days and nights are beginning to run together, but it must be the next day or two, when Bill tries to charm me into cooking a meal for the group. After the Miss Ivory tuna sandwiches, I have not fixed anything else for them to eat. And when Bill tells me how everyone would enjoy one of "your good pork chop suppers," I refuse. I want them to leave! Why on earth would I encourage them to stay by cooking for them?

From then on they cook all of their meals outside. They choose meat from the freezer and whatever else they want from the pantry. Anybody in the group who wants anything from the kitchen comes right on in and helps themselves as they please from the freezer, pantry, or refrigerator.

The loud singing and preaching and reading from Ephesians, according to Bobby's interpretation, goes on every evening. I am invited out every time they start up, but I refuse and continue to sleep on my mother's floor.

Then one Saturday, a few days after my staunch refusal to cook, Billy changes his tactic. That night, he pleads with me again to come out and join their worship. He is sweet and charming, telling me that they just want to sing and play the guitar.

Again I refuse. "I'm sorry, Billy, but I will not participate in anything involving Bobby."

Within minutes, Bobby brazenly storms into the kitchen where I am standing. "You are dishonoring my brother!" he yells. "He asked you to join him in worship and you refused. It is your obligation to follow your husband."

"Bobby, I used to believe that, but there is a limit to all things. He is now under your influence, not God's, and I refuse to comply."

"You, Patsy, have hardened your heart. You, sister-in-law, are worldly and are following the ways of the world."

Again, I muster my courage and say, "You need to leave me and my household alone, Bobby. You are none other than an example to me of an Antichrist!"

He goes outside in a rage and I hear him yelling about "that preacher" and how he is going to that church in the morning to expose that deceiver. "I'm going to walk through that door and down to the pulpit and let those poor sheep know what a fraud and a viper that Miles is!"

I should know better than to confront Bobby. Confrontation is a challenge and he becomes more perverse and determined than ever.

The next morning is Sunday and I call the church at the time I know Brother Miles is in. "Brother Miles, I've got to warn you, Bobby's threatening to enter the church sanctuary and make a scene. I heard him last night. He's going to call you a fraud and accuse you of leading the congregation astray."

"Thank you for calling, Patsy, but don't worry," Brother Miles says. "I already have a plainclothesman here and Bobby will not pass."

It had started to rumble a little thunder earlier, and rain soon taps against the window. I have not heard Bill enter the house; He could hear me talking and has eased into the butler's pantry to eavesdrop on my conversation. As I go to hang up the handset he grabs my wrist and jerks the phone from my hand. "You will go through my brother to use this phone!" he says in a quiet, threatening voice. "In fact, I'll just take it with me."

"But, Billy," I ask, "what about Mother? I might need to call her doctor."

"You can make a medical call. Just go through Bobby first. And you seem to forget I *am* a doctor!"

I decide right then, when Bill takes my phone, that I have had enough.

I am leaving here. What to do? Think fast. I will prepare my mother for my escape.

Soon Bill loses interest in standing around and goes back outside. Through the window I watch him go out to the tent, find no one inside, and head toward the gym. Because of the weather, the group has gone into the workout gym to pass the time and stay out of the rain. They only have the pickup truck, so I think they won't be going to church today. This is good. It's good for me, too, that they are all in the gym, but I must work fast.

After giving Mother breakfast and helping her bathe and change clothes, I ask her, "Are you okay, Mother? Is there anything you need? Be sure, because I have to leave for just a bit and want you to be comfortable. Big Mike will be coming over today, probably before I get back." In a matter of minutes, I know I will be leaving my mother and my home. I kiss her goodbye and head straight for the kitchen, out the back door, and into the rain—carrying not one thin dime nor one possession with me, except my driver's license and the clothes on my back.

It is one of those loud, thundering Texas downpours that could continue for hours, and as I disappear down the side of the hill and toward the ravine, I feel confident my getaway will be clean and undiscovered. For some reason, this confidence doesn't keep me from feeling desperate and half-panicked.

From childhood I remember my way over this area of our ranch to where Wayne and his first wife, Diane (who died about three years ago), had built their house; they had purchased the land from us. Between our house and his, the land is rough and uneven but over the years, it has become even worse than I remember. The bushes, thorns, and barbed-wire fences are different now and every step is uncharted territory for me. As though a wild bobcat were closing in on me, I tear frantically through the brush and crawl under and over barbed-wire fences, ripping my clothes and skin.

When I arrive at Wayne's house I know the door will be open, but that he will probably be at church. As it turns out, Wayne is late leaving home, and when I walk through the door without knocking—my hair stringing and clothes soaking wet—he is astonished. "Patsy, what is going on over there?"

"Wayne, I had to leave the house. I feel my mother and I are in real danger. Bobby wants to kidnap me. But what about Mother? She requires my constant care." I look at my hands and arms. "I didn't know how scratched and bloody I am—but Wayne, I had to get out of there the best way I could, and that was through the ravine. They're all inside the gym because of the rain so I'm sure I wasn't spotted."

Wayne calls Susanne on her cell phone. "She will be on her way to church," he says to me. "Susanne," he says into the phone. "Turn around now. Don't go to church. We've got a situation here, and Patsy needs you. Bring her some clothes, too."

"Wayne, can I please use your phone? Mother is in the house by herself, and I've got to get her out. I'm going to call her doctor. I know Dr. Boling will help me. His mother and my mother were best friends."

"His office number is probably here," Wayne hands me a little blue phone book. "This is Sunday morning, though."

"Thanks. I can reach a doctor on call from this number."

As it turns out, Dr. Boling is the doctor on call this weekend, which is wonderfully convenient for my purposes. When I relate my story, he says, "Let's send her to the hospital and get her out of that house. I will admit her and have an ambulance sent for her. Can you have someone there with her? Because we will need to coordinate all this."

"Yes, I will call her nurse now—you know him, Big Mike—and have him call you. And thank you so much."

I immediately place my call to Big Mike; I have his cell number memorized. "Big Mike, you know our situation. I have escaped to a friend's house but Mother is at home by herself. Dr. Boling is sending an ambulance to our house for her and he's going to admit her to the hospital. I need desperately for you to be with Mother or she will be terrified. Here is Dr. Boling's phone number, please call him and coordinate with him."

"What is the timeline, Patsy?"

"The wheels are turning right now. And Mike, you will need to give Bill an excuse for taking Mother out. Since we are desperate, tell him that she has rails in her lungs and needs to see a doctor. He will understand pneumonia."

"I'm on my way, Patsy. I'll call Dr. Boling and be there in thirty minutes."

On the way to Wayne's, Susanne stopped by her house for everything she thought I would need. When she gets here, she turns his guest shower and bathroom over to me—a first aid kit, too. She gives me a change of clothes and blows out my hair. "Now, Patsy, you look fit to go to the hospital when Big Mike calls you."

"Susanne, I can't thank you enough. You've been wonderful. I need only one more favor, and then I'll be out of your hair."

"Don't be silly," she replied. "We don't want you out of our hair. But what's the favor?"

"I need a quick ride to Charles and Lana Frazier's. I talked to them shortly after that truckload from New Mexico first drove up over a week ago, and Charles wanted me and Mother to come to their house right then. It seemed unrealistic at the time, but now I need to take them up on their generous offer...at least for myself. They have a lot of extra room in case I need to stay a few days—and I probably will."

At their kind insistence, I stay with the Fraziers for a while. They even give me use of one of their cars. I spend much of that time at the hospital, and then at the nursing home, with Mother.

After a while, I run into a neighbor, Jim, at the gas station. He and his wife live across the valley from our house and I know that the loud sounds echo and reverberate around the valley and disturb them—Bobby and his group do everything just as loud as is humanly possible without microphones. I had explained to these neighbors some of what was going on at the house and that I had left temporarily. Therefore when I saw him he said, "That crowd at your house kept up the all night singing and preaching until just a couple of days ago "When it stopped we figured they left. It's so peaceful at your house now, Patsy, we can actually sleep at night." He laughs.

"That is such good news, Jim. Maybe I can finally go home."

I walk out of the store and get Ronnie on the phone. "Our neighbor says it's all clear at the house, Ronnie. I'm taking the Frazier's car to them and I'll need a ride home."

"Let me out here, Ronnie. I want to walk in." He, too, gets out of the car and, with no words between us, we walk down the drive.

The house and the yard look wrecked. We stand on the spot where the campsite had been. They had ripped the Thermadore grill out of my kitchen island and hauled it outside. Here at the campsite they had laid the electric grill over open cooking fires. Billy and I had enjoyed the Thermadore and I used it every day, even for bacon at breakfast. Because it was vented to the outside under our pier and beam construction, the outside air would be filled with delicious cooking aromas when Billy came riding in from work—and he loved it. The grill was now burned and warped beyond repair.

The table and tent are gone, the lanterns are gone, and litter is thick on the ground. My flowers and ferns have not been watered and are withered on the porch. Oil is smeared on every window that I can see—all three stories. We go around to the side of the house and see that the Taj Mahal is partially gone—all the double-duty fencing and the antique tubs for bathing. Only the houses and paved dog runs are left. Ronnie moves on toward the gym and I turn back to the house.

Ronnie then turns around and comes back my way, saying, "Patsy, on second thought, there's the possibility that the house is not structurally sound. If their aim was to wreck it, they may have knocked down a supporting pier. I better come with you."

Not knowing how I might react to what awaits inside, I tell him, "I'll be careful and look out for such things as that. Ronnie, I guess it's my mood, but if you don't mind, I'd like to go in by myself."

Inside the foyer, the large Christmas mirror is broken into shards, and has fallen to the floor. The empty frame with its four hooks looks like a prop from a nightmare—leaning against the wall, bed sheet draped carelessly across the back and through its face. I am numb. Bill had stopped enjoying Christmas, and in the past couple of years Christmas had become evil to him. The memories of joyous Christmas Eve gatherings, reflected in the old mirror, are shattered—symbolically and in fact.

Crunching glass underfoot, I walk through the disheveled dining room, around the dirty table, and watch the crystal chandelier. It is still reflecting light at me and winking bravely. I almost smile. I don't enter, but I do look in the bright adjacent sunroom. With windows around the three outside walls, the midday sun streams in, melting the oil that had been slapped on every glass window pane, as it turns out, in the entire house. Greasy pools of oil have already formed on the sills. Turning through the butler's pantry into my favorite room, the kitchen, I notice first the gaping, clumsy hole in the island. That's where my grill was—where I had enjoyed fixing so many happy family meals. Opening the refrigerator, I see it is empty. Not even a partial jar of anything is left. The freezer, too, is empty—totally. The pantry is void of a single item; not even salt or pepper. I gaze out the tall kitchen window through the smudge of oil, across the deck and out to the swimming pool in the old grove of oaks. *For an instant, time disappears, and I can see our children, laughing and squealing and diving headfirst into the pool.*

Like in a dream, I walk through the house, noticing the handiwork of derangement. The oil on the windows must symbolize something to Bobby. Mirrors—Bobby's accursed icon of vanity—are all covered. The mirrors are draped with sheets, pillowcases, towels, whatever linen will cover them. Every one of them—on the walls, in the bathrooms, and even the full-length mirror upstairs in my closet.

My closet is ransacked. With just a glance, it is obvious that my clothes, at least all the nice clothes, what Bobby deemed the vain and sinful clothes, are gone. A long denim skirt and two or three old, colorless blouses are left hanging.

What else is in my closet, Bobby? You know—the box. The virtual treasure chest, you called it. You opened it, Bobby, that night so long ago. With mock horror you declared its contents vanity: "All this stuff poor Patsy is burdened with…" You wouldn't leave me with all that burdensome stuff, would you, Bobby? With my heart stopped in my chest, and feet unwilling to move, I reach for the shelf, the one I dread to explore…and my fear is confirmed. It's no surprise. This is no screaming "Oh dear God, no!" kind of shock. It's what I expected. I knew it would happen. *And it's what Roland told me he thought would happen.* All the pieces of jewelry are gone; every one. The beautiful tokens of my Daddy's love and skill, given to me on special occasions with all his affection. Daddy, I'm sorry.

The tears don't fall. Move on, Patsy, I tell myself. Move on to the next room. The other place you dread to search.

The storage room is built off the third floor spa, and under the angle of the roof. There is no doubt in my mind that Virginia's Christmas heirlooms are gone. Several years ago, before she died, Virginia had given all the treasured boxes of heirlooms to Billy and me. "Because you and Billy are stable," she said, "and because you love and treasure tradition like I do." I had not told her about her twins burning their grandmother's doll. Should I have? Who then could she have handed her things off to?

I stand before the storage door a moment longer and reminisce. I will never forget our children's joy over Virginia's hand-knitted stockings, presented to them and myself that Christmas long ago. All of the handed-down treasures from Belle and Virginia and my mother that represented love, many hours of dedicated work, and stewardship of their God-given talents—not something that money could buy; will they be there? Please, Bobby, those weren't vanity. Surely they weren't. I open the storage door and discover that everything valuable—that is, everything valuable to me—has been drug out of the room, leaving only useless things scattered and thrown around. I am sure we will find a fire site outside—somewhere close—convenient for tossing our history into. Virginia, I'm sorry.

Ronnie is outside, checking the gym and other outbuildings. I see him and call. He turns to me slowly with a look of sad disbelief. "Patsy, all of Doc's photographic equipment is missing." A few years ago, Bill became interested in photography. That casual interest required that he invest many thousands of dollars in fine equipment. I remember one of his friends commenting, "Bill, you've got more photographic equipment than Gittings Studio."

"We need to look for a fire site, Ronnie, where some of the things might have been burned."

"I've already found that, Patsy. It's in the clearing behind the gym." He motions me to follow. "When I saw the house defaced, I thought they might have burned things. They did not burn that equipment, though. I didn't find any burned metal pieces that I could identify."

No, there are no metal pieces—at least not equipment pieces. No charred or melted gold; no platinum; no silver either. No precious stones can be stirred up from the ashes. What I do find are shards of broken crystal; shattered and burned antique dishes; broken and burned holiday ceramics, dishes, and platters, hand-painted by my mother; Virginia's brass tree, melted into a twisted lump; a few charred buttons; some scorched and charred shreds of fabric. And here are tiny charred beads, lots of them—beautiful little things. They had been sewn in Christmas patterns, by Belle Birge Kingsbery, on the stockings she made for her grandsons. Belle, I'm so sorry.

27. DELIVER ME FROM EVIL

"Though I walk through the valley of the shadow of death, I will fear no evil: for thou art with me; thy rod and thy staff they comfort me."
~ Psalm 23:4

In Texas, the summer heat can linger well into the fall, thankfully disappear for a while, then reappear with a vengeance—even after the welcome cool days predominate. Today is one of those hot fall days, and when the phone rings, I am upstairs in my room with the windows open and the ceiling fan on its highest setting. I grab the phone with a cheery "Hello," expecting a call from my cousin. He will confirm, I hope, my invitation to his family for Thanksgiving dinner here at the ranch.

My spirits sink when I hear Bill's voice on the other end. His soft, gravelly voice that I had once loved, grates in my ear. I practically know without asking that he is in town. Just in time to cloud our Thanksgiving and Christmas.

I stand in the open window, holding the phone in silence and look down at the long drive threading its way through the scattered oaks. It is just at sunset, and the view is bathed in a warm glow so lovely it almost takes my breath away. I inherited this land from my father, and I love it with my whole being. At one time Billy had shared my love of this place. But there came a day when he went away.

It seems like only a moment ago that I stood in this same window, trembling with grief and fear, and watched my husband as he walked down the drive; watched as he took off his shoes and carried them, going barefoot over the stony ground to the end of the driveway; watched him step into the grass and ceremoniously, in biblical fashion, "*shake the dust off his feet.*" At the lane, he turned toward the highway and, never looking back, disappeared from view.

I can see that cruel departure as clearly now as the day it happened; and it hardens my heart. "Where are you?" I say without emotion.

"I'm in town. For a day or two. I need badly to talk you."

I continue to hold the phone in silence. This is not the first time, since he submitted to Bobby's deception, that he has been back in town—it is the second. The first time he returned, he let his brother lay waste to my private belongings and our family heirlooms. The beautiful handiwork of family members—our collective memories and stories—burned in Bobby's "Bonfire of the Vanities."

In light of all that, it probably seems surprising that Bill still has the nerve to call—but I'm not surprised, and I'm actually glad he does call. I need something more from him—his signature on two documents. I must play a careful hand.

"Don't hang up," he pleads. "I don't blame you for being mad at me, but I'm burdened. I need to share some things with you." I almost start to answer, but he continues. "And I'll take my name off the deed. If you want it done, we've got to work fast."

Take his name off the deed! I hesitate, trying to choke back the relief I feel; I don't want him to hear that much joy in my voice. If I had any unkind words for him, they are instantly forgotten.

Years ago, I had let Billy talk me into putting his name on my trust fund and the deed for my land. He is finally going to clear that for me. I am still in the house and hope he will sign the house over to me too.

"Good, Billy, I'm glad to hear it. I will set things up. And I'm not mad; with time, and God's grace, we can overcome a lot. What is your burden?"

As he gathers his thoughts, there is a long moment of silence between us. Then he says in the most humble voice I have ever heard from him, "Patsy, you were right about Bobby, and I was wrong. I will be leaving the country soon, maybe for good, and you need to hear what I have to say."

I really prefer not to hear Bobby's name again as long as I live, but Billy's mood and his urgent tone is compelling to me—besides, I need that signature. "Tomorrow, after school, I can meet you at Central Market—where I used to buy groceries, remember? I need to shop anyway. They have a buffet and we can find a table that's fairly private. You say we have to move fast, then that's the best place."

At four-forty-five, I enter the store, walking briskly with assurance, holding my emotions in check. I try not to be prideful, but considering what Bill has put me through, I do not want the slightest appearance of defeat. I see him immediately, standing right inside the entrance and looking straight at me. He still carries his staff.

Several years ago he made this staff. He carved it beautifully and intricately, and carried it as a symbol—I'm not sure of what. Either it stood for authority or symbolized that he was a Shepherd. I did know that his knee was giving him pain, off and on, at the time, and secretly I felt he needed the staff for walking support.

The beautiful man who was the love of my life looks thin and tired. I feel a great sorrow for him. I feel sorrow not only for Billy, but also for myself, and for what might have been; and sorrow for our children who, in all truth, had no role in this ruinous drama; and sadness for our great, good friends—who grieved with me and lifted me up as things fell apart. Our life together should have been a fairy tale, but it's come to this: Bill, estranged from his children and homeless; and me, penniless except for my small teacher's salary. And my inheritance—what should have buffered us for our lifetime—is squandered.

In the buffet line, Billy looks so puzzled and helpless that I take over and heap his plate with the rib-sticking food that he needs. We had found seats earlier and returned to them, me carrying both plates and Bill with his walking staff and bottles of tea.

Without even looking at the food, he commences his story:

"Patsy, when I lost my position at the hospital I was fed up—with everything. I was tired of explaining things over and over to people. What was the use? No one understood me. So I went to live with my brother."

Uh-huh, I think sarcastically, and he understands you perfectly, and you two get along so well—good choice. But, actually, I guess they had grown to understand each other since Bill yielded to Bobby's ways.

"The Spirit showed me that Bobby was very knowledgeable. He studied the Bible constantly, and had many good insights. My brother is a real man of God. That's what I thought. And he has a good wife and good children. They are all sequestered away—safe and protected from this sinful world."

Was this a dig at me and my refusal to follow him and accept Bobby's way? I held my peace.

"I wanted to depart unto the mountains. I needed to feel the spirit, and I wanted to go and wait on the Lord. I was tired and in danger of losing my way. Sometimes you just have to wait on the Lord. I wanted to let the Lord have his way; let him show me how to live my life according to his will."

I watch Bill and listen as patiently as I can. He is rambling and poetic and he looks and sounds confused. I interrupt, "Billy, I just thought of a question I need to ask. Are you taking the meds for your diabetes?"

He looks at me, puzzled. "I've been healed of diabetes. I thought I told you that."

"Oh. Yes, I guess you did tell me that. I'm sorry—go on." It is amazing to me that Bill, being in medicine, is so oblivious to his own body and its symptoms.

"Where was I? Oh, I wanted to let God speak to me and give me some direction. So I went to Bobby's. But it was the wrong thing to do."

"I hate to interrupt again," I say with concern, "but why don't you go ahead and eat something? Then I have another question."

He stirs his food around and takes his first forkful. "I guess I am hungry." He eats heartily for a few minutes. "What's your question?"

"Well, if I remember correctly, you didn't go straight to Bobby's when you left the clinic. The last time I heard from you, you were preaching in Waco." Actually, he had been in Waco at the same time all the news was focused on the Branch Davidians there. We had worried about Bill being in "Whacko," as some of us called it at the time. "What happened about that? Why did you leave Waco?"

"Nothing happened about that," he says without looking up, his mouth full. "I wasn't feeling well. It was time to move on."

I sense his stay in Waco might be a sore point, and I never bring it up again. As a result, I remain a little curious, to this day, about his time there.

"You said you weren't feeling well. How did you get to New Mexico?" Surely, I think, he didn't hitchhike in his condition.

"I had a little money, so I took the Greyhound to Taos, then got a ride to Ledoux." He starts to shift around and seems impatient with my questions.

"Go on, Billy. If you'll just eat, I won't interrupt."

"I got to Bobby's at the end of March. Bobby said that sometimes there would be a break in the snow in March. I hoped that would be the case. Bobby could bring the truck down to Ledoux. But the snow was still deep. Instead of the truck, he came down on horseback and brought a horse for me."

I know that Billy had a bad experience as a kid and he didn't like to ride horses. "I know you didn't like that," I say.

"Nope. That nine-thousand-foot climb, on horseback in deep snow, was not a good time." Bill continues. "But, when we finally got to the cabin, Bobby's family made it all worthwhile. The kids were jumping up and down like little puppies. I never felt so welcome. Kurina had a hot meal made, and we sang and the kids played guitars and fiddles. Kurina had made a bed for me in the little cabin, and a fire in the stove. That's where I slept, comfortable as could be. Sometimes I listened to wolves howl up and down the mountain at night. When the weather warmed up, I slept in Bobby's old camp tent. You know I enjoy sleeping outside. Up there in the mountains the stars are so clear and close, I felt God magnified in their glory."

"Bill, it sounds like you had a wonderful visit."

"It was good—for a while. I gained my strength back and began to grow clearer. I felt like the outdoorsman that I really am at heart. I believe Bobby and me were born to be mountaineers."

Pilgrim mountaineers, I think, because I doubt he has dropped the moniker given to him by Bobby of "Pilgrim Billy." Bobby had started calling himself "Pilgrim Bob" several years ago.

"You said your visit was great for a while. Then what?" I ask. "I guess things started to turn sour with you and Bobby, as usually happens?"

"Not like usual, Patsy, not at all. But I started to notice things. Gradually. You can't help but observe a family's interactions when you live right in their midst." Bill stirs his food again. He looks like his troubled thoughts are a thousand miles away.

"What did you notice, Billy?

"Lots of things. I noticed that Bobby had started mistreating Kurina, for instance. She is a good, humble woman and deserves better. When he didn't know I was around I heard him be really cruel to her. He could say some mean, belittling things. And words do hurt. They cut to the bone. The truth be known, I think she liked me to be around. As long as I was close by he would control himself. I had never known Bobby to have regular, periodic mean spells; but that's what was happening. When he had these moods, the whole family was afraid of him."

I don't say anything, but I am a little confused. At one time, Billy thought Bobby's total control over his wife and children was admirable. And did he say Bobby had "periodic mean spells"? That sounds an awful lot like a man who drinks. Had Bobby started drinking? I want to ask, but find I am still reticent to ask such a bold question of Billy. I keep my thoughts to myself.

"Anyway, as long as I could help Kurina and the children by just being there, I felt that was good. But I did not come between Bobby and his family in any way. I needed to stay in the mountains for a while, so I kept on Bobby's good side."

I can't imagine Bill not tearing into him—verbally, at least; but, though it's unfortunate, I know it's been years since Bill challenged Bobby. "Let me ask you this, Billy: did he still have the entire household gather at his feet every evening?"

"Oh, yes. And me, too. For at least a year, I sat straight across from Bobby and enjoyed his Bible reading and teaching. The sound of Bobby's reading was therapy to me. I had been preaching in Waco, on   the   streets,   and   I as tired. 'Weary and heavy-laden,' so to speak."

"And you didn't argue with him at all? I'm amazed."

"I told you, I wasn't feeling well. I needed a rest. His way was fine with me; at least, for a while."

And, I think to myself, you've made such a shambles of your life, Billy dear—you had nowhere else to go. You couldn't risk fighting with Bobby. Your brother, in the full sense of the word, was your keeper. "Go on. I'm listening."

"Another thing bothered me…" Billy pauses, looks me in the eye, then drops his gaze and continues. "He would send his children into dangerous situations. I mean, I think he should have sent two boys or even he should have gone himself with one of the boys into the mountains to watch the sheep. He should not send a teenage boy and a teenage girl into the wilds together."

"What are you saying Billy? I don't follow."

"Yes, you do, Patsy. You mentioned it to me yourself that it's not healthy to have teenagers, isolated with no friends from outside the family."

"Yes, you're right, I did say that, several years ago. And you got really torn up that I would even think such a thing."

He continues, "Certainly, I had no idea that Bobby would send his teenage boy and girl into the mountains for days at a time, to watch sheep. Why would a father set his children up like that? There's a verse or something that says, 'Avoid the near occasion of sin.' That tells me to stay out of temptation's way. Seems like he tried to cause them trouble. Maybe as a test? I came to know those kids pretty well. They're good Christian kids, and I'm sure they were fine, but it was no thanks to their dad."

Bill, trying to make sense of Bobby's complex behavior, is pretty much babbling. I can tell he is uncomfortable talking about this subject, but I understand him.

He pauses to take a few bites—so deep in thought that I am loath to interrupt. I wonder why he didn't just say something to Bobby. Considering his dependent situation, though, I guess he was afraid to speak up. In former times, Billy would have been all over Bobby, reminding him that Jesus said, "Lead us not into temptation."

All I manage to say is, "I'm surprised, Billy, that you didn't go with the boys yourself."

"I did—one time. After that, Bobby didn't let me go again."

"Didn't 'let' you go again? I guess you made the mistake of reading a verse to the boy or asking him a question?"

"Exactly! That's what happened. At night, I got out my Bible and we read and talked. But I found out Bobby doesn't want anybody but himself to talk to his children, or teach them a thing. Or, for that matter, be around them or influence them in any way... Not even me. And all those children are programmed to report everything to him. As soon as Bobby heard about me reading the Bible, that was the end of my being alone with the boys. And Bobby makes harsh judgments about people," Billy continued. "John told me that even the few people within riding distance from their cabin who had tried to be neighborly were soon rejected by his dad as *ungodly*. Then the children were told to keep those people off the property and have nothing more to do with them."

"Do you remember, Billy, what I told you I overheard Bobby tell Kurina, when they were planning to leave Fort Worth and go to New Mexico? This is what he said, and I'm quoting: 'Kurina, I can teach people out there, and we can have our own following again.' How, I want to know, could he have his own following if he ran everybody off, like the boy claimed?"

"I don't know what he expected. But I can tell you this—when I went around to the ranches, looking for odd jobs, I discovered, right off the bat, that the people didn't like or trust Preacher Bob. I was surprised. I thought that since they called him 'Preacher' that meant they respected him."

"Not so?" I ask.

"Not at all. These ranchers told me some things I hated to hear. I believed that my brother had been saved and was a man of God, but after a while I began to doubt any of that. One of the ranchers said

Preacher Bob had sent his boys to steal oats and hay from his barn. The man had seen the boys just as they were getting away. 'Hale,' the man said to me. "'Your brother is a menace.'"

"And you believed all this stuff they were saying about Bobby?" I asked.

"I was right in his house observing him and, frankly, it rang true. Of course, I tried to make excuses to this particular rancher—anything I could think of—like they're isolated and might have been desperate, but the man would have none of it. He said he would gladly sell Bobby food for his animals. In fact, he told me he had already given Bobby food and would give more if asked. And his wasn't the only account I heard. These scattered neighbors liked Kurina and felt sorry for her, but they had no use for Bobby or any of his preaching."

"How could they respect him," I ask, "when he stole from them?"

"Yeah, I know, how could they? Your actions have to match your words. And when somebody didn't accept Bobby's preaching, he wrote them off as ungodly. When I finally did ask him why he didn't just buy oats from his neighbors, you might guess what his excuse was." Bill pauses for me to think.

"I think I can guess. But you tell me," I said.

"Bobby said the man wasn't godly, so it didn't matter."

"Uh-huh. He's holding onto that old Gypsy philosophy that Roland warned us of," I recall to Bill. "If someone isn't just like you, then that person doesn't matter, and what you do against them isn't a sin."

Bill doesn't comment on my statement regarding Roland, but he does say, "When Bobby could have bought oats, he chose to steal. And him a man who's been saved? If he had been, he wouldn't act that way."

I don't comment one way or the other. It seems to me that, at last, Billy is figuring things out for himself.

I involuntarily glance at my watch and he asks, "Are you in a hurry?"

"Not really. The traffic rush is in full swing for another hour. I can stay till it clears. Go on."

"Well, I said I went around visiting ranchers, trying to get some work, and I did. I got a big fencing job, too big for one man, on a ranch that some people had just bought. I needed Bobby and one of his boys to help. But Bobby's reputation had gone before him. The new rancher was a nice guy, and we got along fine, but he told me that the only time he wanted Bobby and his boys on his property was when he was there himself.

"I didn't mention that restriction to Bobby, but he's clever and he knew; he could tell the man didn't trust him. It became real obvious one day when the rancher rode out to where we were working, probably a half-mile from his home site, and told us to call it a day. He said he had to drive his wife into Taos. I told him that, if he didn't mind, there were several hours of daylight left and we would like to keep working. The man looked right at Bobby and said, 'I'd just rather you be gone.'"

"Gosh!" I gasp. "What an undisguised insult! I'm surprised Bobby didn't go wild."

"Yeah, me too," Bill said. "But, you know, he just took it in stride; didn't say a thing, and we left. I didn't know what to make of the way he didn't say a word, but after thinking about it, I figure he had been insulted before and just learned to shrug it off."

I can't resist when I say, "Or plot how he could steal from the man, or hurt him some way to get even."

Bill winces at my bit of insight, but he answers, "There're some complicated things going on with my brother—there sure are. It would take more of a psychologist than you or me to figure it out."

Yeah, like maybe Roland, I think.

"But," Bill continues, "might as well tell the whole story. The man was on horseback, and he had a rifle. I know Bobby is quick and tough, but that would be a deterrent even to him."

I am surprised that Bill thought so. I had never seen the man, but I had seen Bobby in action. In my mind, unless the rancher was Paul Bunyan, Bobby could have him off his horse and pinned to the ground in a second. And forget the gun—that would be flung into the woods.

"Anyway," Bill continues, "I think he figured I had heard some other stuff on him because after that job Bobby didn't like me going around visiting by myself. He and the boys and I did a lot of handiwork around the mountains. We put up and repaired many miles of fencing, and roofed two or three houses but after that incident, they either got the jobs themselves or Bobby went with me to find work. And we always worked the jobs together."

"I'm sure you didn't like to be restricted?"

"I hated it. The feeling that he wanted to check my movements. But I didn't have time for it to worry me much. In fact, maybe I liked it better that way. I didn't have to hear people talk about Bobby. Anyway, you can stay busy around their little ranch. I took good care of the animals." At this point Billy chuckles. "I don't doubt for a minute that Bobby has the healthiest sheep herd in New Mexico."

Happy to see him lighten up, I laugh with him. "I bet he does. Those sheep are probably spoiled rotten."

"I'm just telling you what my life was like there," he said.

"I know, Billy. Go on."

"Well, we were out a lot, fencing and roofing. And doing other repair work, like I told you. I was almost always busy. Sometimes I had too much work and got tired. Seems like I was tired a lot. When we weren't working, I enjoyed the children—as long as I didn't read the Bible to them. They're great kids and I think they loved me. I became really close with some of them and loved them very much."

"I'm glad you and the children enjoyed each other. That was a real blessing for you and them."

"Yes, it was. But there's a story I need to tell. One evening, there was an especially beautiful sunset." He pauses, and starts over. "Sometimes there'll be an evening when the sun's rays will turn the mountains red. You were there when that happened, weren't you, Patsy?"

"We all were, Bill, and it was gorgeous! Kurina said the mountains were named Sangre de Cristo—Blood of Christ, because of the red sunsets."

"Right. Well, the weather was turning cold already at that altitude, but with that incredible sunset, I longed to sleep out in the open. With the weather changing I knew it might be my last chance for a while. I often don't bother to pitch a tent, and I didn't that night. The two Pyrenees were my good buddies from the time I arrived, and the compound was always safe with those dogs. That night I felt like the freest man on earth. I fell asleep rejoicing in the beauty of the sunset and the gifts of nature.

"Sometime later I heard a muffled cry from the shed, below where I was. I didn't try to wake up because I figured Bobby was giving one of the children another 'discipline.' It happened pretty often, so I went back to sleep. It couldn't have been long before I heard another muffled scream, a girl's voice with something over her mouth, and a lot of scuffling and banging around. Something didn't seem right. This time I came awake and stood up. For some reason, I don't even know why, I pulled my sleeping bag with me and eased over into the shadows. While I was still wondering what to do, Bobby came out of the shed and closed the door on whoever was in there. He walked at the edge of the clearing—obviously, he didn't want to be seen either—and started up the hill. I watched him but stayed in the shadows. I had no desire to confront him.

"He continued on up toward the cabin, when that uncanny sixth sense of his kicked in. Like lightening, Bobby swung his head and looked straight at me. It was dark and we were both in shadows; but he could see my silhouette—as I could see his. By his stance, I could tell Bobby was shocked that I was outside watching him. He didn't say a word, nor did I. We both stood dead still and stared at each other—waiting, like a standoff."

Billy pauses for effect and sips his tea. I am speechless and wait for him to continue.

"I know it sounds eerie, Patsy, but as we stood there I felt something frightening pass between us. It felt, as best I can describe, like a new being was born at that minute, and I think that new entity was fear. As much as we had argued and threatened each other in the past, Bobby and I had never been afraid of each other.

"I finally broke the impasse and got in my sleeping bag. I tossed around like I was getting settled but wound up watching Bobby. I couldn't turn my back on him—I was scared of him! I felt I needed to watch, to see where he would go or what he would do. He went on up to the cabin, staring back at me as he closed the door. I knew in my heart that we would both have to deal with this other thing now, this new kind of fear. I was troubled then, and couldn't even begin to fall asleep. I had the new, disturbing fear to contend with, and I wanted to know which daughter he had beaten so cruelly. Who was still in that shed? I was afraid it was Naomi, but couldn't imagine what she had done to merit such a discipline. Before long, my question was answered because Naomi came quietly out of the shed and went in the little cabin. Patsy, I have an uncle's affection for Bobby's children and I was heartbroken. A man shouldn't hit a grown woman."

He holds a long pause and I grow impatient. "Yes? Go on."

"Don't jump ahead of me, Patsy. I'm trying to tell this like it happened. I tried to work out some plans for myself during the night but I wasn't able to. I knew I wanted and needed to leave there. But should I take the coward's way out and leave immediately or stay and try to influence Bobby's behavior?"

"Fat chance of that," I blurt out.

Bill ignores my comment. "In my confusion, and till I could make better plans, I decided to act like nothing had happened between us. I hoped Bobby would also decide to ignore it. That seemed like the most comfortable and convenient thing to do. So in the morning, as usual, I went to the cabin for coffee. I had no more than poured my cup when Bobby turned on me, pointing his finger and snarling between clenched teeth, 'Don't you talk to my wife!' "

"Patsy, Bobby said this in a tone he's ever used with me. Poor Kurina looked at me like a whip had cracked over her head."

"Then he turned on her the same way, 'And don't you talk to my brother.'

"He was shaking with rage—you know how mad he can get. Two of his grown boys were in the room. When they saw him turn on me, in an instant, they were on their guard. The atmosphere in that room was so charged that I felt highly threatened—and not just from my brother, but from my nephews, who I had grown close to. I took my coffee and went straight to the door. 'Think I'll skip breakfast this morning,' I said as I went out."

"'I think you better get out of here, you ungodly phony!' he yelled after me.

"I went immediately behind the house and into the woods. I wanted to hide. I was afraid they would come after me. I was extremely confused by all this insanity from Bobby. Nothing, from the beating last night to right now, made sense to me. I walked a long time on the trail behind the house, but it only went deeper into the woods, and my knee was starting to hurt."

When he pauses I want to ask him about his knee, but I'm paying such rapt attention I can't even form the question.

"But at least I had cleared my mind," he says. "I knew what I had to do. With Bobby, abusive and half-crazy and now turning violent on me, and exciting his grown boys against me, I thought, I must leave this place—today. The weather was turning colder and I knew it would be deteriorating during the day. I didn't have my good coat or my license or any of my papers. I had to have those things to survive. And I needed a shot in my knee. I turned back toward the cabin—and almost collided with Bobby. He said to me, with hate in his voice, 'I think you better leave here.'

"Do you know how I felt, Patsy? To hear my identical twin talk to me like that? He was afraid of me—it was clear. Still, I don't have the words to describe how rejected I felt. 'My plans exactly,' I told him. 'I'm just going back for my papers.' He looked like he wanted to kill me. 'I said you better leave here,' he repeated. 'In fact, you better leave this mountain. Now!'

"I stood my ground. I told him first I had to have my papers. 'I worked eight years for that license, and I won't leave without it. And I'm getting a shot for my knee.'

"I know that anger begets anger, and he had more than enough for both of us, so I did not raise my voice. But he knew with certainty that I meant what I said. I followed him back to the clearing.

"When we got to the clearing, not a soul was around, and not a sound. No one was going to see me off.

"'I'll get your shot,' Bobby barked over his shoulder. Patsy, you know that I am the one who stocked the storage cabinets in his tack room, and I kept him supplied with all those medicines and medical supplies—everything he needs for his animals and family; it's practically a pharmacy. Now he won't let me get what I need—which is more than one shot. I was so outraged that if it had only been him and me, and not his boys standing by, I would have taken him on, regardless of the outcome.

"I went on to the little cabin and saw that my few belongings were disturbed—Bobby had already gone through them. I checked to see what he had taken. Amazingly, I accounted for everything, even the little money I kept for myself. While I was in there, two of the boys, James and John, had appeared outside. He was talking to them at the edge of the clearing, right about where I was last night. Bobby came over, handed me the hypodermic and said, calmly this time, 'Get in the truck. They're taking you out.'

"Like nothing had ever happened, he went back to the cabin, and I got in the truck. I almost wanted to say 'thank you.' I had expected to walk out—in my case, with this knee problem flaring, hobble out, so the courtesy truck ride to Ledoux was a big relief.

"On our ride out I tried to keep up a conversation with my nephews the best I could—but they were pretty somber. Usually, if you can't think of anything else to say, you can talk about the weather. But they wouldn't even comment on the coming storm—which I pointed out would be on us within a few hours. Poor guys—I had watched them grow into young men. We had enjoyed each other's company for three years, and today, without a 'how do you do,' I was leaving. I think they hated to see me go.

"Those roads are bone-rattling rough; you know that, and we bounced and crashed along for a while. We weren't on the road I expected, but there's more than one way up and down. Finally, they stopped the truck and got out. And I got out. I started looking through my backpack, hoping I had squirreled away some crackers. I didn't have breakfast, due to my brother losing his mind that morning, and I was famished.

"James asked me (I guess he saw me digging around), 'Do you have something to eat?' After scratching through everything in the backpack, I was able to say, 'Yeah, two granola bars.' I sat down on a rock to have my lunch.

"James watched me, and he looked pretty sorrowful. They do hate to see me go, I thought. He wouldn't look me in the eye, but he came over and handed me a pound hunk of Kurina's homemade cheese and a loaf of her bread, and said, 'Here's some stuff Mother made.' I was grateful for that food, and so moved that Kurina had sent it. The last time I had seen Kurina, she was looking at me, both of us in wide-eyed shock, while Bobby yelled at us like a madman. By his behavior, I knew that James and his mother had had to hide this food from Bobby; maybe from John, too. Maybe it was from emotion, or being weak with hunger, but my hand was shaking so bad I could hardly take the stuff from him. I almost cried.

"James started to walk around then, just looking here and there. I watched him while I unwrapped the food. Then I noticed that John was already back in the truck, looking at me. I figured he wanted to go. Before I could stand up, he saw me looking at him and he started the engine. That's when James, saying nothing to me, started running for the truck. What the heck are they doing? I thought. Then I started to yell and gather my things, but James was already in the truck before I could take a step.

"'For God's sake, boys, wait a minute!' I yelled. But they had that old truck already turned around and they cut out so fast there was no mistaking their intentions. I can't even describe to you, Patsy, the panic that came over me. Now I understood—I was being abandoned.

"I had no animosity toward my nephews. They were only following orders. This abandonment was Bobby's and only Bobby's doing.

"I felt my mind and body failing me. My legs got weak as water. I was shaking all over as I sat back down with my little granola bar and listened to them drive away. I must have sat there a long time. I don't remember what I was thinking. Thirst was what eventually brought me around. I got up and finished the water in my canteen—it was days old—and I tried to focus. I had to have a plan. But I couldn't make my thoughts come together. I needed food, so I ate some of Kurina's provisions."

He's describing diabetes symptoms to me again, I think; something he would recognize in a second in another person.

"Finally reality set in, and panic almost took over again," he continues. "Within hours, I could very well be dead. I looked out over the mountains and watched the gray snow clouds gathering lower in the sky. I had told the boys the snow was on its way as we drove here. We had driven for at least an hour. It would be snowing by the time the truck got back to Bobby's.

"I had to determine where I was. If I didn't sort out this location, I wouldn't make it. When we left the cabin I thought the boys were driving me to town and we would be parting. I had been talking to them. Talking about the weather in fact, and telling them I had enjoyed my stay with them—all kinds of stuff. I even talked about the animals, and how many kids and puppies they might have to sell at the fair next time—anything to keep my mind off Bobby. I was sorry to be leaving my nephews, and they were so quiet that I thought they, too, were sad to see me go. In trying to keep our spirits up, I had failed to watch the trail. I started backtracking in my mind, trying to remember any turns we had taken. We took lots of turns. Turns and—oh dear God! Horrified, I realized that we had been climbing. What had I been thinking? I could still feel the truck pulling. We had been gradually climbing, not descending. At no time do I remember the truck's nose aiming downhill. It was all clear to me. My brother had his boys drive me to the top of this mountain and put me out in the coming storm. Bobby intended for me to die! He knew my knee was bad, and that I get tired. He wanted to kill me. He would let the storm do it for him."

Bill is whispering at me and his beautiful eyes have an unsettled look, questioning, like he wants answers. Involuntarily, the thought comes to me—fratricide, as old as Cain and Able.

"Bill, surely not!" I whisper back, truly horrified. "Are you actually telling me that Bobby wanted to kill you? He wanted you to die?"

"Yes, he wanted to kill me. And I knew for certain that he would succeed. A blizzard was coming and I didn't even know where I was. And I hope, Patsy, that you never experience the terror I felt. I look back on it now, and physiologically, find it interesting. I started shaking and the pit of my stomach gripped in a knot; my legs and knees went numb with weakness and my feet were stinging numb; my neck and face seemed to burn and I got a sudden, splitting headache, which, thank God, didn't last. The fear involved my entire body and, for a minute, took all my attention. I couldn't think—my brain was just chaos."

His eyes have turned sharp with remembering. "I'm so sorry, Billy. I'm sorry that you experienced such an awful thing. And I'm sorry that I can't comprehend all this. Why?"

"Why would he want me dead? It had to do, Patsy, the best I can figure, with whatever went on in that shed the night before. That's when he became afraid of me!"

Bill stops talking then and picks up his knife and fork again.

Trying to process what he has just told me, I also continue with my own neglected meal.

Billy starts up again, getting back to the desperate situation that he had found himself in. "Bobby's place, as you know, since you've been there, is the highest ranch around. It's about nine thousand feet, so he said. I felt I could be at ten thousand easy, even more. No ranches were this high. I had to get down that trail as far as I could before the snow started, and I didn't have long.

"When I started down the trail I discovered the boys had thrown a few of my things out of the truck. I found stuff within fifty feet of where the truck had been parked. Making an instant decision and barely slowing down, I took only my hat and a blanket. I had a flashlight in my backpack but it did me absolutely no good in that blizzard. I never even took it out. I was glad to be wearing the good mountain coat I bought at Luke's before leaving Fort Worth.

"I was walking down the path as fast as I could, rocks rolling under my feet at every step. My biggest fear right then was breaking an ankle. I had my walking staff to steady me, but my knee was painful and tricky. Even though the weather was gaining on me, I did stop long enough to inject that one shot into my knee; doing that, in my state of mind and with my hands shaking, took probably ten minutes. I was desperate now. I kept repeating, please God, please

God, deliver me from evil. It was the only prayer I could manage. For the longest time, I slid and balanced and plodded on, without ever having a coherent thought. Just put one foot in front of the other, hang on to the staff, and don't fall. That's all I could think. I was going downhill and covering, I felt like, a good bit of ground, under the circumstances. The wind was strong with hard gusts, but it was basically at my back; it wasn't slowing me down.

"Then the blizzard struck. The temperature must have dropped ten degrees within seconds. When the flakes came the wind was blowing them horizontally in front of me. I was moving with the wind, though, and going downhill. That was the good part. The bad part was the cold. The wind was blowing so hard I couldn't hold the blanket around me, and my hat had already blown away. My coat had a zip-out hood that I managed, in all that fury, to get unassembled and Velcroed around my head. The hood was a lifesaver; I know as well as I know anything that it was. And I had to think of my hands. They could easily become frostbitten. You know that under normal circumstances I always prepare myself, but now I had no gloves. They must have been in the pile of things the boys threw out. I made the obvious plan to use one hand to hold my staff, and the free hand shoved in my pocket for warmth, and then switch—it was the only way. My pain was so great that I longed for the medications I had brought to the mountains; shelves of it were still sitting in Bobby's tack room.

"But remember, Patsy, I've always had a good sense of direction. I figured I now knew approximately where I was—if I wasn't actually deceived and walking in circles—always a possibility, and a big fear. I had deliberately, and with a plan, left the road when the snow started piling up. With the wind blowing the snow into flurries, I couldn't see the ground or anything else and had to slow down. It would have been impossible to find my way out of there, but I had an ace up my sleeve. From repairing fences, I knew there were hundreds of miles of fencing throughout this mountain. My chances of running into a fence line were pretty good, if I had figured right. When I hit a fence, I would feel my way with my staff and keep walking along it.

"Not being able to see wasn't my biggest problem—the cold was.

The cold would kill me. It had gone through my body into my bones. I was stiff with cold and could barely pitch forward. I knew that I needed to find a fence, and I knew what to do when I found it, but would I live to find it? You know, Patsy, you can get so exhausted and cold that your brain just goes numb. You almost stop caring what happens and start to welcome sleep—death. It's like you wonder about the choice: to live or to die, to live or die—which one will it be? Dying seemed like a real good option; it's so easy. Then, thank God, I ran into the fence.

"With luck and God's help, that fence would be my lifeline. I was surely on the outside of the fence, and that meant a house would be on the inside— probably not too far. I hoped the blowing snow would let me see a light from the dwelling—to see the light for just a second would be enough. I kept looking to my right and forward; that's where I guessed the light would be. Then I saw it. From the aspect of the fence to the light, I realized that I knew this ranch. By staying with the fence I would soon be at the drive. I would make it! I would live! My spirits soared in spite of the cold.

"In less than an hour, I had made my way to the ranch house door. The rancher and the whole family came to the door. After waiting for me to shake the snow off and give my name, they let me in the room. When I pulled back my hood, they recognized me as Preacher Bob's brother. I guess they could see I was freezing because the wife went straight over and dipped me a bowl of soup off the stove. I ate two bowls full and felt like I could finish off the whole pot if she offered it. These were good people and they stayed with me while I ate and warmed up. This was one of the 'ungodly' ranches where Bobby had his boys steal oats.

"I asked if I could spend the night in their barn. That's such a strange request these days that the rancher was reluctant, especially since Bobby didn't live that far away. The rancher said, 'I guess you missed the Preacher's house. You can't see hardly nothing in this kind of weather.'

"They wanted to know what I was doing out in this storm anyway. That's what the wife said, 'What in the world are you doing out in all this?'

"I told them the truth: My brother drove me out in the truck this morning and abandoned me up on the peak. As soon as I said it, I realized that they would now be suspicious of both me and Bobby. I figured they would want to know what I had done to deserve such treatment—being put out in a blizzard. But they didn't even ask. Bobby's reputation is so sordid that if they were surprised, they didn't act it.

"I did insist on sleeping in the barn. I didn't want to interfere with them by sleeping on the floor in that small room, but also, I was hurting. I broke down and took the aspirins the lady offered me, but they had no effect. I felt that if I could nestle down into the hay in the barn it would be much softer than and almost as warm as the floor. And indeed, it wasn't bad. I was so grateful to be alive and safe that I must have slept nine or ten hours.

"The rancher had said to me, 'If you want to sleep out there, go ahead, but come inside in the morning for coffee.' And that's what I did, and they gave me breakfast, too. He helped me figure out the shortest way to Ledoux, which was only a couple of miles down and bearing to the east a little. I had the snow on the ground to contend with, but the weather had pretty much cleared. I knew that, other than my knee, I would have no trouble.

"I made it out, Patsy. I survived. God delivered me from evil. This is one murder attempt of Bobby's that didn't work. I had to tell you, though, that he tried to kill me. And that I'm finished. I won't speak to him again. If he ever contacts you trying to find me, which he probably will because he will be curious when they don't find my body, please don't tell him where I am."

"You can rest assured that your whereabouts will be safe with me, Billy," I say truthfully. "I will never tell him a thing. In fact, I probably won't even take his call. And, Bill, I'm sorry it came to this. Bobby is a curse to everyone who loved him."

We sit quietly, and finish our meal, both of us lost in thought.

I break the silence. "The papers, by the way, are at Milton's office. I called my attorney yesterday, after I heard from you, and set everything up."

He looks at me without speaking. A small dread grips my chest.

Don't let him back out. "You said you would sign them, Billy. Clear your name off the deed?" I'm sure it will be painful for him, I thought. Those signatures will be his final severance. "Think of your children," I say. "My teacher's pay is quite skimpy. I can barely pay the mortgage and taxes. I might need to sell some land to see us through. It's free and clear, and it's all I have left."

We sit a minute longer. He drops his eyes from my face, and stares vacantly across the floor—maybe across the years. "Patsy, I want you to know… Things would have been handled differently…if I hadn't been under Bobby's influence."

Is he trying to apologize? "I know, Billy. Don't even worry about it." I gather my sweater and purse, preparing to leave.

"You're right, Patsy." He fixes his eyes on me—earnest and sad.

In an instant the years fall away: I see him in his James Dean jeans and white shirt, his raven black hair and green eyes, flashing his beautiful smile, choosing me over all the other adoring girls.

"Yeah, you're right," he repeats, "too late to worry now."

"Just sign the documents for me, Billy; that's all I need. They are in Milton's office. He will pick you up—and I do thank you."

I stand, take a few steps, then turn back. His eyes look hopeful for a moment. "And Billy," I say, "I, too, will never speak to Bobby again; so do let me know where you travel."

As it turned out, Billy took his name off everything—the house as well as the land.

And he did travel—around the eastern United States and to Guyana. Bill had told me years ago that he wanted to be a missionary. He was finally allowed into Nicaragua, to serve the poor and treat them and their animals. He died there in 2004. Bill had friends in Esteli and Somoto who cared for his body and buried him quickly, as required by law, for the holy days of Easter were at hand.

28. THE FINAL REQUEST

"The grave; the last inn of all travelers."
~ *William Davenport*

About the time Bobby had decided to move out of the Sangre de Christo Mountains, the ranchers and farmers up and down the mountainside decided they had had enough of Preacher Bob and made a complaint against him. They signed a petition demanding that he leave the area. The leaders of this movement against Preacher Bob gave the petition to the sheriff of Mora County and sent a copy to Jack Nicholson and his business manager. They asked Mr. Nicholson to have the trouble-making preacher and his family vacate the Nicholson property.

All of this trouble coming down on Bobby would in no way have encouraged him to get out. In all probability, it would have caused him to become more entrenched and be more of an undesirable neighbor than before. But he had already started investigating the possibility of getting some government money to homestead in the Alaskan wilderness. He felt that in such a wilderness, he and his family would be left alone to live their lives isolated and safe from the encroaching development they were beginning to encounter in New Mexico. So two years after Bobby put his brother out in one of the worse blizzards of the decade, he took his family from New Mexico to Alaska, seeking ever more insulation from the sinful world.

At some point, after years of abstinence, Bobby began to drink again. This started before he took the family from New Mexico. He would drink hard liquor, and during these spells he could be violent. To add yet another predicament to their lives, after they got to Alaska, Bobby started praying that he and his family would die together.

Bobby talked to Kurina and said something to this effect: "If anything happens to one of us, or if we are invaded and have to leave the way of life we believe in, rather than returning to all the evil around us, it would be better for all of us to just end our lives together." Though this paranoid talk frightened Kurina, she dared not contradict Bobby. He was her father figure, having in effect taken her into isolation at fifteen. He had taught her how to cook, and all the other basics of homemaking, including how to take care of the children. Bobby was the children's doctor and Kurina's doctor, as well as their teacher. Only he had molded Kurina's and the children's belief system. Being so dependent on her husband in every way, she hid her alarm at his suggestions.

In the past, during times of strong, even life-threatening, confrontations with Bobby, Kurina had nowhere to run. With a baby in her arms, one in her tummy and more little hands hanging onto her skirt, going into the cold wilderness was far too dangerous. So when she contemplated or attempted escape, she would always turn back to the cabin to face whatever would be. With Bobby becoming older and sicker, physically and mentally, and him becoming friendly with the idea of the family suicide pact, she had to walk on eggshells more carefully than ever before, hoping to protect her family and not trigger that ultimate violent act in Bobby.

In the springtime, in Alaska, Bobby's life ended. I will not be going there for his final service. I will not experience whatever would await me, and will not be expected to conjure up an emotional response to his death.

I do, however, know some sons who are grieving, and who will attempt to journey all the way there—compelled to close a chapter in their lives.

Near the end of his life, after his and Kurina's children had testified against him in court, and the older children had finally seen through his mask of religion to the evil that lay in his heart, Bobby had started writing to several family members. As Bobby lay dying in jail, he had one final request of the two sons he had ignored almost their entire lives. This request went, absurdly, something like this: "My sons, I want you to come up here and take my body back to Texas. I want you to bury me with my first wife, Kathleen Connally. She is resting in her family's burial plot in her hometown cemetery. She was a sweet, innocent girl. Perhaps by taking this step, I can finally rest in peace."

Some of us in the family are appalled that Bobby made such an impossible and selfish request of his sons. It could serve no purpose other than cause them to feel like helpless failures, unable to carry out their dad's final request. As it turned out, neither of them made it to the funeral.

As Bobby's health declined, he also started writing to me. I had gotten word, now and then, about Bobby and his family from his old friend and mine, Milton; but Bobby and I had not exchanged letters since Bill shook the dust off his feet and walked away from the ranch. I guess Bobby had a lot of time to think about his life, and what might have been, and he had some regrets. In one of his "if only" letters, he wrote: "If only my mother had bought that five acres and a barn for me, I would have stayed in Texas. The circle would have been unbroken. We would have all been together: Billy and you and your children; Kurina and me and our children; my parents; our friends… Our lives would have been entirely different."

But even in his decline, Bobby remained scheming and deceitful. His correspondence was full of statements—devised to redeem himself in my eyes—that I knew for a fact were untrue.

When I didn't answer his letters, he changed his tone with me: "Do you still live in that big house on the hill? Or have you lost it?"

I did still live there at the time, (thanks to my loving and helpful family and friends who helped me clean and refurbish my home after the time of Bobby's Judgment Table), but I am positive, and I mean without any doubt in my mind, he hoped I had indeed lost "that big house." After all, he had done practically everything in his power to cause me ruin.

I never answered any of his letters, including his last letter—addressed to my house but including Katie. "Katie, surely you or your mother could write to me, and tell me what is going on with my brother's family. I long to hear from you." Katie would not even read it.

Today, in Alaska, the private graveside service for Bobby will take place. Just about now the participants will be gathering. They will soon join the procession; driving the distance to his lonely resting place. Though I am not there physically, I will be with Kurina and their children in my thoughts. And, I will say this: My memories, what I've heard of the place, what I know of the family, and also my imagination, count for a lot.

I checked the facts later, and my musings were not far off. The morning announces itself with lingering flashes of lighting and thunderclaps. After battering the town most of the night, the storm seems reluctant to move on. It's as if the heavy clouds wish to hang around and cause additional misery to the little company of mourners who will soon gather in the desolate cemetery five miles removed from town. The atmospheric conditions are so gloomy it's as if the weather were prearranged—symbolically representing the very presence of death.

As I approach the scene, my eyes are locked on the last shovelful of earth being tossed onto the casket of Robert Allen Hale. The desolation of this place overwhelms me. The grave, slightly mounded in gray, stony soil, is surrounded by a small group of people. They are bound together either by being blood kin or a bond linked from their own heart to Bobby's. In my mind's eye, I see the expressions on their faces, and feel that many of the mourners would like to be heard. I think they would have a lot to say. Yes, there are a large range of emotions from the people here. They tell of the good times and the joyful times; the hard times and the bad times—even the very bad times. If they could only voice their feelings, I am sure we would hear those who are truly mourning. Two of them would be the sons who have been unable to travel from California. I focus my thoughts on them. Their intense blue eyes grip me, and I can see in them the inner turmoil and despair of genuinely grief-stricken sons; young men who have waited their whole lives for love and approval from their father, and finally received a few letters at the very end.

The feelings of sorrow, emotional pain, even freedom, and joy might also be represented here. It would be wrong to suggest that all present will mourn the loss of their friend or father with usual sentiment.

I think of the last words the presiding minister will speak: "From dust we come, to dust we return." From what I have heard of the preacher, he will try to communicate with the immediate family. He is plain-spoken and he will comfort them without sugarcoating some of Bobby's life experiences. I imagine him saying, and hope he will say, "Your dad is gone. The deception he was under does not have to be a part of your life. There is a brand-new day for you."

The service will be finished by now. They are a strong family and they will have all made it through. I can almost see Kurina as she hugs the children. They are an interesting assortment, Bobby and Kurina's children: hearty, healthy, blue-eyes and green-eyes, and mostly blond. They are dressed in the modest, long clothes required by their parents, and they reflect a vigorous upbringing. It's hard to imagine the extended lineage to follow Bobby: all of his children, some we don't even know, and their children and grandchildren.

For some reason a familiar tune comes to mind, then the words of a song. It is by fellow Texan Willie Nelson. It pretty much reflects my frame of mind on this occasion: "Yesterday is dead and gone and tomorrow's out of sight..."

All the possibilities for second chances are finished now. Two lives, two men; both exceptionally capable, both with potential beyond the norm. They were well equipped for life, but squandered their God-given talents. They were so alike, but so different. So close, yet so far.

Yes, Bobby, in the end, all was indeed vanity. All of your jealousy, all of your fabricated religion, all of your control, all of your hard work to be poor, all of your deception, all of your rejection of people—good people whose only fault was seeing through your deceit. It is with a heavy heart, Bobby, that I bid you farewell.

Robert Allen Hale   William Kingsbery Hale
Palmer, Alaska, 2008   Somoto, Nicaragua, 2004

"Like the inescapable shadow which follows me, the lead weight of sin haunts me.
Graciously look upon me; your love is my refuge."
~ *James Whitaker*

A True Man

A man like so many men, yet so much greater than most.

A man that was destined to do many great things and change lives.

Yet so many great things go unnoticed, such as all the things we don't give second thoughts about, it was these things that he did.

Though he could make you mad, somehow with one look he could leave you with a smile on your face.

A man that left this earth in the stormy month of April on the 9th day and 2004th year.

This is the man I will remember.

Dedicated to my Grandfather, William K. Hale,

- Taylor Wimberley, 16

TO THE READER: FROM PATSY DORRIS HALE

It must seem to many of you that there is little victory in my story; that I was swept up in a chaotic entanglement of ideas, opinions, and beliefs with little chance of my emerging without injury and doubt. It must have seemed at times that I would not overcome some of the challenges that were my lot on this earth. Fortunately, that is not true. I have overcome many trials and emerged victorious.

Bill, for a season, was steadfast and was able to share in loving and helpful ways with many youth in different studies. He was a leader at church, and we had many large and happy gatherings at our home. These are the memories my family desires to hold onto—Billy as a wonderful husband and father, before he was entrapped in deception and drawn away from us by his brother.

How did Patsy escape the same entrapment, you might ask. It is because I was blessed to have a firm foundation from a young age, and I gratefully acknowledge my dependence on that faith. To be gifted with a strong faith, that will uphold them, is my constant prayer for my family, and all others I come in contact with.

I also believe that my faith helped me understand Bill's real relationship with Bobby and enabled our marriage to last those thirty-five years. In the end, Bill admitted that Bobby did a lot to destroy us and, most of all, to destroy him. He knew we are all responsible for what we do and for the choices we make; however, he did express to me after all was said and done: "Patsy, you know this never would have happened without Bobby pushing. Please forgive me."

I did forgive Bill, gladly and with love.

ACKNOWLEDGMENTS

Patsy thanks:
I would like to thank the following people for their contributions to the completion of this book. I am so grateful for their continual love and support.

I am so thankful for Wilma Martin Turner's emerging writing talent expressed in this memoir; and for our long-term friendship. Her ability to interpret information brought my story to life as a result of many languishing hours lasting sometimes throughout the night on into the early hours of dawn.

My cousin, Paul Ryon has always enjoyed a good spin on a story. He put forth many ideas for the title of this book from my many adventurous entanglements with the Hales. In the end his suggestions were put to use when Mark Kirby chose, HE HEARD HIS BROTHER CALL HIS NAME. I am eternally grateful for your quick wit Paul and cousinship.

My family and friends: Without the long-lasting encouragement and many years of friendship from the time of my childhood in Texas to this present day, I do not think I could have endured without such a strong circle of friends and family. I thank you.

I have sincere appreciation for Carol Anderson and Sue Walker, along with my other dear friends in Destin, Florida who offered their critiques and exhortations from beginning to end.

Open-hearted gratitude is given to Mark Kirby. He has been powerfully consistent in encouraging every step of the way and the book is better because of his insights and details. We cannot thank you enough for being our editor.

Wilma thanks:

My first thought of gratitude goes to Patsy Hale, who has been my friend since we met at NTU in Denton, Texas. There came a time of turmoil when Billy, pushing all of his friends away, caused us to lose touch. After Patsy and I were able to renew our friendship she shared with me one of the most remarkable stories I have ever heard. It is her story and includes the account of those missing years. I listened spellbound, sharing the sentiment with many of her friends: "Patsy, you need to write all this down." I thank Patsy for asking me to help her, for her patience in answering my many questions, and for spending hundreds of hours relating the amazing details of this important memoir.

I must give heartfelt thanks to my wonderful book club, Women of Words, in north Georgia. Each of them, some who are writers themselves, have believed in me and encouraged me every step of the way in this undertaking. They read an early manuscript copy of the book, which resulted in one of the liveliest and most meaningful discussions we've had since I joined their ranks seven years ago.

How could I have finished this project at all without my family's long time friends Jack and Martha Harich? Patsy and I both thank Jack for his many selfless hours of technical help and for always being more than willing to answer any of my computer questions, and solve the many problems I encountered. I thank Martha for agreeing to read and critique the final manuscript of the book. I was more than thrilled when she emailed me saying, "It's almost daylight and I can't put this book down."

And many thanks to my husband, George. He has patiently put up with my late, hours, bad moods, and even my absence from a family vacation. He read the book right along and never failed to renew my flagging confidence.

ABOUT THE AUTHORS

Patsy Dorris Hale

Patsy Hale was born in Ft. Worth, Texas to two wonderful, grateful parents being that she was a child they never thought they could have. At an early age she taught Tottle, a handicapped young-adult, to say her first words and found this to be very inspiring. This inspiration led her to pursuing a degree from North Texas State University with a B.S. in elementary education and a minor in music. While still attending college, she married William K. Hale. After she completed college, they started a family resulting in four beautiful children. For the last four years she has run a tutoring service she started for pre-K to 6th grade. It has been such a great encouragement to see that light of understanding turn on in a child's mind. She presently lives in Destin, Florida, which is truly a paradise.

Wilma Martin Turner

Wilma Turner was born in Atlanta, married young and moved to Texas with her husband, George. Both were students at North Texas State University, where they met and became good friends with Patsy and Billy Hale. This powerful true story is Wilma's first book and was written with Patsy's encouragement and trust. Wilma lives with her husband on a small farm in north Georgia.

Made in the USA
Charleston, SC
12 May 2014